Teaching Pal 2

Authors and Advisors

Alma Flor Ada • Kylene Beers • F. Isabel Campoy
Joyce Armstrong Carroll • Nathan Clemens
Anne Cunningham • Martha Hougen
Elena Izquierdo • Carol Jago • Erik Palmer
Robert Probst • Shane Templeton • Julie Washington

Contributing Consultants

David Dockterman • Mindset Works
Jill Eggleton

Printed in the U.S.A.

ISBN   978-1-328-51725-8

3 4 5 6 7 8 9 10   0868   27 26 25 24 23 22 21 20 19 18

4500737492   A B C D E F G

Navigating the Teaching Pal

The Teaching Pal is a companion to the Teacher's Guide, providing point-of-use instructional notes for using the student texts in *my*Book for different purposes.

Blue Notes
READ FOR UNDERSTANDING

During a first reading of the complete text, use these notes to guide collaborative discussion about the gist of the selection.

 READ FOR UNDERSTANDING

Whose phrase does Flora repeat? What does it mean? Cite evidence from the text to explain your answer. *(Flora reads comics about a superhero named Incandesto who is really the janitor, Alfred T. Slipper. She repeats his famous phrase, "This malfeasance must be stopped." Malfeasance means "misconduct or wrongdoing.")*

ANNOTATION TIP: Have students go back to the text to highlight evidence for their answer.

DOK 2

Purple Notes
TARGETED CLOSE READ

During subsequent readings, use these notes to take a closer look at sections of the text to apply a reading skill.

 TARGETED CLOSE READ

Figurative Language

Have students reread paragraph 40 to look for something that the author exaggerates.

Which part of paragraph 40 shows exaggeration through the use of hyperbole? *(The last part of the paragraph where it says an average squirrel's thought is repeated, "some six or seven thousand times a day" shows exaggeration.)*

How does exaggeration help to describe the squirrel's personality? (It shows that all squirrels think about is getting food to eat.)

DOK 2

Yellow Notes

Use these notes for teaching support on the pages that appear before and after each selection.

Academic Discussion

Vocabulary Network Guide students to think about how each word relates to people's identities as they decide what to add to the Vocabulary Network. Remind students to come back to this page after each selection to add more words.

Red Notes
NOTICE & NOTE

Use these notes to help students deepen their understanding as they learn to look for signposts in the text in order to create meaning.

Notice & Note

Aha Moment

- **Remind students** that an Aha Moment is when a character realizes something significant about himself or herself or the character's world. This causes a change in the character's actions and self-understanding.

- **Have students** identify an Aha Moment on this page. Ask them how this moment changes what Flora thinks about herself. *(As she rushes to the aid of Mrs. Tickham, she realizes that, in spite of being a cynic and much to her surprise, she is a helpful person.)*

ANNOTATION TIP: Have students underline the sentence or sentences where the Aha Moment occurs in the text.

DOK 2

Welcome to *myBook!*

Do you like to read different kinds of texts for all kinds of reasons? Do you have a favorite genre or author? What can you learn from a video? Do you think carefully about what you read and view?

Here are some tips to get the MOST out of what you read and view:

Set a Purpose. What is the title? What is the genre? What do you want to learn from this text or video? What about it looks interesting to you?

Read and Annotate. As you read, underline and highlight important words and ideas. Make notes about things you want to figure out or remember. What questions do you have? What are your favorite parts? Write them down!

Make Connections. How does the text or video connect to what you already know? To other texts or videos? To your own life or community? Talk to others about your ideas. Listen to their ideas, too.

Wrap It Up! Look back at your questions and annotations. What did you like best? What did you learn? What do you still want to know? How will you find out?

As you read the texts and watch the videos in this book, make sure you get the MOST out of them by using the tips above.

But, don't stop there… decide what makes you curious, find out more about it, have fun, and never stop learning!

TABLE OF CONTENTS

7

MODULE 10

Communication Nation

9

Introduce the Topic

- **Read aloud** the module title, *Marvels of Nature.*

- **Tell students** that in this module they will be reading and viewing selections on the topic of Earth's natural wonders.

- **Have students** give an example of something they consider to be a marvel of nature. *(Possible responses: the Grand Canyon, Niagara Falls, or California redwood trees)*

- **Have students** tell what criteria they think something has to have in order to be considered a marvel of nature. *(Possible responses: Something is a marvel of nature because it was formed by nature and is unique.)*

Discuss the Quotation

- **Read aloud** the quotation by Nancy Newhall.

- **Lead a discussion** in which students discuss what they think Newhall's statement means and why. Ask them to consider what the wilderness actually is and why it might hold answers. *(Possible responses: The wilderness is an area of land like mountains or a forest. It may hold answers because many places in nature are yet to be explored.)*

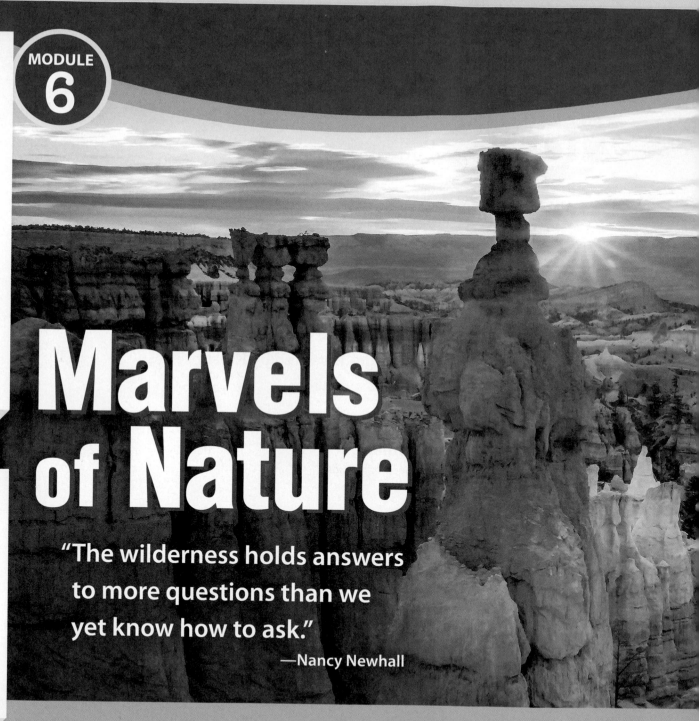

MODULE
6

Marvels of Nature

"The wilderness holds answers to more questions than we yet know how to ask."

—Nancy Newhall

10

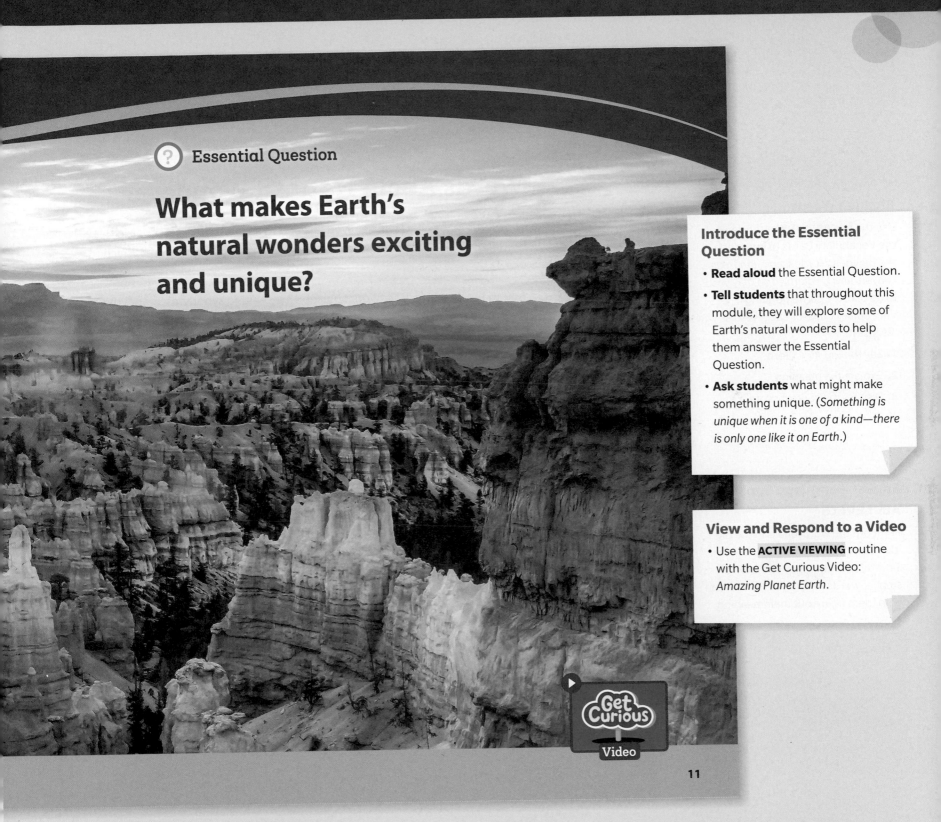

(?) Essential Question

What makes Earth's natural wonders exciting and unique?

Introduce the Essential Question

- **Read aloud** the Essential Question.
- **Tell students** that throughout this module, they will explore some of Earth's natural wonders to help them answer the Essential Question.
- **Ask students** what might make something unique. (*Something is unique when it is one of a kind—there is only one like it on Earth.*)

View and Respond to a Video

- Use the **ACTIVE VIEWING** routine with the Get Curious Video: *Amazing Planet Earth.*

Get Curious
Video

11

Big Idea Words

Use the **VOCABULARY** routine and
the Vocabulary Cards to introduce
the Big Idea Words *scenic, landscape,
canyon,* and *landform*. You may wish
to display the corresponding
Vocabulary Card for each word as you
discuss it.

1. Say the Big Idea Word.

2. Explain the meaning.

3. Discuss the context sentence.

**English Language Support
ALL LEVELS**

Point out the word *land* is in the Big
Idea Words *landscape* and *landform*.
Tell students that they can look for
smaller words in large words that can
help them figure out their meaning.

Words About Natural Wonders

The words in the chart will help you talk and write about the selections in this
module. Which words about the natural world have you seen before? Which
words are new to you?

Add to the Vocabulary Network on page 13 by writing synonyms, antonyms,
and related words and phrases for each word about the natural world.

After you read each selection in this module, come back to the Vocabulary
Network and keep building it. Add more ovals if you need to.

WORD	MEANING	CONTEXT SENTENCE
scenic (adjective)	Something that is scenic has beautiful scenery.	The scenic cliffs towered over the beach.
landscape (noun)	When you look at a landscape, you are looking at the area of land around you.	The landscape of a forest is thick with trees.
canyon (noun)	A canyon is a deep valley that has steep sides.	He felt dizzy as he looked down into the canyon.
landform (noun)	A landform is a natural feature, such as a mountain, of a land's surface.	The tallest landform on the map is Mount Everest.

12

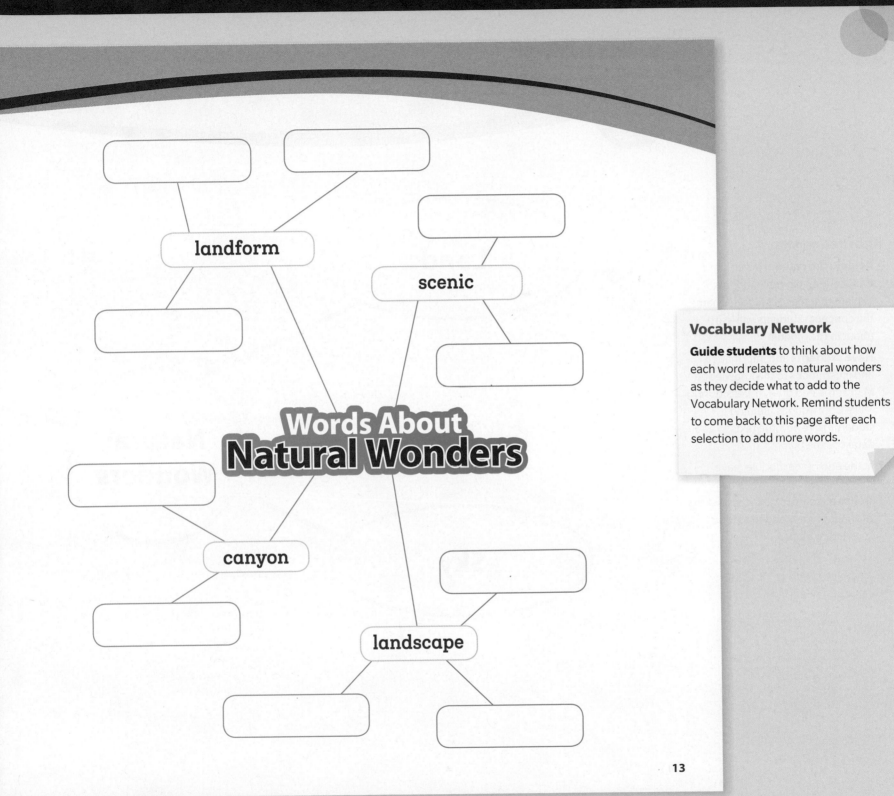

landform

scenic

Words About
Natural Wonders

canyon

landscape

13

Knowledge Map

- **Review the categories** on the Knowledge Map with students. Explain that these categories name the concepts students will learn about in the module.

- **Have students** add information and illustrations to the Knowledge Map at the end of each week during Make Connections. Remind students to review the texts to add details to the map.

- At the end of the module, have students work in pairs or small groups to compare and contrast the information they added to their Knowledge Maps.

Land

Natural Wonders

Sky

14

Water

Short Read

Seven Natural Wonders

wonder

n. **something extraordinary—a marvel**

1 The world is full of wonders—unusual places with amazing landforms. Seven of these natural wonders are unique. They are known as the Seven Natural Wonders of the World.

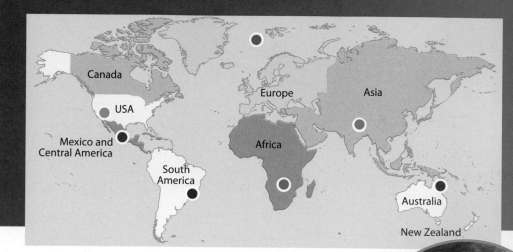

● **Grand Canyon**

2 Arizona's Grand Canyon is more than a mile deep and 200 miles long. The canyon offers spectacular natural views. But its colorful layers of rock aren't just breathtaking to look at; the layers give geologists valuable clues to our planet's past.

● **Paricutín**

3 This natural wonder literally rose from the earth as people watched. In 1943, a Mexican farmer marveled as the landscape of his farm changed before his eyes. A volcano grew from his cornfield. It reached 1,000 feet in just 10 months!

16

Harbor of Rio de Janeiro

4   The Harbor of Rio de Janeiro in Brazil is the world's largest deep-water bay. Majestic mountains fringe the shoreline, providing scenic views. The vertical contrast of towering peaks to golden beaches to deep valleys below is quite dramatic.

Aurora Borealis

5   The Aurora Borealis, or Northern Lights, illuminates the night sky above the North Pole with a natural light show. Charged particles collide with gases in Earth's atmosphere to create the colorful spectacle.

Victoria Falls

6   Victoria Falls in Zambia, Africa, is one of the world's largest waterfalls, stretching over 5,000 feet wide. A thick mist billows over 1,300 feet above the falls. The mist gave the falls its original name, "The Smoke That Thunders."

Mount Everest

7   The peak of Mount Everest is the highest point on the planet. Tectonic activity created the mountain long ago, when two huge plates deep within Earth's crust crashed together. The collision pushed the land above the plates higher and higher. Today only the bravest adventurers dare to climb to the top of the world.

Great Barrier Reef

8   The Great Barrier Reef stretches more than 1,000 miles across the waters off of the Australian coast. The skeletons of tiny sea creatures called *coral polyps* form the reef. The reef is one of the few living things on Earth visible from outer space.

myNotes

READ FOR UNDERSTANDING

Introduce the Text

- **Read aloud** and discuss the genre information. Point out these examples of each text feature:
  - » headings (page 24)
  - » captions (pages 22-23)
  - » text and graphic features (page 20)

- Use Display and Engage **Build Background 6.2**.

- **Tell students** to look for the Critical Vocabulary as they read, and to think about the words' meanings.

ANNOTATION TIP: Have students use the box to note what they want to learn from this selection.

Prepare to Read

GENRE STUDY **Informational texts** give facts and examples about a topic.

- An author's purpose for writing informational texts is to share facts about a topic.

- Authors of informational texts often organize their ideas using headings and subheadings.

- Informational texts include text and graphic features, such as captions, pronunciation guides, maps, and photographs.

SET A PURPOSE **Think about** the title and genre of this text. What do you want to learn about the Mariana Trench? Write your ideas below.

Build Background:
Coral Reefs

CRITICAL VOCABULARY

trench

summit

thrive

prehistoric

vital

glimpse

submersible

remotely

autonomous

MARIANA TRENCH

by Michael Woods
& Mary B. Woods

📖 **READ FOR UNDERSTANDING**

Set a Purpose

- **Have students** skim through *Mariana Trench*, noting some of the graphic features, headings, and sidebars to make predictions.

- **Guide students** to set a purpose for reading. Discuss with them what they think they will learn from this selection.

DOK 2

19

READ FOR UNDERSTANDING

Synthesize

MODEL SYNTHESIZING

💬 **THINK ALOUD** *When I synthesize, I combine what I have learned with what I already know to gain a new understanding. As I read new information, my thinking changes to help me better understand what I read. I can get new information from the text and from the graphic features like photos and captions. When I look at the map, I see the Pacific Ocean and some continents. I know I am reading about the Mariana Trench. I know what a trench is, and I know some facts about oceans. When I read the text, my ideas may change as I synthesize the new information.*

CHINA

JAPAN

MARIANA ISLANDS

PHILIPPINES

MARIANA TRENCH

AUSTRALIA

NEW ZEALAND

PACIFIC OCEAN

UNITED STATES

1 Many people know that the highest point on Earth is at the top of Mount Everest. That famous peak towers 29,035 feet (8,850 m) above sea level. It is in the Himalaya mountains, near the border of China and Nepal. But how many people can name the lowest place in the world? That point is at the bottom of the Mariana Trench, a valley in the floor of the Pacific Ocean. The trench lies just east of the Mariana Islands, southeast of China and Japan.

> **trench** A trench is a long, narrow groove or ditch.

This satellite photo of the Pacific Ocean shows the Mariana Trench as a dark blue crescent.

📖 READ FOR UNDERSTANDING

What information does the text tell you about the Mariana Trench?
(The Mariana Trench is the lowest place on Earth. It is in the Pacific Ocean near the Mariana Islands.)

DOK 1

🔍 TARGETED CLOSE READ

Text and Graphic Features
Have students reread page 21 and connect the text to the map.

How does the map help you understand more about the text?
(It shows the location of the Mariana Trench in the Pacific Ocean as well as neighboring countries.)

ANNOTATION TIP: Have students underline the text evidence. Have them draw an arrow from the text to the location of the Mariana Trench on the map.

DOK 1

21

2   This enormous trench extends for about 1,554 miles (2,500 kilometers) from one end to the other. It could stretch from New York City almost to Denver, Colorado. The trench averages about 45 miles (72 km) wide. A person walking at a brisk pace would need about ten hours to go from one side to the other.

3   Inside that groove in the ocean floor is the Challenger Deep, the deepest spot in the world. It lies 210 miles (338 km) from the island of Guam. It is about 36,000 feet (11,000 m) below sea level—almost 7 miles (11 km) deep. If Mount Everest were placed in the Challenger Deep, the mountain's peak would still be under 7,000 feet (2,134 m) of water.

In this satellite image, the deepest areas of the Mariana Trench appear in dark blue.

Mount Everest, the highest point on Earth, lies on the border between Nepal and Tibet.

 READ FOR UNDERSTANDING

How does the photo help you understand the text on page 22? Why did the author include it?
(Seeing Mount Everest helps me visualize how deep the Mariana Trench is. The text says Mount Everest can fit inside the trench and the peak will still be 7,000 feet under the top of the water. The author included the photo to make clear how deep the Mariana Trench is.)

ANNOTATION TIP: Have students underline the sentence that connects the text to the photo.

DOK 2

23

Synthesize

What do you know so far about the Mariana Trench? *(It is the deepest spot on Earth.)* **What is the most important point the author makes in paragraph 5?** *(It is impossible for anyone to dive down into the Mariana Trench because the water temperature and pressure of the water are too severe.)*

If students have difficulty synthesizing, use this model:

🗨 **THINK ALOUD** *The author gives many details about the water temperature and the pressure in the Mariana Trench, but I can combine all the details to remember the most important point. I can synthesize the new information in the paragraph by saying that the Mariana Trench is too dangerous for divers to dive.*

ANNOTATION TIP: Have students underline the sentences that explain why humans could not survive in the Challenger Deep.

DOK 3

 READ FOR UNDERSTANDING

How does the text feature *Ever Wonder?* add to your understanding of the Mariana Trench? *(It explains why it is so dark in the Mariana Trench and talks about different zones of visibility.)*

DOK 1 **24**

 myNotes

Flashlight fish have glowing patches just beneath their eyes.

WEIRD CREATURES

4   Conditions are very harsh at the **summit** of Mount Everest. Temperatures average –33°F (–36°C), and winter winds howl at more than 100 miles (161 km) an hour. Yet climbers have reached the top and lived to tell about it.

5   But no human, not even an expert diver, could survive the environment of the Challenger Deep. In this pitch-black world, the temperature is about 36°F (2°C). The human body shuts down quickly in water that cold. A person on the ocean floor also would be crushed by the weight of the water. Water is heavy. A 1-gallon (4-liter) milk jug holds about 8 pounds (3.6 kilograms) of water. At the deepest point in the ocean, water would press down with a weight heavier than hundreds of elephants.

summit   The summit of a mountain is its top or highest point.

Ever Wonder?

6   Why is it pitch dark in the deep ocean? In the oceans, deeper means dimmer. Water absorbs and scatters sunlight. So, little light remains after 660 feet (201 m). Beyond that depth is a twilight zone, where the human eye cannot see colors. This zone of faint light goes down to about 3,300 feet (1,006 m). The midnight zone, from there on down, is in total darkness.

An anglerfish uses its natural fishing pole to lure prey into its mouth.

7 However, living things do **thrive** in the Mariana Trench. Some creatures look like deep-sea movie monsters or survivors from **prehistoric** times. These animals and plants are specially built for life in an extreme environment. Some can produce a glowing light, like fireflies. This is called bioluminescence. Creatures use this light to attract prey.

8 Anglerfish have bioluminescent, built-in fishing poles. In some of these fish, the pole is like an antenna growing from the top of the head. This rod glows in the dark water. The anglerfish waves it to attract other fish. When a fish approaches, the angler snaps up the prey in its huge mouth packed with long, needle-sharp teeth.

9 Flashlight fish also live in the Mariana Trench. Like the anglerfish, they are bioluminescent. The flashlight fish lurks in the dark water and turns its light on and off. When a curious fish approaches, it becomes dinner!

10 Certain types of crabs and bacteria thrive in the Mariana Trench. Scientists had never seen some of these until fairly recent deep-sea explorations. This is because the creatures can't exist anywhere else. The extreme temperatures and pressure of the deep ocean are vital to these organisms.

> **"A world as strange as that of Mars."**
>
> —William Beebe, an explorer, describing the deep ocean after setting a world record in 1934 by diving to 3,028 feet (923 m) in a submersible (small submarine)

thrive When living things thrive, they grow well and are healthy.
prehistoric Something that is prehistoric is very old, from a time before history was recorded.
vital If something is vital, it is needed or very important.

Notice & Note

Word Gaps

- **Remind students** that when they read a word that they don't know, they can ask themselves questions or look for clues in the text to help them figure out the word's meaning.

- **Have students** locate and highlight the word *bioluminescent* in paragraph 7. Help students figure out the word's meaning.

- **Have students ask themselves: Do I know this word from somewhere else?** (*Sample answer: No, but parts of the word seem familiar to me.*) **Does it seem like a technical word for this topic? Explain.** (*Yes, it is a word that seems to describe a fish characteristic.*) **Can I find clues in the paragraph to help me understand the word?** (*Yes, in paragraph 8, the text talks about a fish that has a pole that lights up. In paragraph 9, the text describes a flashlight fish that can turn its light on and off. So* bioluminescent *must mean something that lights up.*)

ANNOTATION TIP: Have students underline the words in the text that provide clues to the meaning of *bioluminescent*.

DOK 2

25

CHALLENGER LOOKS DEEP

11 The Mariana Trench was discovered in 1875. Scientists on the British ship HMS *Challenger* used a machine to measure the ocean depth in different places. The machine unreeled a spool of wire with a heavy weight at the end. Dials measured the length of wire let out. When the weight touched bottom, scientists could tell the depth of the ocean floor. With that simple method, they realized that the water near the Mariana Islands was extremely deep.

12 In 1951 the British Royal Navy vessel HMS *Challenger II* returned to the area with a modern measuring device. It is called echo sounding, or sonar. It sends out sound waves that bounce off a surface, such as the seafloor. Scientists measured the time needed for sound waves to bounce back from the seafloor to the ship. This told them the ocean depth. Using echo sounding, *Challenger II* mapped the entire Mariana Trench. The deepest point it found was 35,760 feet (10,900 m). That point was named the Challenger Deep, after the ship.

The Moon over Mariana

13 Twelve U.S. astronauts have been on the moon. They explored the moon's surface in the 1960s and 1970s during the Apollo space program. However, only two people have ever visited the deepest place on Earth. Don Walsh (bottom, right) and Jacques Piccard (top, right) spent just twenty minutes there during their descent in the *Trieste* submersible in 1960.

26

A deep-sea submersible collects samples from the bottom of the Mariana Trench using a robotic arm.

14 People got their first **glimpse** of the Challenger Deep in 1960. That year scientist Jacques Piccard and U.S. Navy lieutenant Don Walsh traveled to the bottom. They rode in the *Trieste* (TREE•est), a **submersible** vehicle. Small submarines of this kind are built to withstand extreme underwater pressure. They usually carry scientific instruments for exploring the deep ocean. Piccard and Walsh found a point deeper than *Challenger II* had found. It was 35,813 feet (10,916 m) below the surface. They also observed small fish near the ocean floor.

15 Since then oceanographers have used other vehicles and instruments to explore the deep ocean. Some are **remotely** operated vehicles, or ROVs. Scientists control these through cables from a ship on the surface. Others are **autonomous** underwater vehicles, or AUVs. These explore on their own without any connection to another ship. AUVs navigate with onboard computers and record data from the areas they explore.

16 In the 1990s, several Japanese ROVs explored the Mariana Trench. They observed shrimp, sandworms, and other living things. The ROV *Kaiko* scooped up samples of mud from the trench floor for scientists to study. Scientists found tiny organisms in those samples that are Earth's deepest living creatures.

---

glimpse   A glimpse is a very quick look at something.
submersible   If something is submersible, it can go or work under water.
remotely   If you use something remotely, you control it from a distance.
autonomous   If something is autonomous, it controls itself.

 TARGETED CLOSE READ

Central Idea

What is the central, or main, idea of the text on page 27? (*Special vehicles have explored Challenger Deep and the Mariana Trench.*)

Evaluate and give two details that support the central idea. (*Possible responses: Scientists ride a submersible vehicle called the* Trieste. *They use remotely operated vehicles and autonomous vehicles without people aboard to explore the Mariana Trench.*)

DOK 2

 TARGETED CLOSE READ

Text and Graphic Features

Have students find the phonetic spelling of the word *Trieste* in paragraph 14. **Why do you think the author adds the pronunciation guide for this word?** (*so that the reader can correctly pronounce the word* Trieste)

DOK 2

27

PLATES SO DEEP

17 The Mariana Trench is so deep because of movement in Earth's surface. Many huge plates of rock make up the surface. Earth's crust, or outer layer, forms the top of each plate. The bottom of each plate is part of Earth's mantle, the thick layer below the crust. The plates float on a layer of puttylike rock in the mantle. While floating, the edges of these plates slide past one another and bump into one another.

18 At the Mariana Trench, a heavy plate of rock on the ocean floor is pressing against a plate of lighter rock. When this happens, the heavier ocean plate plunges downward at a steep angle into Earth's mantle. The bottom of the Mariana Trench is where that heavy plate of rock is moving down into the mantle.

> **"It's like a magic mirror."**
> —Andy Rechnitzer, an oceanographer who planned the first dive into the Mariana Trench in 1960, describing the foreign world of the deep ocean

19 Plate movements have formed more than twenty other deep ocean trenches in different parts of the world. The Puerto Rico Trench, for instance, is the deepest place in the Atlantic Ocean. It lies north of the island of Puerto Rico. The trench is about 5 miles (8 km) deep and 1,100 miles (1,770 km) long.

Mariana Trench Expressway

20 Navy submarines patrolling the world's oceans like to stay in deep water. It is more difficult for enemies to detect them there. That's why U.S., Russian, and other submarines often use the Mariana Trench as an expressway. The trench is the main north-south route for submarines in the Pacific Ocean.

At the Mariana Trench, the movement of ocean plates into Earth's mantle created many underwater volcanoes. This cliff near the Mariana Trench shows layers of light and dark ash that collected on the seafloor during eruptions.

READ FOR UNDERSTANDING

How do the picture and caption help deepen your understanding of the Mariana Trench? *(I can see the layers of the Mariana Trench. The text tells how the Trench changes during plate movement and volcanic eruptions.)*

DOK 2

29

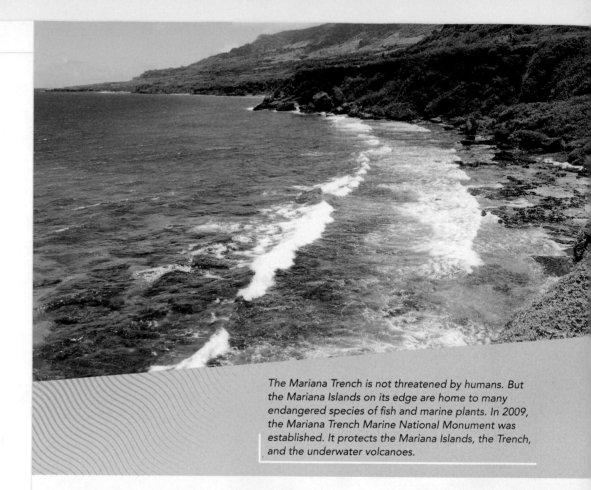

The Mariana Trench is not threatened by humans. But the Mariana Islands on its edge are home to many endangered species of fish and marine plants. In 2009, the Mariana Trench Marine National Monument was established. It protects the Mariana Islands, the Trench, and the underwater volcanoes.

WORRIES ABOUT THE WONDER

21 The future of the Mariana Trench seems very safe. Neither people nor nature threatens its existence. Ships sailing over the area do not cause any damage to the trench. However, movements of Earth's plates may eventually change the Mariana Trench. In millions of years, it may be deeper or shallower. But it is sure to remain a wonder that holds many secrets of the deep.

30

Collaborative Discussion

Look back at what you wrote on page 18. Tell a partner two things you learned from this text. Then work with a group to discuss the questions below. Refer to details and examples in *Mariana Trench* to explain your answers. As your group works together, think carefully about each question and answer.

1 Review page 22. What comparisons do the authors use to explain the size and depth of the Mariana Trench?

2 Reread pages 24–25. What makes creatures that live in the Mariana Trench unusual?

3 What are some of the ways that scientists have explored the trench? Why is it difficult to do research there?

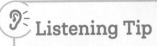

Listening Tip

To be sure you understand, restate in your own mind what a speaker has said. Then ask yourself, "Do I agree with that idea? Is there something else I can add?"

Speaking Tip

Think about what you will say before you speak. Point out the text evidence you used to answer the questions.

Academic Discussion

Use the **COLLABORATIVE DISCUSSION** routine. Have students write responses to the questions. Then have groups apply the Listening and Speaking Tips as they discuss their responses.

Possible responses:

1. *On p. 22, the trench's length is compared to the distance between Denver and New York City. Its width would take a brisk walker ten hours to go from side to side. The deepest part, known as the Challenger Deep, could hold Mount Everest inside of it and still have 7,000 feet of water covering it.* DOK 2

2. *The creatures that live in the Mariana Trench are unusual because they are able to survive in this very harsh environment. The intense pressure and extreme cold creates a place where they thrive. These creatures could not live anywhere else. Flashlight fish and anglerfish are bioluminescent, and their glowing light attracts prey.* DOK 2

3. *Because the Mariana Trench is so deep, so cold, and has such intense pressure, it is difficult for humans to explore. Scientists use sonar or echo sounding to map the trench. Don Walsh and Jacques Piccard used a small submarine to study the deep ocean. AUVs and ROVs are also used to explore the trench.* DOK 3

Write a Personal Narrative

PROMPT

In *Mariana Trench*, you learned about the lowest place in the world. You also learned about Navy Lieutenant Don Walsh's descent into the Challenger Deep, the deepest part of the Mariana Trench.

Imagine that you are Lieutenant Walsh. Use facts and details from the text and your imagination to write a story describing Walsh's dive in the *Trieste* to the deepest place in the world. Tell what he sees, feels, and thinks throughout his experience. Don't forget to use some of the Critical Vocabulary and some science words in your writing.

PLAN

Write facts and details from the text and the sidebars. Then explain one cause-and-effect relationship discussed in the text that Walsh might have seen or felt.

Write About Reading

- **Read aloud** the prompt with students.

- **Lead a discussion** in which students share their ideas about what Lieutenant Walsh sees, feels, and thinks during his dive. Tell students to use text evidence to support their ideas.

- **Then read aloud** the Plan section. Have students use ideas from the discussion in their notes.

Now write your narrative from the point of view of Lieutenant Walsh.

Make sure your narrative

- ☐ introduces the situation and the first-person narrator.

- ☐ uses first-person pronouns, such as *I*, *me*, *my*, and *myself*.

- ☐ uses facts and details from the text to describe Walsh's experience.

- ☐ uses descriptive words and sensory details.

- ☐ ends with a sentence that sums up the experience.

Write About Reading

- **Review with students** the directions and checklist in the Write section.

- **Encourage students** to use their own words as they write facts and details from the text to describe Lieutenant Walsh's experience.

READ FOR UNDERSTANDING

Introduce the Text

- **Read aloud** and discuss the genre information. Point out these examples of each text feature:
  » headings (page 37)
  » causes and effects (page 39)
  » science words (page 39)

- Use Display and Engage <u>Meet the Author 6.6</u>.

- **Tell students** to look for the Critical Vocabulary as they read, and to think about the words' meanings.

ANNOTATION TIP: Have students use the box to note what they want to learn from this selection.

Prepare to Read

GENRE STUDY **Informational texts** give facts and examples about a topic.

- Authors may organize their ideas using headings. Headings and subheadings tell readers what the next section of text will be about.

- Authors of informational texts may organize their ideas by explaining causes and effects.

- Science texts also include words that are specific to the topic. These are words that name things or ideas.

SET A PURPOSE **Think about** rocks you see every day. Then look at the title and the photo on the next page. What types of rocks do you think you will read about? What do you want to learn about these rocks? Write your ideas below.

**Meet the Author:
April Pulley Sayre**

**CRITICAL
VOCABULARY**

eternal

organic

intriguing

34

Weird and Wondrous ROCKS

by April Pulley Sayre

Ask and Answer Questions

MODEL ASKING AND ANSWERING QUESTIONS

THINK ALOUD *I will ask myself a question to help me get an idea of what I will be reading: What do I think this selection will be about? I will use the headings and the photographs and captions to help me answer my question: I think this selection will tell me about unusual and unique kinds of rocks that are in different parts of the country. Now I have more questions: Where are these different rocks? What makes them special?*

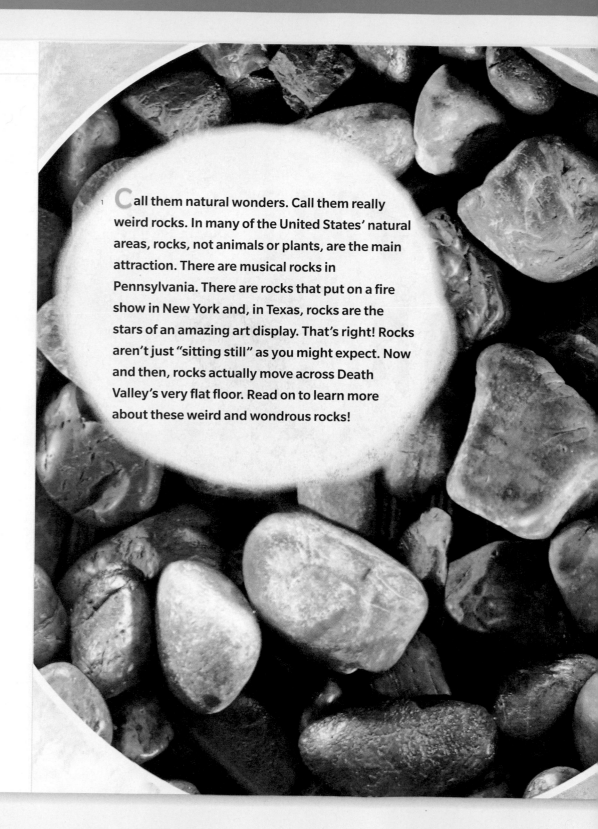

1 Call them natural wonders. Call them really weird rocks. In many of the United States' natural areas, rocks, not animals or plants, are the main attraction. There are musical rocks in Pennsylvania. There are rocks that put on a fire show in New York and, in Texas, rocks are the stars of an amazing art display. That's right! Rocks aren't just "sitting still" as you might expect. Now and then, rocks actually move across Death Valley's very flat floor. Read on to learn more about these weird and wondrous rocks!

Ringing Rocks County Park, Pennsylvania

2 A huge field in eastern Pennsylvania is full of mysterious rocks. When hit with a hammer, these rocks ring like bells. At Ringing Rocks County Park, visitors enjoy tapping the boulders to hear the sounds they make. Several musicians have even included the rocks' strange sounds in concerts!

3 The ringing rocks are made of diabase, a dark, igneous, or volcanic, rock. People used to think that not all of the rocks rang, but scientists have shown that they do. Some of the rocks produce sounds too low for humans to hear.

4 Some scientists think that high levels of iron in the rocks produce the ringing. Another theory points to stress caused by repeated freezing and thawing. The rocks and their sounds still need more study. In the meantime, the musical rocks provide great entertainment.

 myNotes

3

READ FOR UNDERSTANDING

What are the ringing rocks in eastern Pennsylvania made out of? *(They are made out of a dark, volcanic rock called diabase.)* **Do all of these rocks ring? Explain your answer.** *(Yes, they do all ring; however, some ring at such a low level that humans cannot hear them. That is why people used to believe that they did not all ring, but scientists have proven otherwise.)*

ANNOTATION TIP: Have students highlight the sentences that explain the ringing rocks.

DOK 2

TARGETED CLOSE READ

Text Structure

What are two causes for the ringing in the rocks? *(Some scientists believe that the cause of the ringing in the rocks is due to iron levels that are very high. Others believe that "repeated freezing and thawing" causes stress in the rocks which then causes them to ring.)*

What is the author's purpose in using cause and effect here? *(The author wanted to explain why the rocks make the noise.)*

ANNOTATION TIP: Have students underline the causes and then highlight the effect.

DOK 3

What is unique about the waterfall in Chestnut Ridge Park? (*A small fire burns in a grotto, or hollow area, underneath it.*)

What is burning to create the flame? (*The eight-inch flame is produced by natural gas that is formed from organic matter that has decayed.*)

DOK 2

Notice & Note

Contrasts and Contradictions

- **Remind students** that "Contrasts and Contradictions" are times when the author makes readers stop and wonder about something.

- **Guide students** to find a fact or facts on page 38 that contrast or contradict something that they know to be true. (*Normally a flame in a waterfall would immediately go out. So how does this flame hardly ever burn out, and how has it stayed lit for about a thousand years? This doesn't make any sense with what we know about fire and water.*)

ANNOTATION TIP: Have students underline the sentences where the contrast and contradiction occurs.

- Have students reflect on the Anchor Question: *What does this make me wonder about?* and add to their notes.

DOK 3

38

Eternal Flame Falls, New York

5 In Chestnut Ridge Park in western New York, a small fire burns in a grotto, or hollow area, beneath . . . a waterfall? The flame may have been burning, on and off, for a thousand years. Hikers are told to carry barbecue lighters in case the fire goes out. They may need to relight it, because sometimes the flame needs help to be "eternal."

6 The Eternal Flame burns natural gas. The gas forms from decaying organic matter and seeps out from shale rocks. Shale is a type of sedimentary rock that contains fossilized organic matter—the remains of ancient plants. The natural gas produces a flame up to 8 inches (20 cm) tall. The grotto protects the flame from wind and water.

7 Long-lasting flames burn in other places, too. Many are linked to mines or volcanoes. Where natural gas burns, it usually forms from super-hot underground shale. Still, a flame burning under a massive waterfall makes Eternal Flame Falls truly unique and wondrous!

eternal	If something is eternal, it has no end and lasts forever.
organic	If something is organic, it is made up of living matter.

Caverns of Sonora, Texas

8   At first you might think you are on another planet. What surrounds you can't possibly be on Earth! The Caverns of Sonora is a seven-mile-long system of beautiful caves that lie beneath a Texas ranch. Legend says that a dog found the entrance to the caverns around 1900. In 1955, cavers crossed a ledge above a deep pit. They found passages leading to strange shapes and sparkling with crystals.

9   The caverns were formed by slow-moving water under the ground. The water dissolved the limestone layer and carried it away, forming the caverns. Water trickling through the cave walls over thousands of years has created some pretty amazing rock formations.

10 The water contains dissolved minerals. Drip by drip, as the water falls from the cave ceilings and walls, the minerals build up to form stalagmites and stalactites. Stalagmites grow up from cave floors. Stalactites grow downward from ceilings like icicles. Helictites are stalactites that grow in branching shapes. They can resemble teeth, drinking straws, or wings. Some of the deposits on the cave walls look like coral or popcorn. It can take centuries for these cave deposits to form, and the process continues today!

Helictites growing on cave wall ▶

 myNotes

📖 READ FOR UNDERSTANDING

What are stalagmites, stalactites, and helictites? Where do they grow? *(Stalagmites and stalactites are formed from a buildup of dissolved minerals in the water that drips from cave walls and ceilings. Stalagmites grow upward from the cave floor, while stalactites grow downward and hang from cave ceilings. Helictites are branches of stalactites.)*

DOK 2

📖 READ FOR UNDERSTANDING

Ask and Answer Questions

After reading page 37, what questions do you have? *(Sample questions: What is a cavern? Are the Caverns of Sonora safe to visit? How deep do they go?)*

How will you find the aswers to your questions? *(I will reread page 39 to answer my questions. I can do research if the text does not answer them.)*

If students have difficulty asking and answering questions about the text, use this model:

Q **THINK ALOUD** *I am wondering: Are the Caverns of Sonora safe to visit? I reread the text to see if the author answers my question. If not, I can do research to get the answer. Asking and answering questions helps me understand things that are unclear.)*

DOK 3

Sailing Stones, Death Valley National Park, California

11 In Death Valley National Park, rocks seem to move on their own. They leave parallel tracks in the thick, deep mud of a remote playa, a dry lakebed. The rocks, which vary in weight from a few ounces to hundreds of pounds, can stand still for years at a time. Then, suddenly, hundreds of pebbles and boulders drift across the playa all at once. The only problem was that no one had ever seen this happen—they had only seen the puzzling tracks. Until recently, even scientists didn't know how the rocks moved!

12   To unlock this mystery, scientists set up a weather station to measure wind speed and rainfall. They installed tracking devices in rocks in a range of sizes up to about 36 pounds. They left time-lapse cameras in place to record movement.

13   Over time, rain and snow created a temporary pond a few inches deep. A thin layer of ice formed on top, trapping the rocks. Sunlight melted the ice enough to break it into large floating sheets. Then a mild wind pushed the ice sheets, which slowly dragged the rocks, leaving the telltale tracks. Mystery solved!

Notice & Note

Contrasts and Contradictions

Remind students that when the author is comparing and contrasting things, they should ask themselves why this comparison is important.

- **Have students** read paragraph 11 and determine what the author is comparing. (*The text says that the rocks in Death Valley National Park "seem to move on their own." The text also says the rocks "stand still for years at a time." I know that a rock cannot move all by itself. I wonder, then, what it is that is causing these rocks of all different weights to move? I will read further to see if I can find out.*)

- **ANNOTATION TIP:** Have students highlight the text that contrasts the rocks.

- **Have students** reflect on the Anchor Question: *What does this make me wonder about?* and add to their notes.

DOK 3

40

myNotes

41

myNotes

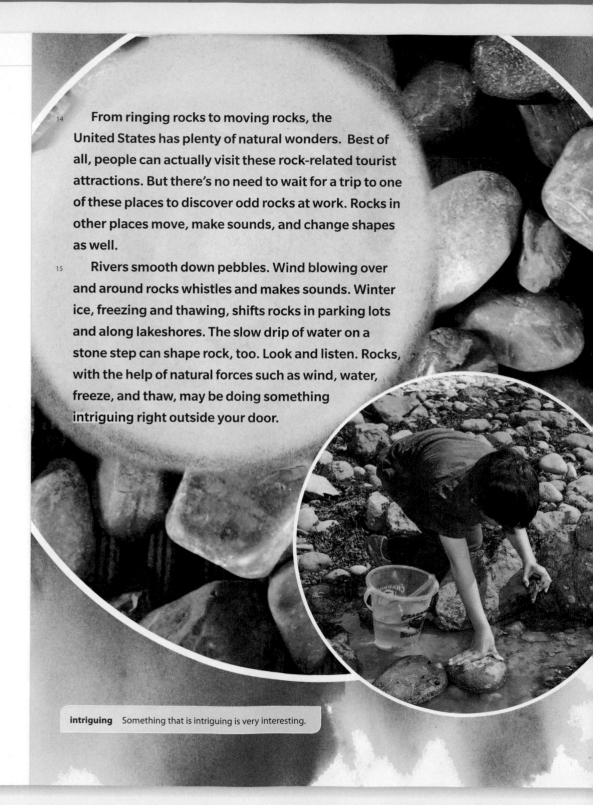

14 From ringing rocks to moving rocks, the United States has plenty of natural wonders. Best of all, people can actually visit these rock-related tourist attractions. But there's no need to wait for a trip to one of these places to discover odd rocks at work. Rocks in other places move, make sounds, and change shapes as well.

15 Rivers smooth down pebbles. Wind blowing over and around rocks whistles and makes sounds. Winter ice, freezing and thawing, shifts rocks in parking lots and along lakeshores. The slow drip of water on a stone step can shape rock, too. Look and listen. Rocks, with the help of natural forces such as wind, water, freeze, and thaw, may be doing something intriguing right outside your door.

intriguing   Something that is intriguing is very interesting.

42

Collaborative Discussion

Look back at what you wrote on page 34. Tell a partner what you learned in this text. Look for details in *Weird and Wondrous Rocks* to support your ideas as you make notes on the questions below. Then discuss the questions with a group. Keep the discussion moving forward by linking each new idea to what has been said.

1 Reread page 37. What details help you understand how the rocks were formed?

2 Reread page 38. Why do the flames need help to be "eternal" sometimes? Why is the word *eternal* in quotation marks?

3 Review page 39. What comparisons does the author use to help you picture the stalactites and other rock formations?

Weird and Wondrous ROCKS
by April Pulley Sayre

Listening Tip

As you listen to each speaker's ideas, think about how your own ideas connect to or build on them.

Speaking Tip

Before you speak, point out how your comment will connect to or build on what another speaker has said. Cite evidence in the text that supports your comment.

Academic Discussion

Use the **COLLABORATIVE DISCUSSION** routine. Have students write responses to the questions. Then have groups apply the Listening and Speaking Tips as they discuss their responses.

Possible responses:

1. *These rocks were formed by volcanic or igneous rock known as diabase.* DOK 2

2. *On page 38, the text says that "sometimes the flame needs help to be 'eternal,'" because on occasion, it will briefly go out. That's why hikers are asked to carry lighters with them in case this happens. The word eternal is in quotation marks because the flame is not consistently lit all of the time, which would be the true meaning of the word eternal. Another clue tells us that for a thousand years, this "flame may have been burning, on and off."* DOK 3

3. *On page 39, the author compares stalactites to icicles. Branches of stalactites are then compared to coral, popcorn, drinking straws, wings, and teeth.* DOK 1

Write a Description

PROMPT ···

In *Weird and Wondrous Rocks,* you learned about unusual rocks in the United States and what makes them weird and wonderful.

Imagine that your class is making a book called *Weird Science Facts* for younger students. Choose one of the types of rocks from *Weird and Wondrous Rocks.* Write a description to help a younger student understand what the rocks look like and what makes them weird and wondrous. Add a drawing or other diagram to show your ideas. Don't forget to use some of the Critical Vocabulary words in your writing.

PLAN ···

Make notes of important details about your chosen rocks. Then explain what causes the rocks to be weird and wondrous.

Write About Reading

- **Read aloud** the prompt with students.
- **Lead a discussion** in which students share their descriptions of the rocks from *Weird and Wondrous Rocks.* Tell students to use text evidence to support their ideas.
- **Then read aloud** the Plan section. Have students use ideas from the discussion in their notes.

Now write your description of your rocks.

✓
Make sure your description

☐	introduces the topic clearly.
☐	uses facts and details from the text to show why the rocks are unusual.
☐	uses precise language and vocabulary.
☐	clearly defines or explains new vocabulary or scientific terms.
☐	includes a drawing, diagram, or other visual element that helps readers better understand the information.

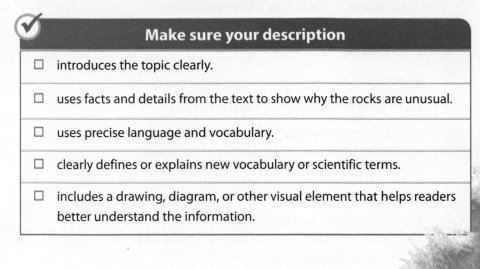

Write About Reading

- **Review with students** the directions and checklist in the Write section.

- **Encourage students** to use their own words as they write details from the text to describe their chosen rocks and explain why they are weird and wondrous.

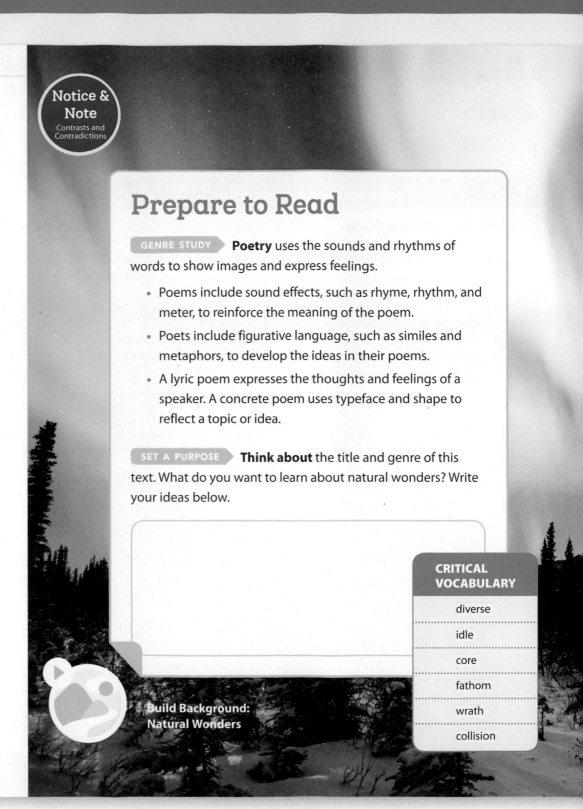

Prepare to Read

GENRE STUDY **Poetry** uses the sounds and rhythms of words to show images and express feelings.

- Poems include sound effects, such as rhyme, rhythm, and meter, to reinforce the meaning of the poem.
- Poets include figurative language, such as similes and metaphors, to develop the ideas in their poems.
- A lyric poem expresses the thoughts and feelings of a speaker. A concrete poem uses typeface and shape to reflect a topic or idea.

SET A PURPOSE **Think about** the title and genre of this text. What do you want to learn about natural wonders? Write your ideas below.

Build Background:
Natural Wonders

CRITICAL VOCABULARY
diverse
idle
core
fathom
wrath
collision

 READ FOR UNDERSTANDING

Introduce the Text

- **Read aloud** and discuss the genre information. Point out that this selection includes informational text along with poetry. Each poem is about a natural wonder, and for each poem there is informational text about the same natural wonder.
- Use Display and Engage **Build Background 6.8**.
- **Tell students** to look for the Critical Vocabulary as they read, and to think about the words' meanings.

ANNOTATION TIP: Have students use the box to note what they want to learn from this selection.

46

Nature's Wonders

Poetry About Our Amazing Earth

 READ FOR UNDERSTANDING

Set a Purpose

- **Have students** read the titles of each nature poem while also glancing at the photographs and informational text that is provided. Ask them what they would like to learn about in each poem.

- **Guide students** to set a purpose for reading. Discuss with them how they think these types of poems are connected.

DOK 2

47

Ask and Answer Questions

MODEL ASKING AND ANSWERING QUESTIONS

THINK ALOUD *I ask myself a question to help me understand. Paragraph 1 says that the reef is "a diverse mix of marine life." What do these words mean? The definition of diverse says "things that are different from each other." In the photo, I see colorful coral, other plants, and different fish. I now understand that this phrase must mean that there are many kinds of plants and animals living in the reef.*

Notice & Note

Contrasts and Contradictions

- **Remind students** that the author may make you stop and wonder about something by writing something that goes against, or contradicts, what you already know. **Have students** identify a comparison in paragraph 1. *(the reef with a rainforest)*

- **Ask students** why this comparison contradicts what they know about these places. *(Reefs are underwater, and rainforests are on land.)* Ask what the author means by this comparison. *(They both have a huge variety of living things in them.)*

DOK 3

 myNotes

The Great Barrier Reef is the world's largest system of coral reefs. It lies off the northeast coast of Australia. The reef is a living thing, made up of small tube-shaped animals called *coral polyps* and their limestone skeletons. The reef is home to the most **diverse** mix of marine life on earth. Because of this, it is sometimes called "the rainforest of the sea."

diverse   If something is diverse, it is made up of things that are different from each other.

The Great Barrier Reef

In the Coral Sea, off the coast of Queensland, Australia

2 It's sixteen hundred miles long
along the Queensland coast,
the barrier reef whose name is "Great,"
and that's no idle boast.

3 It's sixteen hundred miles long
and every inch alive.
Perhaps you'd like to have a look?
You do not need to dive

4 or even get your swimsuit wet
to see this awesome place;
the reef's so huge it's visible
by astronauts in space.

5 To think, you can be orbiting
the earth while looking at
a teeming turtle, dolphin, whale
and porpoise habitat.

6 Your eyes will tell the story
and you will not doubt its moral:
There's hardly anything on earth
more beautiful than coral.

—Robert Schechter

> **idle** If something is referred to as idle, it is not doing anything. An idle boast is bragging about something that cannot happen.

myNotes

49

 TARGETED CLOSE READ

Author's Craft

What words tell how the poet feels about the Great Barrier Reef? Cite evidence from the poem to show how his voice comes through. (*The poet feels a sense of awe about the Great Barrier Reef. He uses words such as* great, awesome, *and* beautiful.)

ANNOTATION TIP: Have students highlight words or phrases that tell how the speaker feels about the Great Barrier Reef.

DOK 2

READ FOR UNDERSTANDING

Ask and Answer Questions

What questions do you have while reading the poem? (*Responses may include: What does the author mean when he says that you don't need to dive to see the reef?*) **How did you answer your questions?** (*Responses may include: I read on to understand that you can view the reef from space because he mentions the reef being visible to astronauts.*)

If students have difficulty thinking of a question, use this model:

> **THINK ALOUD** *As I read, I need to ask questions about things I'm unsure of. When I read about looking at the reef without getting wet, I wonder how I could do that, so I read on to answer my question.*

DOK 2

1 The Mariana Trench is the lowest point in the world. It lies beneath the deep waters of the Pacific Ocean. The first people to explore the Mariana Trench were Don Walsh and Jacques Piccard. They traveled in a steel capsule made to withstand the crushing pressure, tens of thousands of feet below the sea.

The Mariana Trench

Western Pacific Ocean, east of the Mariana Islands

2 In all the oceans, nowhere else so deep,
So dark with secrets men won't let it keep:
It yields to human eyes in submarines
And then, full of itself, goes back to sleep.

3 You wouldn't dream that hidden at its core
Life would go on as it has done for more
Than most of time, though seven heavy miles
Of water press down upon its floor.

4 To fathom it at last, to put on show
All that it holds, laid out in a neat row,
May happen sooner than to do that to
The mind of someone whom you think you know.

—X.J. Kennedy

> **core** The core of something is its center.
> **fathom** If you fathom something, you understand it.

1 Located in the Himalayas in South Asia, Mount Everest is 29,035 feet above sea level, which makes it the highest peak in the world. Everest was formed when the Indian tectonic plate pushed against the Asian plate. Each year, Everest grows a little over an eighth of an inch. This is due to the fact that the Indian plate continues to move against the Asian plate.

2 In the 1920s, British expeditions made multiple attempts to climb to the top of Mount Everest. On May 29th, 1953, Sir Edmund Hillary and Tenzing Norgay were the first recorded people to make it to the summit. However, British explorers George Mallory and Andrew Irvine may have reached the summit first. In 1924, they disappeared while attempting the climb. To this day, no one knows whether or not they made it to the summit.

— myNotes

Mount Everest

Himalaya Mountains, on the border between Tibet and Nepal in Asia

3   Eyes
        travel up
       to the skies,
     following the path
    of the mountain's rise;
    the wind's wrath whips
  through our tents, as my heart skips
  and trips. We hush our fears through the night;
 rushing gusts of wind and snow frighten us in jest, as we wait
for that warming sight, the morning light, and continue this quest,
to a point higher than the rest, a height that will be conquered by only the best,
the strength of muscle will be put to test—to climb to the top of Mount Everest.

—Carol R. Baik

wrath   Wrath is strong anger.

 TARGETED CLOSE READ

Author's Craft

How does the poet use imagery to tell you about the experience of climbing Mount Everest? *(The poet uses imagery to tell how the mountain climbers felt and what they thought as they climbed Mount Everest.)*

ANNOTATION TIP: Have students highlight the words and phrases in the poem that express the feelings and thoughts of the mountain climbers.

DOK 3

TARGETED CLOSE READ

Elements of Poetry

What is the subject of the poem on page 51? *(climbing Mount Everest)*
How is the poem arranged? *(The lines form a triangle or cone, from the longest line at the bottom to the top word. The rhyming words appear within the lines instead of at the ends of them.)*
What is the effect of this arrangement? *(The arrangement mirrors the shape of the poem's topic: Mount Everest.)*

ANNOTATION TIP: Have students trace a line around the shape of the poem to highlight its triangular shape.

DOK 3

myNotes

READ FOR UNDERSTANDING

What details are the same in the text and the poem? What details are different? (*Both tell how the Aurora Borealis looks. The text explains that the Aurora Borealis happens when electrically charged particles from the sun enter the atmosphere.*)

DOK 2

READ FOR UNDERSTANDING

Ask and Answer Questions

What questions do you have as you read this poem? How are you able to answer your questions? (*Responses may include: How can there be a curtain in the sky? I read on and learned that the curtain is a curtain of lights, not an actual curtain.*)

DOK 2

READ FOR UNDERSTANDING

Wrap-Up

Revisit the purpose students set before they read the selection. Have students explain what they learned, and have them cite evidence from the text and the poems.

DOK 2

1 The shifting, flickering lights of the Aurora Borealis are a wonder to see. The light show of the Aurora Borealis comes from the **collision** between electrically charged particles from the sun as they enter the earth's atmosphere. Typically seen near the northern polar region, some of the best places to view the Aurora Borealis in North America are Alaska and the Canadian Yukon.

Aurora Borealis

2 Over the shores of Labrador
a certain rippling purple curtain
scatters light throughout the night.
(Wait—the color's now a duller
hue of violet-turning-blue!)
This arctic veil, a breaching whale
could peer behind, and still be blind
as anyone. The northern sun
has bent to drape her gauzy cape
across the skies, and left my eyes
to stare and stare at the glittering air.

—Steven Withrow

collision   A collision happens when a moving object crashes into something.

Collaborative Discussion

Nature's Wonders

Look back at what you wrote on page 46. Tell a partner two things you learned in this text. Then work with a group to discuss the questions below. Use *Nature's Wonders* to support your ideas. Take notes for your responses. When you speak, use your notes.

1 Reread the poem "The Great Barrier Reef." How does the poet feel about the reef? How do you know?

2 Review the poem "Aurora Borealis." What images do the speaker's words create in your mind?

3 How does the informational passage with each poem add to your understanding?

 Listening Tip

Listen to each speaker's ideas. What questions do they raise in your mind?

Speaking Tip

Ask questions related to what another speaker has said. Listen carefully to the responses, and add your own ideas.

Academic Discussion

Use the **COLLABORATIVE DISCUSSION** routine. Have students write responses to the questions. Then have groups apply the Listening and Speaking Tips as they discuss their responses.

Possible responses:

1. *The author repeats the line, "It's sixteen hundred miles long" to show how important the size of the reef is. It got its name as the **Great** Barrier Reef because it is "the world's largest system of coral reefs." In this case, great means "massive or humongous." The author feels that this reef is an awesome place to look at, whether you are diving in it or looking at it from space.* DOK 2

2. *I can visualize the colors changing from purple to violet and then to blue before my eyes. The Aurora Borealis is described, through the use of metaphors, as a curtain, a cape, and a veil, covering the sky, so I can picture that as well.* DOK 3

3. *The informational passages help me understand each poem, which in turn, helps me enjoy them more. I am not sure that I would understand the poems without this helpful information.* DOK 2

53

Write an Opinion Paragraph

PROMPT

In *Nature's Wonders,* you read poems and some facts about four natural wonders.

Imagine that your class has a literature blog. Write an opinion paragraph about the natural wonder you feel is the most amazing. Include a statement describing how the poem about that natural wonder supports your opinion. Support your reasons with specific details from the poem and the informational text. Be sure to use some of the Critical Vocabulary words in your writing.

PLAN

Create a web with words describing the natural wonder you choose. Include words or phrases from the poem and informational text that support your opinion that this natural wonder is the most amazing.

WRITE

Now write your opinion paragraph about the most amazing natural wonder.

Make sure your opinion paragraph

- [ ] clearly states your opinion.

- [ ] provides reasons from the text that support your opinion about your chosen natural wonder.

- [ ] links your opinion and reasons with words and phrases such as *for instance, in order to,* and *in addition.*

- [ ] provides a concluding sentence that is related to your opinion.

Write About Reading

- **Review with students** the directions and checklist in the Write section.

- **Encourage students** to use their own words as they write details from the poem and informational text to support their opinions.

READ FOR UNDERSTANDING

Introduce the Text

- **Read aloud** and discuss the genre information. Point out that literary nonfiction uses literary techniques, such as figurative language, to tell a true story. Literary nonfiction texts tell an accurate story in chronological order and often use scientific words that relate to the topic.

- Use Display and Engage Meet the Author 6.11.

- **Tell students** to look for the Critical Vocabulary as they read, and to think about the words' meanings.

ANNOTATION TIP: Have students use the box to note what they want to learn from this selection.

Prepare to Read and View

GENRE STUDY **Literary nonfiction** tells a factually accurate story using literary techniques.

- Literary nonfiction presents events in sequential, or chronological, order.

- Science texts include words that are specific to the topic.

- Authors of literary nonfiction may use figurative language such as similes and metaphors to describe real places or events.

SET A PURPOSE **Look through** the images in this selection. What images interest you the most? What would you like to learn about these parts of the Grand Canyon? Write your ideas below.

Meet the Author:
Linda Vieira
Meet the Illustrator:
Christopher Canyon

CRITICAL VOCABULARY

shatter

sentries

chasm

glistens

embedded

eroding

GRAND CANYON

A Trail Through Time

by Linda Vieira

illustrations by
Christopher Canyon

 READ FOR UNDERSTANDING

Set a Purpose

- **Have students** look at the first few pages of *Grand Canyon: A Trail Through Time* to note some of the plants and animals they see in the illustrations.

- **Guide students** to set a purpose for reading. Discuss with them what they think they will learn about the Grand Canyon from this selection.

DOK 2

57

READ FOR UNDERSTANDING

Where does this selection take place? *(It takes place in the Grand Canyon National Park.)*

How does the text begin like a story? *(The author uses a lot of descriptive words to set the scene and describe the storm.)*

DOK 2

1   Apredawn storm rumbles over Grand Canyon National Park. Cracks of lightning shatter the dark sky, flashing above an enormous plateau of peaks, valleys, and trenches where ancient mountains once stood. The deepest trench is called the Grand Canyon, one of the Seven Natural Wonders of the World.

shatter   When things shatter, they explode or suddenly break into pieces.

58

2 **D**awn comes, bringing daylight to spires and buttes standing like sentries on the plateau, worn down by weathering and erosion. Coyotes teach their pups to hunt for food in thick forests along the edges of the Canyon.

3 Thousands of visitors from all over the world have come to view the splendor of the Grand Canyon. In campgrounds and lodges near the north and south rims, they prepare for the day's activities.

sentries Sentries are guards or lookouts who stand in a place to keep watch.

myNotes

 READ FOR UNDERSTANDING

Make Inferences

MODEL MAKING AN INFERENCE

THINK ALOUD *When I make an inference, I use clues from the text and what I already know to draw a conclusion. I know **where** this narrative takes place—in the Grand Canyon. I also know that a key part of the setting is **when** the narrative takes place. In the illustration on page 59, I see two children and an adult who are dressed in modern-day clothing and who are carrying backpacks. I can infer, then, that this narrative takes place in the present day. I can tell that it's early one morning in the Grand Canyon, using the clues from paragraphs 1 and 2.*

TARGETED CLOSE READ

Author's Craft

What are two examples of how the author uses descriptive language to help readers picture the view of the Grand Canyon? *(The author uses the simile "Standing like sentries" to compare the buttes to soldiers keeping watch over the Canyon. I can picture tower-like rocks guarding the area around them. In paragraph 3, the mention of thousands of people as well as campgrounds and lodges helps me picture people getting their backpacks packed and ready for a hike.)*

DOK 3

59

READ FOR UNDERSTANDING

Make Inferences

Why do you think people take a pack mule down to the deepest part of the Canyon? *(Because it takes a mule five hours to get to the bottom. It would likely take longer for a hiker.)*

If students have difficulty making an inference, use this model:

Q **THINK ALOUD** *When I think about visiting the Grand Canyon, I think about hiking, so I was surprised to learn that people actually take a mule down instead. Although the author doesn't say exactly why people take a mule instead of hiking, I can infer that the hike is a difficult one.*

DOK 3

Q TARGETED CLOSE READ

Author's Craft

Have students reread paragraph 5.
How does the author use sensory language to help you visualize what is happening in the text?
(Instead of saying that the sun rises, the author talks about it chasing shadows away. This language helps me picture what is happening. Also, the author describes the path to the riverbed as a "twisted, ten-mile trail." This helps me visualize how difficult the trek into the Canyon is.)

DOK 2

60

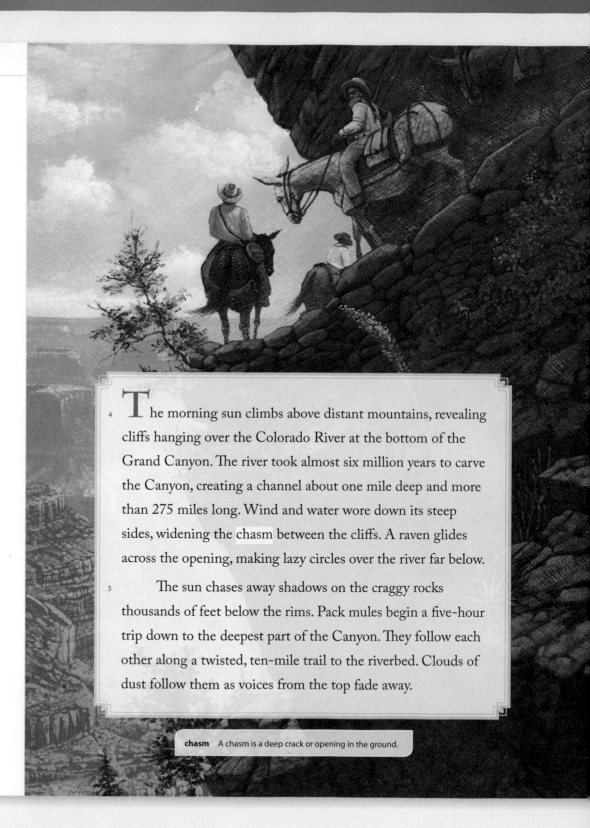

4 The morning sun climbs above distant mountains, revealing cliffs hanging over the Colorado River at the bottom of the Grand Canyon. The river took almost six million years to carve the Canyon, creating a channel about one mile deep and more than 275 miles long. Wind and water wore down its steep sides, widening the chasm between the cliffs. A raven glides across the opening, making lazy circles over the river far below.

5 The sun chases away shadows on the craggy rocks thousands of feet below the rims. Pack mules begin a five-hour trip down to the deepest part of the Canyon. They follow each other along a twisted, ten-mile trail to the riverbed. Clouds of dust follow them as voices from the top fade away.

chasm A chasm is a deep crack or opening in the ground.

6 Canyon visitors along the trail peer with curiosity at symbols of people and animals that were painted on a boulder by Havasupai Indians long ago. Havasupai still live in the Canyon today, tending their flocks and farms in the summertime, hunting small game and gathering nuts and berries in the winter months.

7 As the sun moves higher in the sky, smaller side canyons with rocks layered like multicolored ribbons come into view. Bighorn sheep walk easily along the steep walls of the canyons, looking for food in hidden pockets of soil. Wildflowers stand around them in patches of purple and pink.

TARGETED CLOSE READ

Ideas and Support

How does the author use evidence to support the ideas presented about the Havasupai Indians? *(The author talks about paintings that were made on a boulder by the Havasupai tribe a long time ago. She then presents evidence that the tribe still lives in the Canyon today. She tells of how they farm, hunt, gather, and tend to their flocks.)*

DOK 2

🔍 **TARGETED CLOSE READ**

Simile and Metaphor

Have students reread page 61 to find an example of a simile.

Identify a simile on page 61. What is compared with this figurative language? *(In paragraph 7, there is a simile: "smaller side canyons with rocks layered like multicolored ribbons." It compares the rocks to colorful layers of ribbon using the word like.)*

ANNOTATION TIP: Have students underline the sentence that has a simile.

DOK 2

61

Marvels of Nature **61**

READ FOR UNDERSTANDING

What does the trail show visitors about the history of the Grand Canyon? *(The layers of rocks along the trail show riders millions of years of geological history. Riders can see fossils of fish teeth and seashells in the rocks.)*

DOK 2

🔍 **TARGETED CLOSE READ**

Ideas and Support

What evidence supports the idea that the layers of rock on the trail have been around for millions of years? *(The author tells readers that a canyon wren flies "past fossils of fish teeth and seashells." This evidence confirms the fact that these layers of rock show the history of the Canyon since I know that fossils are from very long ago.)*

DOK 2

62

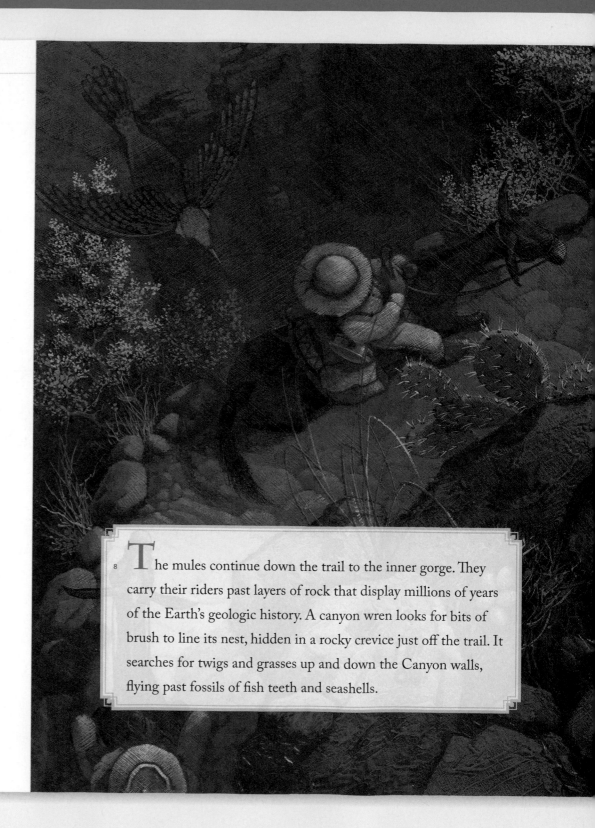

8 The mules continue down the trail to the inner gorge. They carry their riders past layers of rock that display millions of years of the Earth's geologic history. A canyon wren looks for bits of brush to line its nest, hidden in a rocky crevice just off the trail. It searches for twigs and grasses up and down the Canyon walls, flying past fossils of fish teeth and seashells.

myNotes

The noonday sun glistens on a hidden creek near a granary built into the Canyon wall by Anasazi Indians almost 1,000 years ago. Squirrels chase through the now-empty granary, where crops and plants had been stored for food and trade.

¹⁰ A lizard scurries off the trail. It climbs over fossils of prehistoric trilobites, embedded in layers of shale millions of years ago when the land was covered by a primeval sea. After the mules pass, the lizard creeps out from its hiding place to soak up the warmth of the sun.

glistens If something glistens, it sparkles or shines.
embedded If a thing is embedded, it is firmly set into something else that surrounds it.

63

 READ FOR UNDERSTANDING

What does the word *granary* mean? *(a place where plants and crops are stored)*

ANNOTATION TIP: Have students highlight the sentence that explains what a *granary* is.

DOK 1

TARGETED CLOSE READ

Author's Craft

Have students reread paragraph 10, looking for sensory words that contribute to the author's voice or style of writing.

What words does the author use that help you see how lizards act in the Canyon? *(The words* scurries *and* creeps *help me to understand that the lizards are busy animals that seem to be more timid around the other animals.)*

DOK 2

64

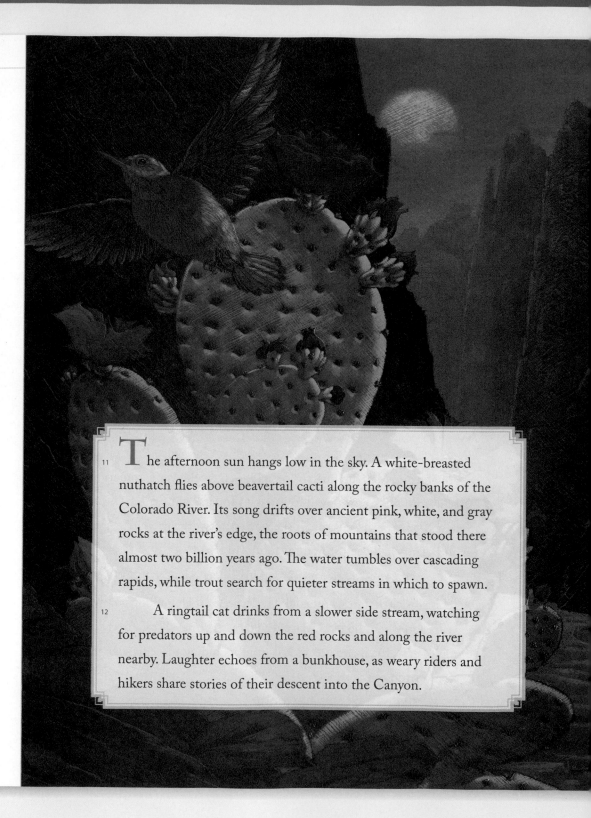

11 The afternoon sun hangs low in the sky. A white-breasted nuthatch flies above beavertail cacti along the rocky banks of the Colorado River. Its song drifts over ancient pink, white, and gray rocks at the river's edge, the roots of mountains that stood there almost two billion years ago. The water tumbles over cascading rapids, while trout search for quieter streams in which to spawn.

12 A ringtail cat drinks from a slower side stream, watching for predators up and down the red rocks and along the river nearby. Laughter echoes from a bunkhouse, as weary riders and hikers share stories of their descent into the Canyon.

13 The endless cycles of eroding rock and moving water carved the Grand Canyon millions of years ago. Blustering wind and pounding rain continue to widen it, grinding down rocks that used to be mountains and volcanoes. The rushing Colorado River deepens this natural wonder, dragging rocks and mud along its path through ancient plains and lava flows.

eroding If something is eroding, it is slowly wearing away, often from wind or water.

65

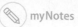
14 The mules rest for the night in a corral near the river, awaiting tomorrow's seven-hour trip back up to the top. Weather and erosion make tiny changes every day in the rocky walls along the trail. Millions of years into the future, the same forces of nature will continue to reshape the Grand Canyon, digging even deeper into the history of our planet.

 READ FOR UNDERSTANDING

Make Inferences

What inference can you make after reading paragraph 14?
(Responses may include: If I were to visit the Grand Canyon in the future, it would look very different than it does now.)

What text evidence supports your inference? (The author says that nature will continue to reshape the Canyon.)

DOK 3

 READ FOR UNDERSTANDING

Wrap-Up

Revisit the purpose students set before they read the text. Have students summarize the selection in order. Have them tell what they learned about the Grand Canyon, citing text evidence.

DOK 2

66

Collaborative Discussion

Look back at what you wrote on page 56. Tell a partner two things you learned from this text. Take notes to answer the questions below. Refer to details and examples in *Grand Canyon: A Trail Through Time* to explain your answers. Then work with a group to discuss the questions. When you speak, use your notes.

1 Reread page 60. How big is the Grand Canyon? Why did it take so many years to form?

2 What plants and animals might you see living in the Canyon?

3 How have moving water and erosion worked together to create the Grand Canyon?

Listening Tip

Don't do all the talking! Notice when others in your group have not shared their opinions and ideas, and ask them to do so.

Speaking Tip

Add new ideas to the conversation, speaking loudly enough so that everyone can hear easily.

Academic Discussion

Use the **COLLABORATIVE DISCUSSION** routine. Have students write responses to the questions. Then have groups apply the Listening and Speaking Tips as they discuss their responses.

Possible responses:

1. *The Grand Canyon is over 275 miles long and one mile deep. It took almost six million years for water and wind to wear down the sides of the cliffs to create this Canyon. It took so long because the wind and rain had to grind away mountains.* DOK 3

2. *Anasazi Indians lived in the Canyon a thousand years ago. Today, Havasupai Indians still live there along with many animals: ravens, bighorn sheep, canyon wrens, squirrels, lizards, nuthatches, ringtail cats. Coyotes live near the edge of the Canyon. Also, mules carry tourists up and down the Canyon each day.* DOK 2

3. *Millions of years ago, moving water and wind eroded rock to carve out the Canyon in endless cycles. Pounding rain and intense winds grind the rocks still. The rushing waters of the Colorado River drag rocks and mud through the Canyon, which continues to deepen it even further.* DOK 2

67

Write a Travel Guide

PROMPT

Did reading *Grand Canyon* make you want to visit and experience its wonders for yourself? If so, you're not alone. More than five million people visit the Grand Canyon every year.

Use what you learned from the text to write a travel guide for people who would like to visit the Grand Canyon. Provide information about what they can see and do, as well as facts about the canyon itself. Remember that a travel guide should encourage people to visit the location. Include a drawing or map to make your guide more interesting and informative. Don't forget to include some of the Critical Vocabulary words in your writing.

PLAN

Make notes about the features of the Grand Canyon using some of the sensory words in the selection. Think about features that might attract visitors to the Grand Canyon.

Now write your travel guide about the Grand Canyon.

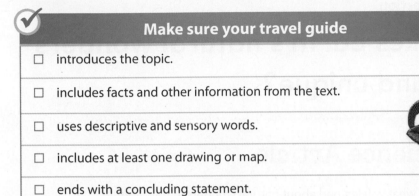

Make sure your travel guide
☐ introduces the topic.
☐ includes facts and other information from the text.
☐ uses descriptive and sensory words.
☐ includes at least one drawing or map.
☐ ends with a concluding statement.

Revisit the Essential Question

• **Read aloud** the Essential Question.

• **Remind students** that the texts in this module about Earth's natural wonders can help them answer the question.

Write a Science Article

• **Guide students** to think about what they learned about natural wonders in this module.

• **Review the features** of a science article using the checklist. Tell students to use the checklist as they draft, revise, and edit their articles.

? Essential Question

What makes Earth's natural wonders exciting and unique?

Write a Science Article

PROMPT Think about what you learned about natural wonders in this module.

Imagine that you are writing an article for a science magazine for kids about Earth's natural wonders. Choose two natural wonders you read about in this module. Explain how these unique places were formed. Be sure to use evidence from the texts. In your article, compare and contrast the ways in which the two natural wonders were formed.

I will write about _____.

✓ **Make sure your article**

☐ provides an introduction that states the topic clearly.

☐ supports each central idea with facts, details, and examples from the texts.

☐ groups related information into paragraphs.

☐ uses linking words and phrases, such as *also, in addition, but*, and *however,* to show similarities and differences.

☐ has a conclusion that sums up the information.

What details from the selections will help you compare and contrast the natural forces that shaped each place? Review your notes and look back at the texts as necessary.

As you plan, look for details about the how each natural wonder was formed. Think about which details are the same and which are different. Use a Venn diagram to record your information.

My topic: _____

Plan

- **As needed, guide students** to think of details that will help them compare and contrast the formation of each natural wonder.

- **Encourage them** to use information from the texts they read in this module as they complete the Venn diagram.

- **Encourage students** to include Big Idea Words and Critical Vocabulary in their articles, as appropriate.

_____   **Both**   _____

71

DRAFT ·· **Write your article.**

Write a strong **introduction** that clearly states your central idea and lets readers know what your article will be about.

Draft

- **Read aloud** the directions, referring back to the checklist as you do so.

- **Suggest** that students tell the two natural wonders they will be comparing, if they are having trouble generating an introduction.

- **Have students** refer to their Venn diagrams to construct sentences about how two of the natural wonders they read about were uniquely formed.

In the **body paragraph**, use your Venn diagram to explain how the two natural wonders were formed. Use facts and details from the texts.

In your **conclusion,** restate your overall central idea.

REVISE AND EDIT · Review your draft.

The revision and editing steps give you a chance to look carefully at your draft and make changes. Work with a partner to determine whether you have explained your ideas clearly. Use these questions to help you evaluate and improve your article.

PURPOSE/ FOCUS	ORGANIZATION	EVIDENCE	LANGUAGE/ VOCABULARY	CONVENTIONS
☐ Does my article state a clear central idea? ☐ Have I stayed on topic?	☐ Does my article have a clear introduction? ☐ Have I provided a strong conclusion?	☐ Does the text evidence from the selections support my ideas?	☐ Did I use linking words to show how ideas are similar and different?	☐ Have I spelled all the words correctly? ☐ Did I use prepositions correctly? ☐ Did I use correct capitalization?

PUBLISH · Share your work.

Create a Finished Copy Make a neatly written final copy of your science article. You may wish to include photos or illustrations. Consider these options to share your writing:

1 Post your article on a school or class science blog and ask for feedback from your classmates.

2 Add your article to a *Natural Wonders* magazine in the classroom.

3 Give an oral presentation of your article to your class. Use visuals to support your presentation.

Revise and Edit

- **Guide students** to use the checklist as they work with partners to improve their articles.

- **Remind students** to refer back to the texts in the module to be sure their details are accurate.

Present

- **Students can copy** their revised drafts using their best handwriting. For handwriting models, see the resources section in the back of this Teacher's Guide.

- **Students can use** a computer to input their revised drafts. See Literacy Centers Printable **Keyboarding 6.1, 6.2, and 6.3** for keyboarding lessons.

73

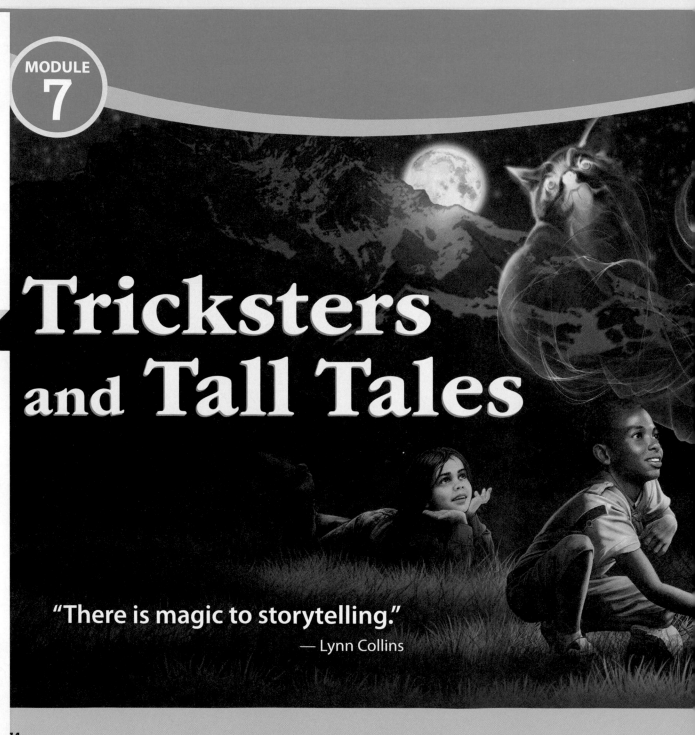

MODULE 7

Tricksters and Tall Tales

"There is magic to storytelling."

— Lynn Collins

Introduce the Topic

- **Read aloud** the module title, *Tricksters and Tall Tales.*

- **Tell students** that in this module they will be reading and viewing selections about traditional tales.

- **Have students** tell what they know about traditional tales.

- Then ask students to name the types of traditional tales they predict they will read in this module. *(trickster tales and tall tales)* Then ask students to name any trickster tales or tall tales they have read previously.

Discuss the Quotation

- **Read aloud** the quotation by Lynn Collins.

- **Lead a discussion** with students about storytelling. Have students tell whether or not they agree with the quote and provide reasons for their opinions. *(Responses will vary. Example: I agree that there is magic to storytelling because it takes an author's talents to tell stories where readers are transported to other time periods and can get inside the minds of characters to understand their views.)*

- **Have students** name authors that they enjoy reading and who, in their opinions, have mastered the magic of telling stories. Encourage students to share examples of ways those authors have shown their talents in storytelling.

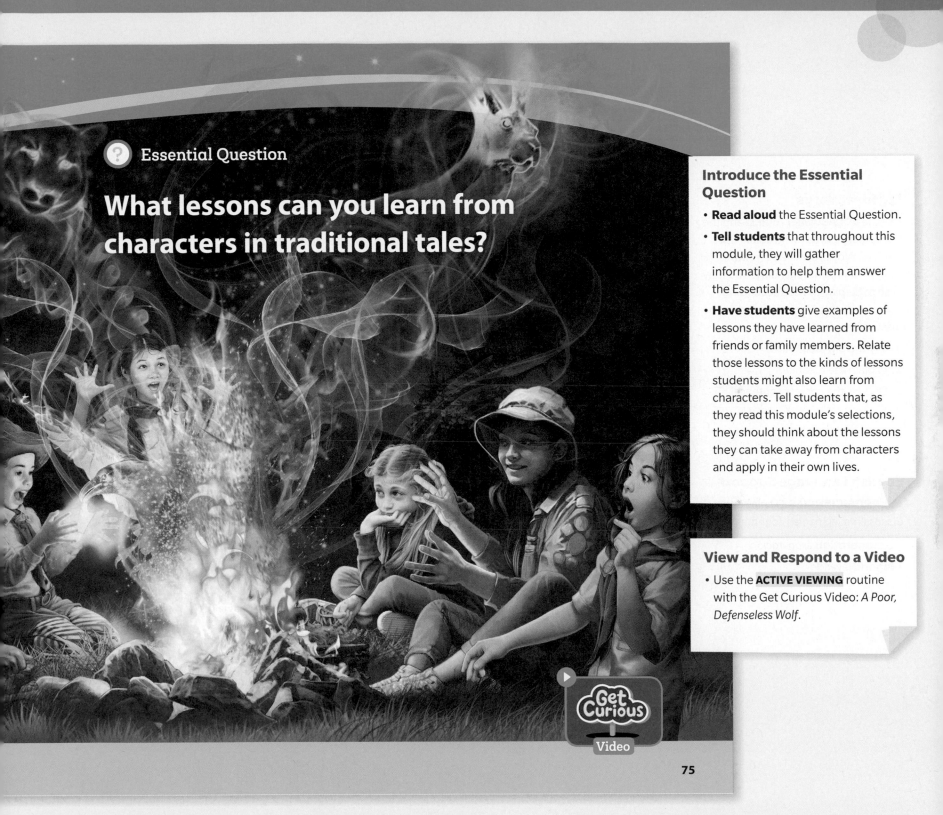

Essential Question

What lessons can you learn from characters in traditional tales?

Introduce the Essential Question

- **Read aloud** the Essential Question.

- **Tell students** that throughout this module, they will gather information to help them answer the Essential Question.

- **Have students** give examples of lessons they have learned from friends or family members. Relate those lessons to the kinds of lessons students might also learn from characters. Tell students that, as they read this module's selections, they should think about the lessons they can take away from characters and apply in their own lives.

View and Respond to a Video

- Use the **ACTIVE VIEWING** routine with the Get Curious Video: *A Poor, Defenseless Wolf.*

Get Curious Video

75

Words About Traditional Stories

The words in the chart will help you talk and write about the selections in this module. Which words about traditional stories have you seen before? Which words are new to you?

Add to the Vocabulary Network on page 77 by writing synonyms, antonyms, and related words and phrases for each word about traditional stories.

After you read each selection in this module, come back to the Vocabulary Network and keep building it. Add more ovals if you need to.

WORD	MEANING	CONTEXT SENTENCE
trickster (noun)	A trickster is a character who deceives or tricks others, usually to get something from them.	The fox is often portrayed as a crafty trickster in folktales.
shrewd (adjective)	Someone who is shrewd is able to quickly understand a situation to gain an advantage.	Her shrewd decisions helped us get out of a difficult situation.
exaggeration (noun)	An exaggeration describes something as more important or larger than what it really is.	Saying that your sister is twice as tall as you are is an exaggeration.
legendary (adjective)	If something is legendary, it is very famous and has had many stories told about it.	Many people have read the legendary story of Hercules.

76

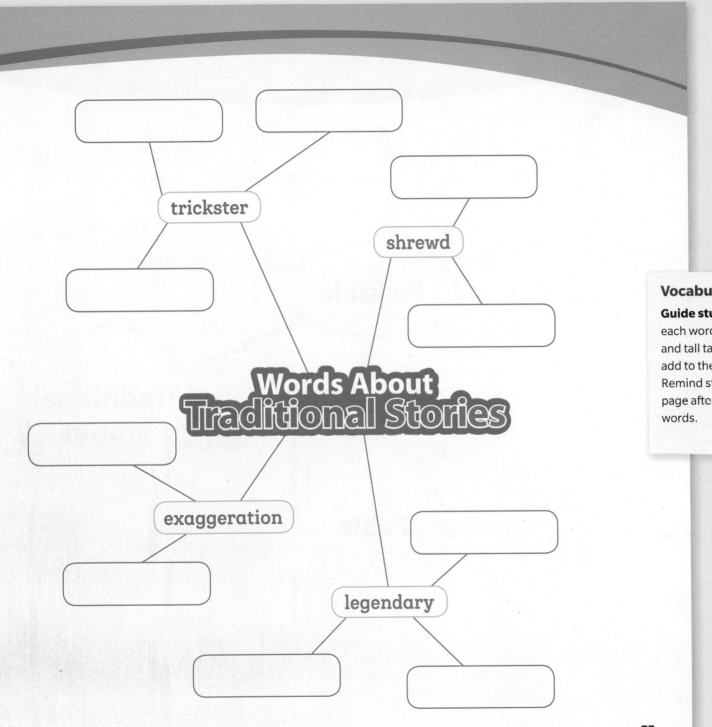

trickster

shrewd

Words About Traditional Stories

exaggeration

legendary

77

Knowledge Map

- **Review the categories** on the knowledge map with students. Explain that these categories name the concepts students will learn about in the module.

- **Have students** add information and illustrations to the knowledge map at the end of each week during Make Connections. Remind students to review the texts and video to add details to the map.

- At the end of the module, have students work in pairs or small groups to compare and contrast the information they added to their knowledge maps.

Folktale

Traditional Stories

Fable

78

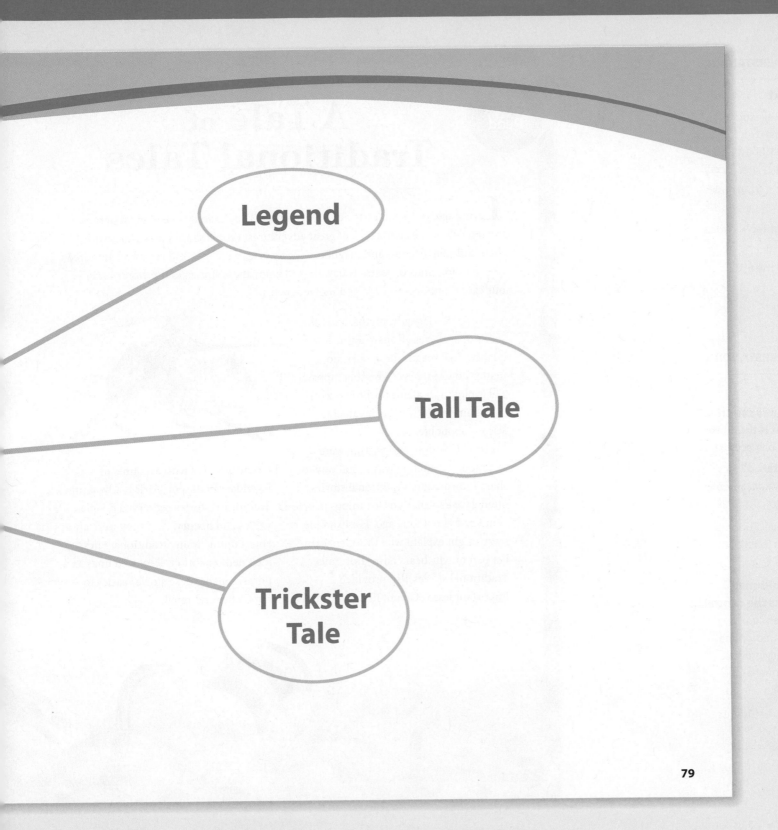

Legend

Tall Tale

Trickster
Tale

79

myNotes

Introduce the Text

Read aloud the title. Tell students that this is informational text. Discuss with students what they know about informational texts. *(They give facts.)*

- **Guide students** to set a purpose for reading.

- **Point out** the highlighted Big Idea Words.

- **Have students** read the text.

 READ FOR UNDERSTANDING

Central Idea

- **What is the topic of this selection?** *(traditional tales)* **What is the central idea?** *(timeless tales teach lessons)*

- **Is the central idea stated?** *(yes)* **Where?** *(in the first two paragraphs and the last paragraph)*

ANNOTATION TIP: Have students highlight the sentences that tell the central idea.

- **What is it about traditional stories that supports the central idea? Cite text evidence.** *(They existed before reading and writing were even invented. They provide entertainment, explanations, and teach life lessons.)*

ANNOTATION TIP: Have students underline the text evidence that supports the central idea.

DOK 3   **80**

Short Read

A Tale of Traditional Tales

1   Long ago, people told stories to each other. They shared tales of great heroes, of larger-than-life characters, of great adventures. People shared these tales with their children, friends, and neighbors. The stories were told and retold for hundreds or even thousands of years. Today, we still enjoy these stories in our libraries, in our classrooms, and on TV and movie screens.

2   Folktales, legends, myths, and other traditional stories all share a timeless quality. That means these tales, no matter how old, never lose their appeal. Their plots and themes continue to entertain people and teach valuable lessons about life.

3   Before reading and writing were invented, storytelling was a vital way to share information. Traditional stories often gave explanations for things people wondered about long ago. For example, a story might explain why thunderstorms happen or why bears have short tails. Traditional stories also provided important lessons about life. They might dazzle listeners with accounts of legendary battles or fearless adventurers. Traditional stories preserved people's values and history. And they were always entertaining. Many traditional tales included repetition. Repeated lines and phrases made these stories easier to remember and retell.

4   Today, we still share ancient traditional stories because of the lessons, or morals, they teach about life. The famous fables of the ancient Greek storyteller Aesop are often about animals, but they include morals that humans would be wise to keep in mind. In Aesop's "The Ants and the Grasshopper," hardworking ants gather food for the winter while their friend the grasshopper lazes about. When winter comes, however, the grasshopper has to beg the ants to share their food. The lesson seems clear and makes sense even today: Work hard and plan for the future—or else!

5   Traditional tales usually feature characters with traits we all can recognize. Some are wise, some are silly, some are greedy, and some are generous. The stories include **exaggeration** not only to entertain us but also to draw attention to extraordinary behavior. Larger-than-life traits hold a mirror to real human behavior. They teach readers the value of virtue and the dangers of acting badly.

6   One type of exaggerated character is the **trickster**. The trickster is usually a **shrewd**, or clever, fun-loving animal character who loves to play tricks on others. Sometimes, the trickster is the one who gets tricked. Either way, the trickster always teaches a valuable lesson.

7   The humor and life lessons in traditional tales make them just as relevant today as they were long ago and will be in the future. Which one is your favorite?

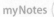 **READ FOR UNDERSTANDING**

Central Idea

- **What text evidence about fables supports the central idea?** *(Many of these ancient tales are still told today because of the morals or lessons that they teach.)*

ANNOTATION TIP: Have students underline the text evidence that supports the central idea.

DOK 2

  READ FOR UNDERSTANDING

Central Idea

- **How does the author organize the text to support the central idea?** *(Paragraph 3 focuses on traditional stories, while paragraph 4 is about fables. The fifth paragraph talks about character traits and exaggeration used in traditional tales. The next paragraph focuses on trickster characters and the last paragraph summarizes the text. All of these paragraphs together support the central idea.)*

DOK 2

81

**Notice &
Note**
Again and Again

 READ FOR UNDERSTANDING

Introduce the Text

- **Read aloud** and discuss the genre information. Point out that tall tales are exaggerated stories that include main characters with super-human abilities. Explain that students should look for unbelievable solutions to problems as well as numerous exaggerations of both characters and events.

- **Have students look** at the illustration and explain anything they notice that fits with the tall tale genre. (*I notice that the character has unusually long braids.*)

- Use Display and Engage **Meet the Author and Illustrator 7.2**.

- **Tell students** to look for the Critical Vocabulary as they read, and to think about the words' meanings.

ANNOTATION TIP: Have students use the box to note what they would like to know about the main character in the story.

DOK 2

Prepare to Read

GENRE STUDY **Tall tales** are exaggerated stories that are meant to be entertaining.

- Tall tales include a main character who is larger than life and who often has super-human abilities.

- The main character in a tall tale solves problems in a funny way that is hard to believe.

- Authors of tall tales use exaggerated descriptions of characters and events.

SET A PURPOSE **Think about** what you know about tall tales. What are some things you'd like to know about the main character in this story? Write your ideas below.

Meet the Author:
Jerdine Nolen
Meet the Illustrator:
Kadir Nelson

CRITICAL VOCABULARY

recall

vividly

accentuated

partial

splendor

resourceful

disposition

commendable

devastation

82

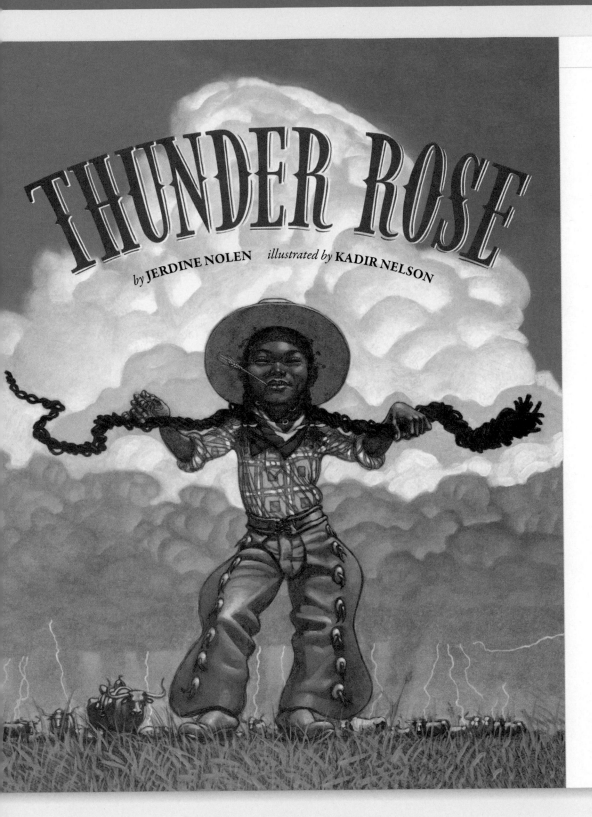

THUNDER ROSE

by JERDINE NOLEN   *illustrated by* KADIR NELSON

myNotes

 READ FOR UNDERSTANDING

Set a Purpose

- **Have students** read the title and look at the illustrations through page 85.

What kind of character do you think Thunder Rose is? Explain with evidence from the illustrations. *(I think she's a tough character. The look on her face and the way she is standing make her look tough. The illustrations show a lot of thunder and lightning, so that must have something to do with her name.)*

- **Guide students** to set a purpose for reading. Discuss with them what they think this selection will be about.

DOK 2

83

1   Rose was the first child born free and easy to Jackson and Millicent MacGruder. I recall most vividly the night she came into this world. Hailing rain, flashing lightning, and booming thunder pounded the door, inviting themselves in for the blessed event.

2   Taking in her first breath of life, the infant did not cry out. Rather, she sat up and looked around. She took hold of that lightning, rolled it into a ball, and set it above her shoulder, while the thunder echoed out over the other. They say this just accentuated the fact that the child had the power of thunder and lightning coursing through her veins.

3   "She's going to grow up to be good and strong, all right," Doc Hollerday said.

4   The child turned to the good doctor with a thoughtful glance and replied, "I reckon I will want to do more than that. Thank you very kindly!"

> **recall** If you recall something, you tell about something you remember.
> **vividly** If you remember something vividly, you have a clear, detailed memory of it.
> **accentuated** If something is accentuated, it has attention drawn to it.

84

READ FOR UNDERSTANDING

What do Rose's ma and pa do to show how happy they are about their baby girl's birth? *(They watch over Rose, and they sing her a lullaby from "the beginning of time." They do this because they are so overcome with love for her.)*

ANNOTATION TIP: Have students underline the text evidence that show ma's and pa's happiness.

DOK 2

5   Shifting her gaze to the two loving lights shining on her, which were her ma and pa, she remarked, "Much obliged to you both for this chance to make my way in the world!" Then she announced to no one in particular, "I am right partial to the name Rose."

6   So much in love with this gift of their lives, her ma and pa hovered over her in watchful splendor. Overcome with that love, they lifted their voices in song, an old song and a melody so sweet and true—a lullaby passed down from the ages, echoing since the beginning of time.

READ FOR UNDERSTANDING

Retell/Summarize

MODEL RETELLING

 THINK ALOUD *I will retell or summarize what has happened so far in this story. A baby girl named Rose is born during a thunderstorm. Rose is healthy and strong. She seems to have extraordinary abilities because she can already sit up and talk.*

> **partial**   If you are partial to something, you prefer it more than other things.
> **splendor**   The splendor of something is its great beauty or impressive appearance.

85

READ FOR UNDERSTANDING

What does the illustration show you about the characters?
(The shocked expressions of the doctor, ma, and pa make me think that they are surprised by Rose. She is sitting up even though she was just born. Also, she has just spoken to all of them. That makes me think she has some extraordinary abilities.)

DOK 2

🔍 **TARGETED CLOSE READ**

Figurative Language

Have students reread paragraph 8.

What does the phrase "rattling the rafters" mean? *(It means that someone or something is making a sound or a noise that is so loud that one might think the roof will shake. Rose is snoring so loudly on her first night that it seems to her parents that the beams in the roof are shaking.)* **What kind of figurative language is this?** *(exaggeration; no one snores loudly enough to rattle the roof)*

DOK 3

86

myNotes ✏

7   "There is a music ringing so sweetly in my ears," the newborn exclaimed. "It's giving me a fortunate feeling rumbling deep in the pit of me. I'll register it here at the bull's-eye set in the center of my heart, and see what I can do with it one day!"

8   Rose snored up plenty that first night breathing on her own, rattling the rafters on the roof right along with the booming thunder. There was nothing quiet about her slumber. She seemed determined to be just as forceful as that storm. With the thunder and lightning keeping watch over her the rest of the night, her ma and pa just took to calling her Thunder Rose.

9   The next morning, when the sun was high yellow in that billowy blue sky, Rose woke up hungry as a bear in spring, but not the least bit ornery. Minding her manners, she politely thanked her ma for the milk, but it was not enough to quench her hungry thirst. Rose preferred, instead, to drink her milk straight from the cow.

TARGETED CLOSE READ

Figurative Language

What simile does the author use in paragraph 9? (*"Rose woke up hungry as a bear in spring."*) **Why is this comparison a good choice to describe Rose?** *(In spring, bears wake up from their winter sleep. Comparing Rose's hunger to that of a bear in spring shows that she is very hungry.)*

What exaggeration, or hyperbole, does the author use in this paragraph? *(Rose drinks milk straight from the cow.)*

ANNOTATION TIP: Have students highlight the simile in the text. Tell them to highlight other similes they may find in the text as they read further.

DOK 2

📖 READ FOR UNDERSTANDING

What more do you learn about Rose? How does she get her nickname? *(Rose does not sleep very quietly. She is a very hungry and thirsty baby and likes to drink her milk directly from the cow. She is also polite and determined. She is named Thunder Rose because there was a huge storm on the night she was born.)*

ANNOTATION TIP: Have students underline sentences that tell more about Rose and explain how she got her nickname.

DOK 1

10   Her ma was right grateful to have such a resourceful child. No other newborn had the utter strength to lift a whole cow clear over her head and almost drink it dry. In a moment's time, Rose did, and quite daintily so. She was as pretty as a picture, had the sweetest disposition, but don't let yourself be misled, that child was full of lightning *and* thunder.

11   Out on that paper-bag brown, dusty dry, wide-open space, Rose often was found humming a sweet little tune as she did her chores. And true to her word, Rose did *more* than grow good and strong.

12   The two-year-old became quite curious about the pile of scrap iron lying next to the barn. Rose took a good-sized piece, stretched it here, bent and twisted it there. She constructed a thunderbolt as black as pitch to punctuate her name. She called it Cole. Wherever she went, Cole was always by her side. Noticing how skilled Rose was with the metal, her pa made sure there was an extra supply of it always around.

13   At the age of five, Rose did a commendable job of staking the fence without a bit of help. During her eighth and ninth years, Rose assembled some iron beams together with the wood blocks she used to play with and constructed a building tall enough to scrape the sky, always humming as she worked.

14   By the time she turned twelve, Rose had perfected her metal-bending practices. She formed delicately shaped alphabet letters to help the young ones learn to read.

resourceful	If you are resourceful, you are good at solving problems quickly.
disposition	Your disposition is the way you tend to act or feel.
commendable	If you do something commendable, you do it well and earn praise.

For his birthday, Rose presented her pa with a branding iron, a circle with a big *M-A-C* for MacGruder in the middle, just in time, too, because a herd of quick-tempered longhorn steer was stampeding its way up from the Rio Grande. They were plowing a path straight toward her front door.

15   Rose performed an eye-catching wonder, the likes of which was something to see. Running lightning-fast toward the herd, using Cole for support, Rose vaulted into the air and landed on the back of the biggest lead steer like he was a merry-go-round pony. Grabbing a horn in each hand, Rose twisted that varmint to a complete halt. It was just enough to restrain that top bull and the rest of the herd.

 READ FOR UNDERSTANDING

What are the cause-and-effect relationships in the last paragraph? *(The lead steer halts (effect) because Rose jumps on its back and is able to control it (cause). The steer halting then causes the entire herd to stop (effect), instead of destroying the family ranch in a stampede.)*

ANNOTATION TIP: Have students highlight examples of cause and effect in the text.

DOK 3

89

Retell/Summarize

Retell what has happened since the herd stampeded toward Rose's front door. *(Rose uses her super-strength abilities to stop the stampede and make a pen to hold the steer.)*

If students have difficulty retelling/summarizing, use this model:

 THINK ALOUD *There are many details that explain what Rose does, but when I summarize, I focus on just the main ideas. The main idea is that Rose stops the stampede and makes a pen to keep the steers in. Rose's super-human abilities help save the day.*

DOK 2

 TARGETED CLOSE READ

Characters

Have students reread page 90 to look for ways the characters changed.

How does Tater change as a result of his interaction with Rose? Give examples from the text. *(Tater goes from being an uncooperative steer to being a gentle creature, as seen by his playfulness with Rose.)*

ANNOTATION TIP: Have students underline the parts of the sentences that explain how Rose interacts with Tater.

DOK 3

90

myNotes

16   But I believe what touched that critter's heart was when Rose began humming her little tune. That cantankerous ton of beef was restless no more. He became as playful as a kitten and even tried to purr. Rose named him Tater on account of that was his favorite vegetable. Hearing Rose's lullaby put that considerable creature to sleep was the sweetest thing I had witnessed in a long, long time.

17   After the dust had settled, Ma and Pa counted twenty-seven hundred head of cattle, after they added in the five hundred they already had. Using the scrap iron, Rose had to add a new section to the bull pen to hold them all.

18   "What did you do to the wire, Rose?" Ma asked, surprised and pleased at her daughter's latest creation.

📖 **READ FOR UNDERSTANDING**

How does the story explain how barbed wire came to be? Use the illustration and clues from the text to explain your answer. *(According to the text, Rose was staking a fence while also watching over a baby girl named Barbara Jay. She made a special twisting pattern with the wire that made the child laugh. Rose called it Barbara's wire, which eventually came to be known as barbed wire.)*

DOK 2

19   "Oh, that," she said. "While I was staking the fence, Pa asked me to keep little Barbara Jay company. That little twisty pattern seemed to make the baby laugh. So I like to think of it as Barbara's Wire."

20   "That was right clever of you to be so entertaining to the little one like that!" her ma said. Rose just blushed. Over the years, that twisty wire caught on, and folks just called it barbed wire.

91

92

21   Rose and her pa spent the whole next day sorting the animals that had not been branded. "One day soon, before the cold weather gets in," she told her pa, "I'll have to get this herd up the Chisholm Trail and to market in Abilene. I suspect Tater is the right kind of horse for the long drive northward."

22   On Rose's first trip to Abilene, while right outside of Caldwell, that irascible, full-of-outrage-and-ire outlaw Jesse Baines and his gang of desperadoes tried to rustle that herd away from Rose.

23   Using the spare metal rods she always carried with her, Rose lassoed those hot-tempered hooligans up good and tight. She dropped them all off to jail, tied up in a nice neat iron bow. "It wasn't any trouble at all," she told Sheriff Weaver. "Somebody had to put a stop to their thieving ways."

24   But that wasn't the only thieving going on. The mighty sun was draining the moisture out of every living thing it touched. Even the rocks were crying out. Those clouds stood by and watched it all happen. They weren't even trying to be helpful.

25   Why, the air had turned so dry and sour, time seemed to all but stand still. And there was not a drop of water in sight. Steer will not move without water. And that was making those bulls mad, real mad. And when a bull gets angry, it's like a disease that's catching, making the rest of the herd mad, too. Tater was looking parched and mighty thirsty.

📖 **READ FOR UNDERSTANDING**

By looking closely at the illustration, how can you tell that there is a drought? *(The ground looks like it is extremely dry and cracked. Tater hangs his head down low and looks very thirsty. Also, Rose has a piece of grass in her mouth that looks dry. It is a sunny day, and it does not look like it will rain soon.)*

DOK 2

93

READ FOR UNDERSTANDING

What is the problem? *(There is a drought and the animals and Rose are thirsty. The animals are getting angry and will not move.)* **What does Rose do? Explain using cause and effect.** *(With her super-human abilities, Rose lassos the clouds and then squeezes them as she hums her song. This causes rain to fall gently (effect), but it is not enough to help. Rose's actions and words cause the clouds to get angry, so they create a tornado (effect). This causes Rose to become angry which then causes lightning and thunder to come from her body (effect).)*

ANNOTATION TIP: Have students highlight a cause and its effect using different colors for each.

DOK 3

TARGETED CLOSE READ

Characters

What does Rose do about the drought? *(She squeezes the clouds to make them rain.)* **What words or phrases give readers clues to Rose's determination to make it rain?** *(Words like "riled" and phrases like "eyes flashed lightning" and "gnashed thunder" show that Rose will not let the clouds win this battle.)*

ANNOTATION TIP: Have students circle words and phrases on the page that paint a picture of Rose during this event in the tale.

DOK 2

26   "I've got to do something about this!" Rose declared.

27   Stretching out several iron rods lasso-fashion, then launching Cole high in the air, Rose hoped she could get the heavens to yield forth. She caught hold of a mass of clouds and squeezed them hard, real hard, all the while humming her song. Gentle rain began to fall. But anyone looking could see there was not enough moisture to refresh two ants, let alone a herd of wild cows.

28   Suddenly a rotating column of air came whirling and swirling around, picking up everything in its path. It sneaked up on Rose. "Whoa, there, now just hold on a minute," Rose called out to the storm. Tater was helpless to do anything about that sort of wind. Those meddlesome clouds caused it. They didn't take kindly to someone telling them what to do. And they were set on creating a riotous rampage all on their own.

29   Oh, this riled Rose so much, she became the only two-legged tempest to walk the western plains. "You don't know who you're fooling with," Rose called out to the storm. Her eyes flashed lightning. She bit down and gnashed thunder from her teeth. I don't know why anyone would want to mess with a pretty young woman who had the power of thunder and lightning coursing through her veins. But, pity for them, the clouds did!

30   Rose reached for her iron rod. But there was only one piece left. She did not know which way to turn. She knew Cole

📖 **READ FOR UNDERSTANDING**

How does the illustration show how strong the storm is?
(The illustration shows a large, dark cloud coming out of very thick, dark clouds. We also see many objects have been picked up by the tornado.)

DOK 2

🔍 **TARGETED CLOSE READ**

Characters

How does Rose react to the approaching tornadoes? *(Rose has to think quickly. She seems unsure how this event will end up.)* **What causes Rose to feel "weighted down"?** *(her thirst and the storm)* **How does her reaction to the approaching tornado compare to her reaction to the steer stampede earlier?** *(Rose was very sure of what she had to do when the stampede happened. She did not seem to question her ability to stop the stampede. However, she seems unsure how to stop the tornado. She is not sure if her abilities can help her.)*

DOK 2

alone was not enough to do the job right. Unarmed against her own growing thirst and the might of the elements, Rose felt weighted down. Then that churning column split, and now there were two. They were coming at her from opposite directions. Rose had some fast thinking to do. Never being one to bow down under pressure, she considered her options, for she was not sure how this would all come out in the end.

95

READ FOR UNDERSTANDING

Reread the first two sentences of paragraph 31. What do you think "fork in the road" means?

(The phrase means that Rose will either be a hero and fight the storm or the storm will be tougher than her.)

DOK 3

Notice Note

Again and Again

- **Remind students** that authors may repeat something over and over again in the text. If students find an example of this, they should stop and take note of it as being significant.

- **Have students** determine what phrases or actions have been repeated by the author again and again. *(When Rose got a "fortunate feeling rumbling deep in the pit of me," I remembered that Rose had used this phrase after she is born and hears the lullaby.)*

- **Have students** reflect on the Anchor Question: *Why might the author bring this up again?* and add to their notes.

DOK 2

96

31   "Is this the fork in the road with which I have my final supper? Will this be my first and my last ride of the roundup?" she queried herself in the depths of her heart. Her contemplations brought her little relief as she witnessed the merciless, the cataclysmic efforts of a windstorm bent on her disaster. Then the winds joined hands and cranked and churned a path heading straight toward her! Calmly Rose spoke out loud to the storm as she stood alone to face the wrack and ruin, the multiplying devastation. "I *could* ride at least *one* of you out to the end of time! But I've got this fortunate feeling rumbling deep in the pit of me, and I see what I am to do with it this day!" Rose said, smiling.

devastation   Devastation is terrible damage or complete destruction.

32　　The winds belted at a rumbling pitch. Rose squarely faced that storm. "Come and join me, winds!" She opened her arms wide as if to embrace the torrent. She opened her mouth as if she were planning to take a good long drink. But from deep inside her, she heard a melody so real and sweet and true. And when she lifted her heart, she unleashed *her* song of thunder. It was a sight to see: Rose making thunder and lightning rise and fall to the ground at her command, at the sound of *her song*. Oh, how her voice rang out so clear and real and true. It rang from the mountaintops. It filled up the valleys. It flowed like a healing river in the breathing air around her.

Adages and Proverbs

What does the adage "as thunder follows lightning, and sun follows rain" mean in this tall tale? *(Since thunder always follows lightning and the sun always follows the rain, we should remember Rose and her good heart when we are in difficult times.)*

DOK 3

📖 **READ FOR UNDERSTANDING**

Retell/Summarize

Have students retell the tall tale.

(Rose is born to loving parents who help her realize her unique talents and abilities. When Rose is born, she is able to sit up and talk. When she is two, she makes a pile of scrap iron into a thunderbolt. She stakes the fence on the farm by herself at age five. When she is twelve, Rose shows her super-human abilities by stopping a stampede of steer. She stops thieves in a local town and fights a tornado. In the end, Rose realizes that she has her own powerful song that she should never doubt.)

DOK 3

📖 **READ FOR UNDERSTANDING**

Wrap-Up

Revisit the purpose students set before they read the text. Have them explain how this tale fits the genre of a tall tale. Tell students to cite evidence to support their reasoning.

DOK 2

✏️ myNotes

33 Those tornadoes, calmed by her song, stopped their churning masses and raged no more. And, gentle as a baby's bath, a soft, drenching-and-soaking rain fell.

34 And Rose realized that by reaching into her own heart to bring forth the music that was there, she had even touched the hearts of the clouds.

35 The stories of Rose's amazing abilities spread like wildfire, far and wide. And as sure as thunder follows lightning, and sun follows rain, whenever you see a spark of light flash across a heavy steel gray sky, listen to the sound of the thunder and think of Thunder Rose and *her* song. That mighty, mighty song pressing on the bull's-eye that was set at the center of her heart.

Collaborative Discussion

Look back at what you wrote on page 82. Tell a partner two things you learned about Rose. Then work with a group to discuss the questions below. Refer to details from *Thunder Rose*. Take notes for your responses. When you speak, use your notes.

1 Review pages 84–85. What is unusual about Rose on the night she is born?

2 What events in the story show that Rose is a larger-than-life character?

3 Review pages 96–98. What does Rose do to stop the two tornadoes? How is she able to do this?

Listening Tip

Listen to each speaker's ideas. What detail or example can you add?

Speaking Tip

Restate a speaker's idea and share another detail or example that is related to it.

Academic Discussion

Use the **COLLABORATIVE DISCUSSION** routine. Have students write notes to answer the questions. Then have groups apply the Listening and Speaking Tips as they discuss their responses.

Possible responses:

1. *Rose sits up, and she talks to the doctor and her parents after she is born. She also takes hold of the lightning and rolls it into a ball.* DOK 1

2. *Rose is a larger-than-life character when she holds a cow above her head and drinks from it, when she makes Cole out of scrap iron by twisting and bending it, when she builds fences and buildings, and when she tames a steer.* DOK 2

3. *Rose calms the storm by singing her sweet melody. She is able to do this with the love from her parents that she has carried with her all along.* DOK 2

Write About Reading

- **Read aloud** the prompt with students.
- **Lead a discussion** in which students share their ideas about elements of tall tales, including character traits, the setting, and events in the story. Tell students to use text evidence to support their ideas.
- **Then read aloud** the Plan section. Have students use ideas from the discussion in their notes.

Write a Blog Post

PROMPT

In *Thunder Rose*, you read a tall tale about a larger-than-life character who does incredible things.

Imagine that you have a blog where you share ideas about writing and books. You plan to write about characters and events in tall tales. Write a blog post explaining what makes a story a tall tale, using *Thunder Rose* as an example. Don't forget to use some of the Critical Vocabulary words in your blog post.

PLAN

List examples of exaggeration in *Thunder Rose*. These may include character traits, the setting, and the events in the story.

Now write your blog post about tall tales.

Make sure your blog post

☐ introduces the topic.

☐ presents information in an easy-to-follow way.

☐ provides specific examples and details from the text.

☐ uses relative pronouns correctly.

☐ ends with a concluding sentence.

Write About Reading

• **Review with students** the directions and checklist in the Write section.

• **Encourage students** to use their own words as they write their blog posts about tall tales.

Notice & Note
Aha Moment

Introduce the Text

- **Read aloud** and discuss the genre information. Point out that folktales include the ideas and beliefs of a culture and are shared from one generation to the next. Through a conflict and a resolution, the plot unfolds. Folktales also include a lesson to be learned, or a moral.

- Use Display and Engage **Meet the Author 7.6**.

- **Tell students** to look for the Critical Vocabulary as they read, and to think about the words' meanings.

ANNOTATION TIP: Have students use the box to note what they would like to know about the characters.

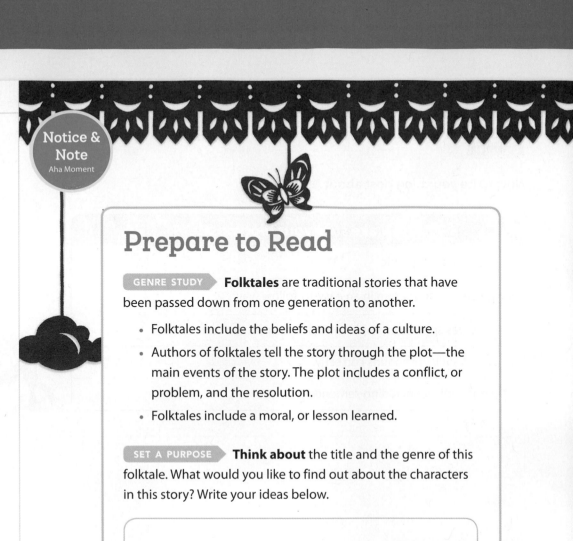

Prepare to Read

GENRE STUDY **Folktales** are traditional stories that have been passed down from one generation to another.

- Folktales include the beliefs and ideas of a culture.

- Authors of folktales tell the story through the plot—the main events of the story. The plot includes a conflict, or problem, and the resolution.

- Folktales include a moral, or lesson learned.

SET A PURPOSE **Think about** the title and the genre of this folktale. What would you like to find out about the characters in this story? Write your ideas below.

CRITICAL VOCABULARY

thrifty
generous
character
fascinated

Meet the Author:
Joe Hayes

In the Days of KING ADOBE

as told by Joe Hayes
illustrated by Ute Simon

103

1   There was once an old woman who lived all alone in a tiny house at the edge of a village. She was very poor, and all she had to eat was beans and tortillas and thin cornmeal mush. Of course, she ate a few vegetables from her garden, but most of them she took into the village on market day to sell or trade for what little she needed for her simple life.

2   But the old woman was very thrifty, and by saving carefully—a penny a day, a penny a day—she was able to buy herself a big ham. She kept it hanging from a hook in a cool, dark closet behind the kitchen, and she only cut a thin slice from the ham on very special days—or if she was lucky enough to have company join her for a meal.

> **thrifty**   If you are thrifty, you save your money and buy only what you need.

3 One evening a couple of young men who were traveling through the country stopped at the old woman's house and asked if they could have lodging for the night. The old woman had no extra beds, but she offered to spread a blanket on the floor for the young men to sleep on. They said that would be fine and thanked the old woman for her kindness.

4 "It's nothing," the old woman told them. "I'm happy to have the company. I'll get busy and make us all a good supper."

5 She got out her pots and pans and then went to the closet and cut three slices from the ham—two thick, generous slices for the travelers and a thin one for herself.

6 The young men were delighted to see the old woman preparing ham for their supper. Seldom were they offered such good food in their travels. But those two young men were a couple of rascals, and right away a roguish idea came into their minds. They decided to steal the ham that night while the old woman was asleep.

generous A generous amount of something is larger or more plentiful than is usual or necessary.

105

READ FOR UNDERSTANDING

Make and Confirm Predictions

What do you predict the old woman will do after she finds out that the two men have stolen her ham? Why do you think so?
(Responses will vary. Sample response: The old woman will catch them, get her ham back, and teach them a lesson about stealing; this is a trickster tale and trickster tales alway have a lesson.)

If students have difficulty making predictions, use this model:

THINK ALOUD *This is a trickster tale, so I can make a prediction that the old woman is going to get her ham back before the men wake up. I can confirm my prediction by reading further on in the text.*

ANNOTATION TIP: Have students note their predictions in the margin.

DOK 2

READ FOR UNDERSTANDING

What do the men's actions tell you about them? *(They are dishonest and greedy.)*

Are you surprised by their actions? Why or why not? *(Responses will vary. Sample: I am not surprised that the men try to steal her ham because the story says that they are rascals, but I am surprised that they stick around after they steal the ham.)*

DOK 1

106

7   After they had all eaten their fill, the old woman spread out a bed for the young men on the floor. She said good night and wished them good dreams and then went into her own room to sleep.

8   Of course, the young men didn't go to sleep. They lay on the floor joking and talking about how nice it was going to be to have a whole ham to eat. When they felt sure the old woman was asleep, the young men got up and crept to the closet. They took the ham down from the hook and wrapped it in a shirt. One of the young men put the ham in his traveling bag. Then the two young men lay down to sleep with smiles on their faces. They had very good dreams indeed!

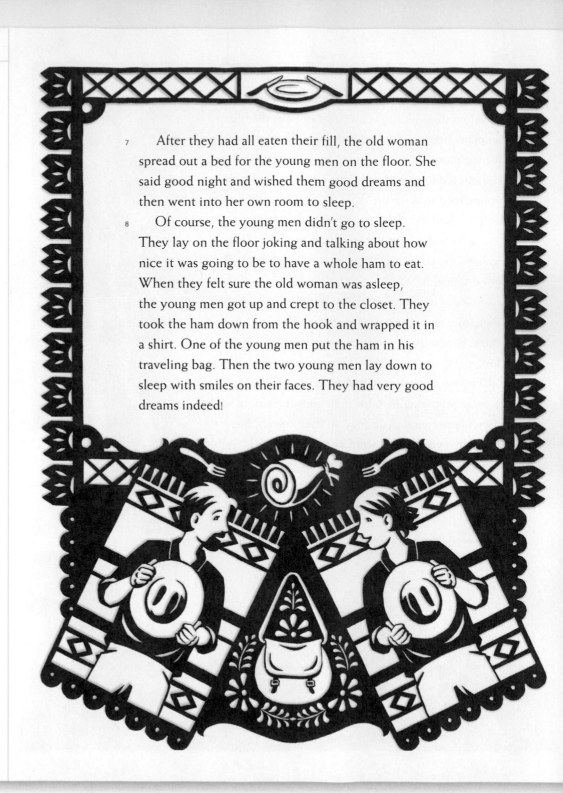

9   But the old woman hadn't gone to sleep either. In the many years of her life she had become a good judge of character, and she had noticed the rascally look in the young men's eyes. She knew she had better be on her guard. When she heard the young men getting up from their pad on the floor, she went to the door and peeked out. She saw everything the young men did.

10   Later that night, when the young men were sound asleep, the old woman crept from her room. She took the ham from the traveling bag and hid it under her bed. Then she wrapped an adobe brick in the shirt and put it in the traveling bag.

11   When the young men awoke in the morning they were anxious to be on their way. But the old woman insisted they stay for a bite of breakfast. "It will give you strength," she told them. "You have a long day of walking ahead of you. And you may not have anything else to eat all day."

character   A person's character is the kind of person he or she is.

myNotes

Notice & Note

Aha Moment

- **Remind students** that an aha moment is when characters realize something significant. This causes a change in their actions and their understanding of the world around them.

- **Have students** explain why they might use the strategy when reading page 107. (*The old woman notices the rascally look in the men's eyes, so she is on her guard during the night.*)

- **Have students** reflect on the Anchor Question: *How might this change things?* and add to their notes.

DOK 2

📖 **READ FOR UNDERSTANDING**

Do you think the old woman is a trickster? Cite evidence to support your answer. (*The old woman is a trickster. She wraps up an adobe brick inside a shirt in place of the ham and puts it in the men's bag.*)

ANNOTATION TIP: Have students underline the text that shows the old woman's character.

Why do you think the old woman asks the men to stay for breakfast rather than sending them on their way? (*I think it is part of the trick she is playing on them.*)

107

DOK 2

READ FOR UNDERSTANDING

How is the old woman's dream the same and different from the travelers' dreams? *(The travelers make up dreams about a king named Hambone the First. They are sitting under a tree in a beautiful land called Travelibag, eating good food. The old woman's dream also has a king named Hambone in the country of Travelibag. However, King Hambone is overthrown and replaced by Adobe the Great. Some people would go hungry for some time.)*

What you think those "dreams" really mean? *(The men are making fun of the old woman by saying they had these "dreams." They are really saying that because they stole the ham, they will now have food to enjoy. The old woman is wise to their stories and adds that Hambone the First has been overthrown by Adobe the Great, which refers to the brick she switches for the ham.)*

DOK 2

12   One of the young men winked at the other as he sat down at the table and said, "You're probably right, *abuelita*, but who knows? Last night I dreamed that today my friend and I would be eating good food all day long."

13   "Is that right?" the old woman replied. "Tell me more about your dream. I'm fascinated by dreams. I believe they are sometimes true."

14   The young man thought he'd really make fun of the old woman. He smiled at his friend and then said, "I dreamed we were sitting under a tree eating. It was in a beautiful land. And the king of that country was named Hambone the First."

15   "Aha!" spoke up the second young man. "Now I remember that I had the same dream. And I remember that the land in which Hambone the First was king was named Travelibag."

16   The young men had to cover their mouths to keep from bursting out laughing. But the old woman didn't seem to notice. In fact, she seemed to be taking them very seriously.

17   "I had a similar dream last night myself!" she exclaimed. "I was in a land named Travelibag, and Hambone the First was king of that country. But then he was thrown out by the good people and replaced by a new king named Adobe the Great. And for some people, that meant a time of great hunger had begun."

fascinated   If you are fascinated by something, you are very interested in it.

108

18   "Isn't that interesting," the young men said, biting their lips to keep from laughing. "Oh, well, it was just a dream." They hurried to finish their breakfast and then went on their way, laughing at the old woman's foolishness.

19   All morning long the two rascals joked about the old woman as they traveled down the road. As midday approached, they began to grow tired. They sat down under a shady tree to rest.

20   "Well, now," said the first young man as he leaned back and closed his eyes. "Don't you think it's time for dreams to come true? Here we are sitting under a tree, just as I dreamed. Open up the land of Travelibag. My stomach tells me I need to visit the king of that land."

READ FOR UNDERSTANDING

What does it mean when the first young man asks, "Don't you think it's time for dreams to come true?" Use text evidence to answer. *(Since the men are sitting under a tree just like they were in their "dreams," it means they should open up the land of Travelibag (their bag) and visit (eat) the king (the ham). They want to enjoy a fine meal.)*

DOK 2

READ FOR UNDERSTANDING

Make and Confirm Predictions

Was your prediction from the beginning of the story correct? If not, what are the differences between your prediction and what actually happens? *(Responses will vary. Sample response: My prediction was incorrect. I thought the men would be the tricksters, but the old woman is really the one who is the trickster.)*

DOK 2

109

Aha Moment

- **Have students** identify an aha moment on this page, explaining how the characters' actions change. *(The men realize that the old woman is more clever than they thought. They don't play any tricks the next time they meet a kind old woman.)*

DOK 2

 my Notes

🔍 TARGETED CLOSE READ

Theme

What is the problem and how does the old woman solve it? *(The woman has been generous, but the men try to steal her ham. She tricks them with an adobe brick.)*

What is the author's message or lesson to be learned from this trickster folktale? *(Do not be greedy, or you may end up with nothing.)*

What details in the text support your idea? *(The men greedily steal the ham, and they end up with a brick.)*

DOK 3

📖 READ FOR UNDERSTANDING

Wrap-Up

Revisit the purpose students set before they read the text. Have students explain how this text fits the genre of a folktale, and cite evidence from the text to support their reasoning.

DOK 2

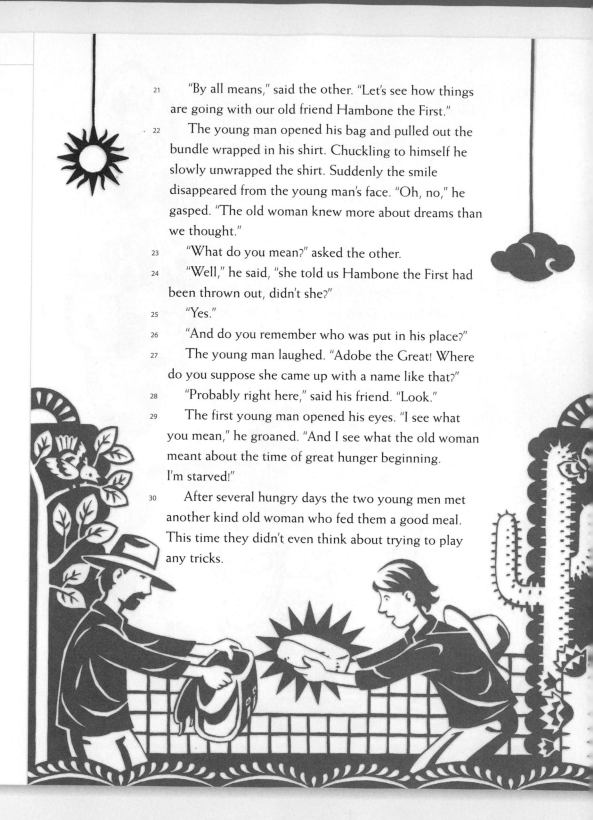

21 "By all means," said the other. "Let's see how things are going with our old friend Hambone the First."

22 The young man opened his bag and pulled out the bundle wrapped in his shirt. Chuckling to himself he slowly unwrapped the shirt. Suddenly the smile disappeared from the young man's face. "Oh, no," he gasped. "The old woman knew more about dreams than we thought."

23 "What do you mean?" asked the other.

24 "Well," he said, "she told us Hambone the First had been thrown out, didn't she?"

25 "Yes."

26 "And do you remember who was put in his place?"

27 The young man laughed. "Adobe the Great! Where do you suppose she came up with a name like that?"

28 "Probably right here," said his friend. "Look."

29 The first young man opened his eyes. "I see what you mean," he groaned. "And I see what the old woman meant about the time of great hunger beginning. I'm starved!"

30 After several hungry days the two young men met another kind old woman who fed them a good meal. This time they didn't even think about trying to play any tricks.

Collaborative Discussion

Look back at what you wrote on page 102. Tell a partner two things you liked about this folktale. Then work with a group to discuss the questions below. Refer to details and examples in *In the Days of King Adobe* to explain your answers. Take notes for your responses. When you speak, use your notes.

1 Reread page 104. What clues does the author give that tell you what the old woman's life is like?

2 Review pages 108–109. What goal does each character have for sharing his or her dream?

3 What details in the text suggest that the old woman is clever?

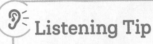

Listening Tip

Listen for important points that other speakers make and the evidence they use to support those ideas.

Speaking Tip

After a speaker presents an idea and evidence, restate it and tell why you agree or disagree.

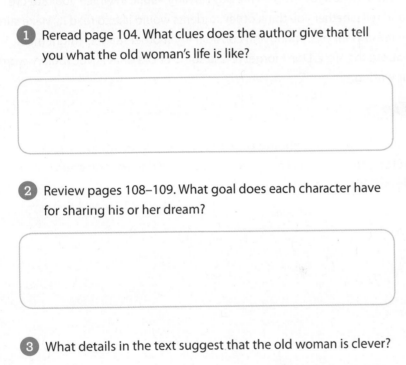

Academic Discussion

Use the **COLLABORATIVE DISCUSSION** routine. Have students write notes to answer the questions. Then have groups apply the Listening and Speaking Tips as they discuss their responses.

Possible responses:

1. *The author tells us that the old woman is very poor. She lives all alone, at the edge of a village, in a very small house. The only foods she eats are cornmeal mush, a few vegetables, and beans and tortillas. She is "very thrifty" and only buys what she truly needs. She saves her pennies to buy a big ham to eat on special occasions.* DOK 1

2. *The two young men each share their dream to make fun of the old woman. She, on the other hand, shares her dream to warn them that they would soon go hungry because she has tricked them by taking back her ham.* DOK 2

3. *The old woman is wise to the young men's tricks and knows that they are up to no good. She watches them steal her ham and then steals it back. She is very clever to replace the ham with an adobe brick so that the bag weighs roughly the same. Also, the dream that she tells them about is very clever.* DOK 2

111

Cite Text Evidence

Write a Review

PROMPT

In the Days of King Adobe is a folktale that tells the story of two young men who try to trick a kind woman.

Imagine that your class has a website where classmates post reviews of stories read in class. Write a review of *In the Days of King Adobe* in which you rate the story and tell whether you think other students would like to read it. Make sure to give reasons for your rating and consider what other readers might most enjoy about the story. Don't forget to use some of the Critical Vocabulary words in your writing.

PLAN

Make notes about the theme of the story as well as the plot and characters. Note things that you like about the story and things that you do not like.

Now write your review of *In the Days of King Adobe*.

Make sure your review

☐ begins by giving a brief summary of the folktale.

☐ clearly states your opinion of the folktale.

☐ gives reasons for your opinion.

☐ uses transition words to connect ideas.

☐ ends with a conclusion that tells readers whether you recommend the folktale or not.

Write About Reading

- **Review with students** the directions and checklist in the Write section.

- **Encourage students** to use their own words as they write a review of *In The Days of King Adobe*.

Notice &
Note
Again and Again

READ FOR UNDERSTANDING

Introduce the Text

- **Read aloud** and discuss the genre information. Point out that fables are short stories that teach a lesson that readers should be able to apply to their lives. Trickster tales are imaginative stories that include a clever character who knows more than he or she lets on to trick another character.

- **Have students** look at the illustration and predict who might be tricksters in these trickster fables. *(I think the fox will be a trickster. Foxes are often tricky characters.)*

- Use Display and Engage **Meet the Author 7.8**.

- **Tell students** to look for the Critical Vocabulary as they read, and to think about the words' meanings.

ANNOTATION TIP: Have students use the box to note what they would like to know about the characters.

Prepare to Read

GENRE STUDY A **fable** is a short story meant to teach a lesson. **Trickster tales** are imaginative stories in which one character tricks another character.

- Fables teach a lesson, called a *moral,* that people should apply to their lives. Sometimes the moral is stated at the end of the fable.

- Characters in fables are usually animals.

- Trickster tales include a clever character who knows more than he or she lets on.

SET A PURPOSE **Look at** the pictures of the characters in the two stories. What are some things you would like to know about these characters? Write your ideas below.

CRITICAL VOCABULARY

succulent

clamped

Build Background:
Trickster Tales

A Pair of Tricksters

illustrated by
Maribel Lechuga and Jui Ishida

115

myNotes

📖 **READ FOR UNDERSTANDING**

What does the Crow have that the Fox wants? *(a piece of cheese in its beak)*

ANNOTATION TIP: Have students underline the detail in the text.

DOK 1

📖 **READ FOR UNDERSTANDING**

In what way does Master Reynard speak to the Crow? Cite evidence from the text to explain your answer. *(Master Reynard, or the Fox, gives the Crow many compliments and even refers to her as the "Queen of Birds.")*

What does the Fox ask the Crow to do? *(sing a song)* **Why does he do this?** *(Because then the Crow will have to open her mouth and will drop the cheese.)*

ANNOTATION TIP: Have students underline examples of some of the compliments that the Fox gives the Crow.

DOK 2

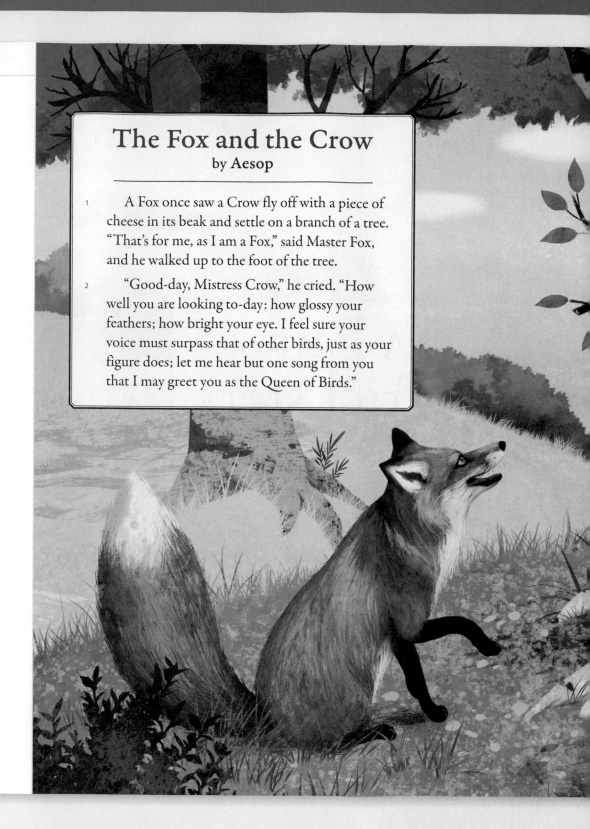

The Fox and the Crow
by Aesop

1   A Fox once saw a Crow fly off with a piece of cheese in its beak and settle on a branch of a tree. "That's for me, as I am a Fox," said Master Fox, and he walked up to the foot of the tree.

2   "Good-day, Mistress Crow," he cried. "How well you are looking to-day: how glossy your feathers; how bright your eye. I feel sure your voice must surpass that of other birds, just as your figure does; let me hear but one song from you that I may greet you as the Queen of Birds."

116

3   The Crow lifted up her head and began to caw her best, but the moment she opened her mouth the piece of cheese fell to the ground, only to be snapped up by Master Fox.

4   "That will do," said he. "That was all I wanted. In exchange for your cheese I will give you a piece of advice for the future.

5   *Do not trust flatterers.*"

 READ FOR UNDERSTANDING

What does Master Fox offer in exchange for the cheese? *(The Fox gives the Crow some advice about not trusting flatterers, in exchange for his meal.)*

What is the author's message? *(Do not trust flatterers because they may want something from you.)*

DOK 3

TARGETED CLOSE READ

Characters

What type of character is the Fox? Give examples from the text to support your answer. *(The Fox is a sly, cunning trickster. He pays the Crow so many compliments, but he really only wants her cheese. He then gives her advice to not trust flatterers like him.)*

How might this experience change Crow? Why do you think so? *(I think Crow might not trust anyone as easily anymore and will now know not to trust flatterers because of the way Fox tricks her.)*

DOK 2

117

READ FOR UNDERSTANDING

Make and Confirm Predictions

Read the first paragraph and then make a prediction about the fate of Raven and the crayfish, based on what you know about the structure and genre of trickster tales. (*Responses will vary. Sample response: The crayfish will somehow trick Raven and will escape safely. Raven will learn a lesson.*)

If students have difficulty making predictions, use this model:

 THINK ALOUD *By using the illustrations and what I have already read, I can make a prediction that the crayfish will trick Raven and will get away safely. I can then confirm my prediction by reading further on in the text.*

ANNOTATION TIP: Have students write their prediction on the page.

DOK 2

TARGETED CLOSE READ

Who is the trickster? Explain. (*Crayfish; she flatters Raven with so many compliments about him and his family that he opens his beak to respond and accidentally sets her free.*)
What does this tell you about Raven? (*This tells me that Raven can be easily tricked.*)

DOK 2

118

Raven and Crayfish
by John and Caitlín Matthews

1 Flying home to his nest one day, Raven spied a succulent crayfish swimming in the lake below. He swooped down and caught the fat crayfish in his beak, thinking of the feast he would have when he came to his treetop home.

2 Crayfish was terrified. Knowing that she was seconds away from becoming a raven's dinner, she began to speak as calmly and sweetly as she could: "Oh, great and powerful Raven! I'm so pleased to meet you. You know, I had supper with your father and mother a little while ago. What a delightful couple!"

3 "Ugoo," said Raven, because his beak was firmly shut, holding tight to his dinner.

4 "And I have often noticed how enchanting your brothers and sisters are. What a handsome family!" continued Crayfish.

> **succulent**   If food is succulent, it is juicy and tasty.

myNotes

Notice & Note

Again and Again

- **Remind students** that when they are reading and something happens over and over again, they should stop to take note of this as being significant.

- **Have students** identify what has been repeated in both tales. *(In both tales, one character gives compliments or flatters the other character over and over again. The trickster character is used over again as well.)*

ANNOTATION TIP: Have students list the things that are repeated in both stories.

- **Have students** reflect on the Anchor Question: *Why might the author bring this up again and again?* and add to their notes.

DOK 2

119

Figurative Language

How does the author use alliteration in the text? Why? *(The author uses alliteration in the phrase, "the cleverest creature of all creatures since the world's creation." The alliteration makes the readers slow down, and it catches their attention. They realize Crayfish is being a flatterer, just like Fox in the previous story.)*

How does the author use assonance, or repeated vowel sounds, in that phrase? *(The words creature, creatures, and creation all share the same long e vowel sound.)*

Why does the author repeat the alliteration and assonance at the end of the story? *(The author wants us to know that even though Raven is the most clever of all, he is able to be tricked and has to go hungry in the end.)*

DOK 3

Wrap Up

Revisit the purpose students set before they read the text. Have students explain what they learned about trickster tales and cite text evidence.

DOK 3

120

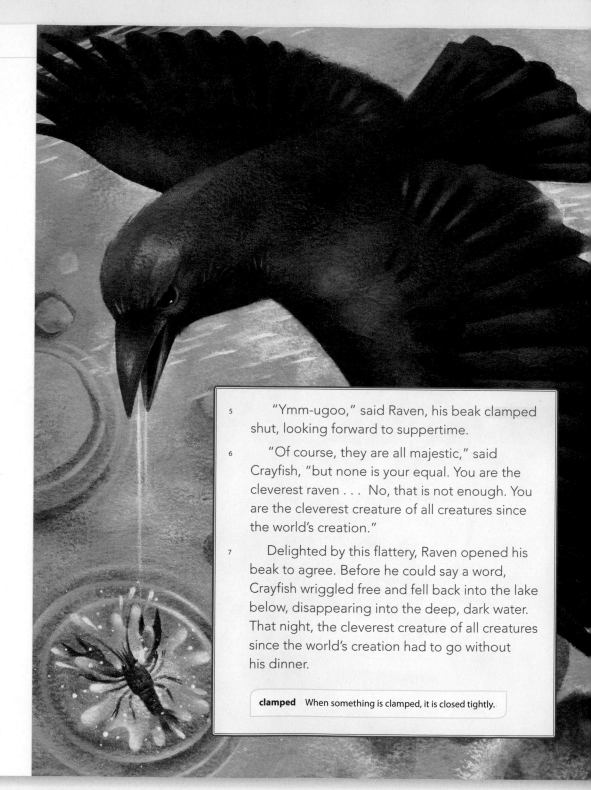

5   "Ymm-ugoo," said Raven, his beak clamped shut, looking forward to suppertime.

6   "Of course, they are all majestic," said Crayfish, "but none is your equal. You are the cleverest raven . . .   No, that is not enough. You are the cleverest creature of all creatures since the world's creation."

7   Delighted by this flattery, Raven opened his beak to agree. Before he could say a word, Crayfish wriggled free and fell back into the lake below, disappearing into the deep, dark water. That night, the cleverest creature of all creatures since the world's creation had to go without his dinner.

clamped   When something is clamped, it is closed tightly.

Collaborative Discussion

Look back at what you wrote on page page 114. Tell a partner two things you learned about the characters. Then work with a group to discuss the questions below. Refer to details and examples in *A Pair of Tricksters* to explain your answers. Take notes for your responses. When you speak, use your notes.

1. Reread page 116. What do you learn about Fox from what he says to Crow?

2. Review pages 118–120. Who does Crayfish talk about first? Why does she call Raven "the cleverest creature of all creatures"?

3. In what ways are these two stories alike? In what ways are they different?

Listening Tip

Think about the conclusions you can draw from what another speaker has said. Does the speaker's statement change or support your ideas?

Speaking Tip

Say each word clearly and use complete sentences and correct grammar when expressing ideas and supported opinions.

Academic Discussion

Use the **COLLABORATIVE DISCUSSION** routine. Have students write notes to answer the questions. Then have groups apply the Listening and Speaking Tips as they discuss their responses.

Possible responses:

1. *We learn that Fox is a flatterer and gives Crow numerous false compliments in order to try and trick her. Fox is very clever and sly.* DOK 2

2. *Crayfish first talks about Raven's parents in a very flattering way. Next, she compliments Raven's siblings. She tells Raven that he is "the cleverest creature of all creatures" with the hope that he would respond to her compliment by opening his beak and setting her free.* DOK 2

3. *Both stories are fables with trickster characters. They both have animals as characters, and the trickster character flatters the other one. Both fables teach a lesson at the end as well. In contrast, the fables have different characters. Fox is trying to get food away from Crow, while Raven is trying to make Crayfish his dinner. The fables have different settings and morals, also.* DOK 3

121

Write a Compare and Contrast Paragraph

PROMPT

In *A Pair of Tricksters*, you read two versions of a fable in which a Crow and Raven learn a valuable lesson.

Imagine that you are writing for your school literary website. Write a paragraph that compares and contrasts the two versions of the fable. Briefly summarize each fable and show how each is similar and different. Don't forget to use some of the Critical Vocabulary in your writing.

PLAN

Make notes about the characters and the language used in each version of the fable.

WRITE ....

Now write your compare and contrast paragraph.

✓	**Make sure your paragraph**
☐	introduces both fables.
☐	tells about the main characters and story events.
☐	tells the lesson that Crow and Raven learn and how they learn it.
☐	uses pronouns correctly.
☐	ends with a concluding sentence.

Write About Reading

- **Review with students** the directions and checklist in the Write section.

- **Encourage students** to use their own words as they summarize the two fables to show how each is similar and different.

Notice &
Note
Aha Moment

Introduce the Text and Video

- **Read aloud** and discuss the genre information. Point out that legends cannot be proven true and often explain how things came to be. Explain that students should look for a character who is a hero overcoming an obstacle.

- **Explain to students** that they will read the story *Ten Suns* and watch a video, *The Ten Suns*. Tell students they will have an opportunity to compare the two versions of the story.

- Use Display and Engage **Meet the Author 7.11**.

- **Call attention** to the Critical Vocabulary. Tell students to listen for these words as they read the text and watch the video.

ANNOTATION TIP: Have students use the box to note what they expect this story to be about. Encourage them to also note how they think the text and video will differ from each other.

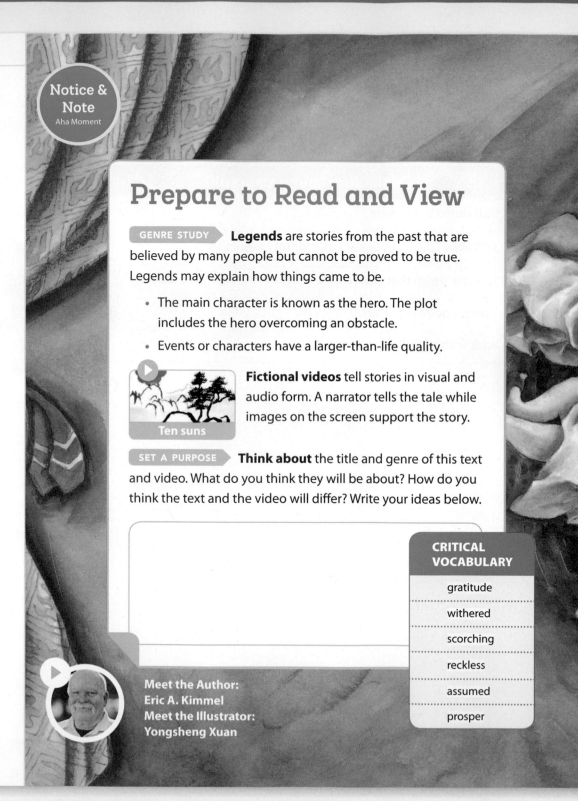

Prepare to Read and View

GENRE STUDY **Legends** are stories from the past that are believed by many people but cannot be proved to be true. Legends may explain how things came to be.

- The main character is known as the hero. The plot includes the hero overcoming an obstacle.

- Events or characters have a larger-than-life quality.

Fictional videos tell stories in visual and audio form. A narrator tells the tale while images on the screen support the story.

Ten suns

SET A PURPOSE **Think about** the title and genre of this text and video. What do you think they will be about? How do you think the text and the video will differ? Write your ideas below.

Meet the Author:
Eric A. Kimmel
Meet the Illustrator:
Yongsheng Xuan

CRITICAL VOCABULARY

gratitude

withered

scorching

reckless

assumed

prosper

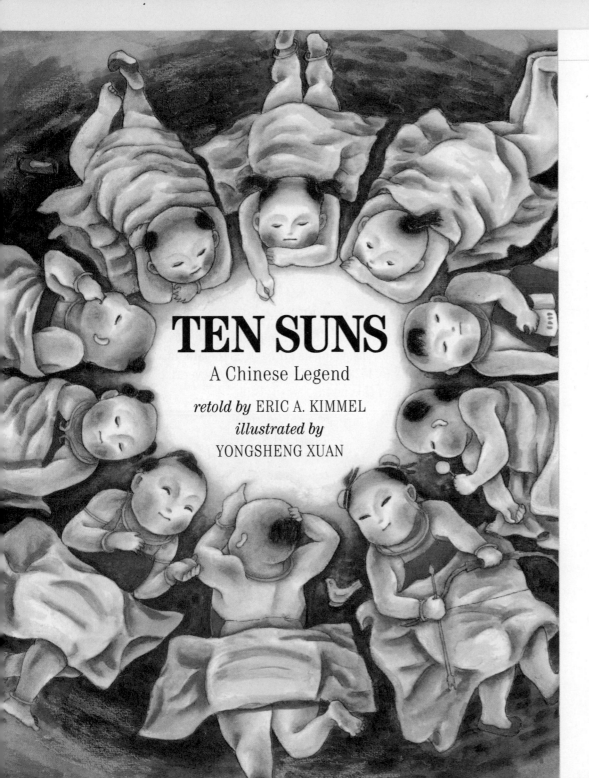

TEN SUNS

A Chinese Legend

retold by ERIC A. KIMMEL

illustrated by
YONGSHENG XUAN

myNotes

READ AND VIEW FOR UNDERSTANDING

Set a Purpose

- **Have students** look at the illustration and read the title and subtitle on this page.

- **Guide students** to set a purpose for reading and viewing. Discuss with them what they think the selection will be about.

DOK 2

125

1 The story of the Ten Suns is one of the oldest Chinese myths, going as far back as the Shang dynasty (c. 1523 BC–1027 BC). There are several versions of this myth.

126

Synthesize

MODEL SYNTHESIZING

THINK ALOUD *I can combine what I know with what I read to synthesize or create a new understanding of the text. I know legends often explain why something is the way it is in the world. The text on page 127 describes a grand palace at the top of a very tall mulberry tree where a god lives who rules the part of the sky where the sun rises. I synthesize these pieces to know the text is describing an imaginary setting with characters that have exceptional powers.*

2   Long ago, when the world was new, a giant mulberry tree grew on the far side of the sea, on the edge of the eastern horizon. Its roots plunged deep into the earth. Its branches scraped the sky.

3   Nestled in the topmost branches of this tree stood a jade palace. Hammered sheets of gold formed its roof. Its windows were made of the thinnest panes of amethyst and lapis lazuli. This was the palace of Di Jun, the eastern emperor, the god who ruled the regions of the sky where the sun arises.

127

myNotes

Why didn't the children walk across the sky together? *(They would produce too much heat.)*

What effect does one sun have on the people on earth? *(He brings warmth and light, so the people offer thanks.)*

ANNOTATION TIP: Have students underline the text evidence in paragraphs 4 and 5 that they use to answer the questions.

DOK 2

4   In those days there were ten suns: the children of Di Jun and his wife, Xi He. They never walked across the sky together. That would produce too much heat for the world to bear. Instead, every morning before dawn, Xi He would awaken one of her sons. They would climb into her dragon chariot and drive to a point on the eastern horizon where Xi He's son would begin his walk.

5   Each day one of the suns would walk across the sky from east to west. When the people on earth saw the sun crossing the heavens, bringing warmth and light, they offered thanks to Di Jun, Xi He, and their family.

128

📖 **READ FOR UNDERSTANDING**

Why do the boys find their task boring? *(It is always the same routine with no one to talk to and nothing to do besides walk the same path across the sky.)*

DOK 1

6   But the gratitude of the earth's people and the importance of their work meant nothing to the boys. They found their task boring. Day after day, year after year, century after century, they followed the same path across the sky. There was no one to talk to, nothing new to see, nothing to do except follow that same weary track over and over again.

> **gratitude**   When you show gratitude, you show that you are thankful.

129

Synthesize

Discuss your understanding of the suns' decision. *(The heat from all ten of them walking together will probably burn up things on earth.)*

If students have difficulty synthesizing, use this model:

 THINK ALOUD *I want to synthesize the information on pages 128 and 130 to help me understand the story. The text tells me that the ten suns never walk together because the world would not be able to handle all of the heat that they would produce. This information, along with knowing that the boys want to all walk together, helps me understand the possible consequences of their decision.*

DOK 3

🔍 **TARGETED CLOSE READ**

Literary Elements

Have students reread pages 129 and 130 to identify what causes the boys to walk together.

Why do the boys decide to change their routine of walking across the sky? *(They think that if they walk together it would be much more fun.)*

Why do the boys get up early? *(They get up early so as not to have their parents stop their fun.)*

DOK 2

130

 myNotes

One night, as Di Jun's boys lay in bed, they began talking. Huo Feng Huang, the oldest, said, "I would not mind walking the path so much if I had some company."

"I feel the same way," Pi Li Xing, the youngest, replied. "Tomorrow, let's do something different. Why don't we all get up early, take the dragon chariot, and walk across the sky together?"

The others agreed. "A splendid idea!"

In the dark of night, while their parents slept, the boys arose, put on their brightest garments, hitched the dragon to their mother's chariot, and rode across the star-swept sky to the eastern horizon. Laughing, chattering, with their arms around one another's shoulders, they began their walk.

¹¹ When dawn came, the people who lived on earth were astonished to see ten suns appear above the horizon. The blazing heat of ten suns shining down at once was more than the world could bear. Crops withered in the fields. Forests caught fire. Lakes and rivers dried up. Mountains shattered to pieces. The sea began to boil. People and animals grew faint. They stretched themselves on the scorching ground and waited to die.

> **withered**   If a plant has withered, it has dried up and died.
> **scorching**   Something that is scorching is very, very hot.

📖 **READ FOR UNDERSTANDING**

Why are the people on earth astonished when dawn came?
(There are ten suns in the sky instead of one.)

DOK 1

🔍 **TARGETED CLOSE READ**

Literary Elements

What problems do the suns' actions cause? *(Crops wither, forests burn, lakes and rivers dry up, mountains shatter, the sea boils, and people and animals grow faint.)*

ANNOTATION TIP: Have students circle at least four text details that show the effect of the suns' actions.

DOK 1

131

12   The great emperor Shun, who ruled the nations of the world, cried to eastern god Di Jun.

13   "Why are you punishing us? What have the creatures of earth done to deserve this terrible fate? Have we not followed the proper rites? Have we not offered the correct sacrifices? Why have you sent your sons to destroy us?"

132

14   The great emperor's cries woke Di Jun and Xi He. They looked out the window of the jade palace. In the distance, they saw their ten sons marching together across the sky. Di Jun and Xi He called to them, "Come back at once! Go no further!"

15   But the boys did not listen. Earth was far below. They could not see the damage they were causing. Higher and higher they climbed, until they reached the place where the sun stands at noon.

16   Di Jun could not allow the world to be destroyed. The existence of all living things depended on him. If his sons would not abandon their reckless walk, he would have to stop them. Di Jun summoned Hu Yi, the Archer of Heaven.

> **reckless**   Someone who is reckless does not care how his or her actions affect others.

Notice & Note

Aha Moment

- **Remind students** that in an aha moment, a character realizes something that shifts or changes the way the character acts.

- **Have students** explain what causes Di Jun to have an aha moment. (*The boys do not listen to their parents. They do not stop walking together. Their actions will destroy the world.*)

ANNOTATION TIP: Have students underline text evidence that leads to the aha moment.

- **Have students** reflect on the Anchor Question: *How might this change things?* and add to their notes.

DOK 2

133

17   Hu Yi had once been a man. He introduced the science of archery to the world by inventing the bow and arrow. As a reward for his discovery, the gods placed him in the heavens among the constellations.

18   Di Jun presented Hu Yi with a magic bow and ten magic arrows. With tears filling his eyes, he told Hu Yi, "Shoot down the ten suns—my sons—who are burning up the earth."

19   Hu Yi refused. "How can I harm your boys? They are like my children. I taught them to shoot with a bow and arrow. We both still love them, even when they disobey."

 READ FOR UNDERSTANDING

Why does Di Jun have tears in his eyes? *(He is telling the archer to shoot down his sons, who he loves, before they destroy the earth.)*

How does Hu Yi feel about this task? *(He refuses because he loves the boys, too.)*

DOK 2

134

myNotes

TARGETED CLOSE READ

Text and Graphic Features

How does the illustration in the printed text fit the description of Hu Yi? *(He had once been a man smart enough to introduce archery to the world. He was honored by the gods as a reward. The illustration shows an extremely strong godlike man holding a bow and arrow.)*

How is this character portrayed in the video *The Ten Suns*? *(He is introduced as the most brave and clever archer.)*

What description does the narrator give of Yi in the video? *(The narrator says that Yi is dressed in his thick cloth uniform to protect himself from the heat of the suns.)*

DOK 2

135

20 "I love the creatures of the earth, too. I must protect them," Di Jun told Hu Yi. "Do not be afraid. You will not harm the boys. My sons will not be hurt, but they will be changed. Never again will they cross the sky as suns. They will be gods no more. Hurry! Do as I command. There is no time to spare. The earth is dying."

21 Hu Yi took Di Jun's bow and magic arrows. He rode the wind down to earth. Taking his place on top of White Mountain, he planted his feet firmly and took careful aim.

 READ FOR UNDERSTANDING

How will the boys be changed according to Di Jun? *(The boys will no longer be gods. They will not cross the sky as suns.)*

DOK 1

Hu Yi released the bowstring. The magic arrow streaked across the sky. It struck the first of the ten suns, shattering it to pieces.

22   One by one, Hu Yi's arrows found their mark. Each sun exploded, filling the sky with blinding light. The boys fell to earth, but they did not die. Instead, they turned into black-feathered birds. They became crows.

READ FOR UNDERSTANDING

What effect does the magic arrow have on each sun? *(The arrow causes each sun to explode and the son to become a crow.)*

DOK 1

READ FOR UNDERSTANDING

Synthesize

Remind students that as they read, it is important to synthesize the information. Have students determine what problem could happen if Hu Yi shoots down every sun. *(Responses may include: The sky will be dark. There will be no heat and light from a sun.)*

DOK 2

137

Notice & Note

Aha Moment

- **Remind students** that a word such as *suddenly* often introduces an aha moment.

- **Have students** explain what the emperor Shun suddenly realizes. (*That there would be no heat or light if all the suns were destroyed.*)

ANNOTATION TIP: Have students underline text evidence in paragraph 23 that leads to the aha moment.

- **Have students** reflect on the Anchor Question: *How might this change things?* and add to their notes.

DOK 2

🔍 TARGETED CLOSE READ

Literary Elements

Think about the sequence of events in the legend. With a partner retell the events in sequence. Which events surprised you? (*Beginning: Boys find their task boring and decide to walk together. Middle: Earth is dying from the heat of ten suns. Emperor appeals to Di Jun. Di Jun tells Hu Yi to shoot down the suns. End: Before Hu Yi shoots down all the suns, the messenger takes his last arrow. The boys are changed into crows.*)

DOK 2

23   The emperor Shun watched the suns exploding in the sky. Suddenly he realized that if Hu Yi destroyed all the suns, there would be no heat or light. The earth would be plunged into icy darkness.

24   There was no time to spare. The emperor Shun summoned his fastest messenger.

25   "Go to the top of White Mountain. Find Hu Yi. Remove one arrow from his quiver to make sure he does not shoot down all the suns."

26   The messenger mounted his horse. He rode faster than he had ever ridden in his life, all the way to the top of White Mountain. There he saw Hu Yi. By now, only one sun remained in the sky. Shun's messenger plucked the last arrow from Hu Yi's quiver just as the Archer of Heaven reached for it. Finding no more magic arrows, Hu Yi assumed his work was done. He unstrung his bow and rode the wind back to the stars.

assumed   If you assumed something, you believed it without proof.

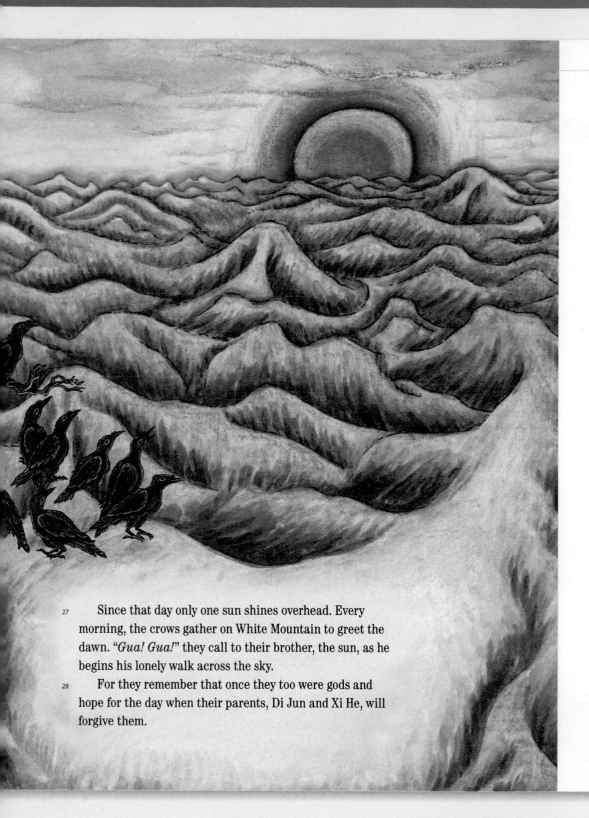

myNotes

²⁷ Since that day only one sun shines overhead. Every morning, the crows gather on White Mountain to greet the dawn. "*Gua! Gua!*" they call to their brother, the sun, as he begins his lonely walk across the sky.

²⁸ For they remember that once they too were gods and hope for the day when their parents, Di Jun and Xi He, will forgive them.

🔍 **TARGETED CLOSE READ**

Media Techniques

How are the illustrations in the video different from those in the text? (*They are simpler black and white illustrations rather than the colorful and detailed illustrations in the text.*) **How do the sound effects and visuals in the video add to this tale?** (*The music gives viewers a feeling as if they are in China, and the visuals show events as they happen.*)

DOK 2

🔍 **TARGETED CLOSE READ**

Text and Graphic Features

How does the video compare to the print version of this tale? What is the same? (*The basic story is the same about the ten suns wanting to travel together.*) **What is different?** (*The ending is very different. In the video, the archer uses his shield to reflect the heat back to the suns instead of shooting arrows. He breaks them apart, and the bits and pieces become stars.*)

DOK 2

📖 **READ FOR UNDERSTANDING**

Wrap-Up

What lesson can be learned from this traditional tale? (*Obey your parents. Consider others over yourself.*)

DOK 3

VIEW FOR UNDERSTANDING

How did your understanding of the legend change as you watched the video? *(I thought that the suns had a good idea to walk together, but then, as I viewed the video, I realized that they hadn't really thought their plan through carefully.)*

DOK 3

 TARGETED CLOSE READ

Text and Graphic Features

What connections can you make between the text and the video, *The Ten Suns*? *(Each version of the story has the same outcome when the suns decide to walk together.)*

DOK 2

 TARGETED CLOSE READ

Media Techniques

How does the animation in the video help you understand this legend? *(The animation is simple. It helps me focus on the story and its message. It helps me see how one change in nature can impact so many.)*

DOK 2

The Ten Suns

As you watch *The Ten Suns,* notice how sound and images work together to tell the story. How is this story told differently from the legend you just read? How is the story supported by the images and music? Write your ideas below.

Listen for the Critical Vocabulary word *prosper*. Pay attention to clues in the images that help to explain the word's meaning. Take notes in the space below about how the word was used.

prosper If you prosper, you succeed and do well.

Collaborative Discussion

Look back at what you wrote on page 124. Tell a partner something you learned about the text and video. Work with a group to discuss the questions below. Use details from the text and video to support your answers. Take notes for your responses.

1 Review pages 130–131. Why does the suns' decision to travel together cause problems for the people on the Earth?

2 Review pages 138–139. What problem will Earth have if the archer shoots down the ten suns? What is Di Jun's solution?

3 How is the ending in each version of the legend similar and different?

 Listening Tip

Notice how each speaker uses gestures and facial expressions that help support their ideas.

 Speaking Tip

When you speak, make eye contact with group members to help you know that they understand your ideas.

Academic Discussion

Use the **COLLABORATIVE DISCUSSION** routine. Have students write notes to answer the questions. Tell students to use the Critical Vocabulary and content-area words in their responses, as appropriate. Then have groups apply the Listening and Speaking Tips as they discuss their responses.

Possible responses:

1. *The suns' decision to travel together causes problems because together they give off too much heat at once. The heat causes bodies of water to dry up and sources of food and plants to die.* DOK 2

2. *The earth will have no light or heat. Di Jun's solution is to turn 9 of the 10 suns into crows, leaving one sun in the sky.* DOK 2

3. *In both versions, only one sun remains in the sky. In the text version, the other suns become crows. In the video version, the other suns become stars in the sky.* DOK 1

Write a Legend

PROMPT

In *Ten Suns*, you read a Chinese legend. You also watched another version of this legend presented as a video.

Imagine that your class is creating a book with different versions of this legend. Write a new version of this legend. Don't forget to use some of the Critical Vocabulary words in your writing.

PLAN

Make notes about the sequence of events in the text and video. Then make inferences about the events that you can use to write a new version of the legend.

Write About Reading

- **Read aloud** the prompt with students.

- **Lead a discussion** in which students share their ideas for new versions of the legend, *Ten Suns*. Tell students to use text evidence to support their ideas.

- **Then read aloud** the Plan section. Have students use ideas from the discussion in their notes.

Now write your new version of *Ten Suns*.

✓ Make sure your legend

- ☐ begins with an introduction.

- ☐ includes dialogue and descriptions to show what happens.

- ☐ describes events in the order in which they happen.

- ☐ tells how the problem of the ten suns was solved.

- ☐ uses transition words and phrases to help readers follow the events.

Write About Reading

- **Review with students** the directions and checklist in the Write section.

- **Encourage students** to use their own words as they describe the events in their new versions of the legend.

Revisit the Essential Question

- **Read aloud** the Essential Question.

- **Remind students** that the lessons they learned from the characters in the traditional tales that they read and viewed in this module can help them answer the question.

Write a Trickster Tale

- **Guide students** to think about the characters and the lessons in the module's trickster tales before choosing a lesson to write about in their own trickster tale.

- **Review the features** of a trickster tale using the checklist. Tell students to use the checklist as they draft, revise, and edit their stories.

? **Essential Question**

What lessons can you learn from characters in traditional tales?

Write a Trickster Tale

PROMPT Think about the stories you read in this module.

Imagine that your class has a story-hour podcast. Write your own trickster tale to read aloud for the show. Think about the lesson you want to share with your listeners. Then, write a new story to teach this lesson. Use what you have learned about trickster tales from *A Pair of Tricksters* and *In The Days of King Adobe* to teach your lesson.

I will write a story about _____.

✓ Make sure your trickster tale
☐ introduces the characters and setting.
☐ has a plot that teaches a lesson.
☐ tells events in a logical order.
☐ uses dialogue, description, and sensory details.
☐ has a conclusion that wraps up the story and reminds readers of the lesson.

Who will be the trickster in your story? Who will the trickster try to fool? Why does the trickster want to fool this character? What lesson will you teach? Look back at your notes and revisit the texts as necessary.

In the chart below, write about your characters and the problem they face, as well as the lesson or moral of the tale. Use Critical Vocabulary words where appropriate.

My Trickster: _____

Characters	How Is the Character Tricked?	What Really Happens?	Lesson or Moral

Plan

- **As needed, guide students** to think about the characters and the events for their stories.
- **Encourage them** to use plot elements from trickster tales read in the module to help them choose a lesson or moral for their stories.
- **Encourage students** to include Big Idea Words and Critical Vocabulary in their stories, as appropriate.

145

DRAFT ·· Write your story.

Write a strong **beginning** that describes the setting and characters. Describe the problem that your trickster wants to solve.

Draft

- **Read aloud** the directions, referring back to the checklist as you do so.
- **Suggest** that students brainstorm the main events of their story with a partner before they begin their story maps.
- **Have students** refer to their chart as they construct the beginning, middle, and ending sentences of their stories.

In the **middle** of your story, tell about how the trickster will solve this problem in an order that makes sense.

Write an **ending** for your story that shows how the problem is solved. Make sure you include the lesson that the characters learn.

REVISE AND EDIT · Review your draft.

The revision and editing steps give you a chance to look carefully at your writing and make changes. Work with a partner to determine whether your characters and events are clearly described for readers. Use these questions to help you evaluate and improve your story.

✓	PURPOSE/ FOCUS	ORGANIZATION	EVIDENCE	LANGUAGE/ VOCABULARY	CONVENTIONS
	☐ Have I told about a problem the trickster wants to solve? ☐ Have I included a lesson?	☐ Does my story have a clear beginning, middle, and ending? ☐ Did I tell the events in an order that makes sense?	☐ Did my trickster act like those in the selections? ☐ Did I include dialogue and sensory details to explain what happens?	☐ Did I use words such as *first, later,* and *finally* to show the order of events?	☐ Did I use correct spelling? ☐ Did I indent each new paragraph? ☐ Did I use prepositional phrases correctly?

PUBLISH · Share your work.

Create a Finished Copy Make a final copy of your story. You may want to include illustrations or present your story in a graphic novel format. Consider these options to share your story:

1. E-mail your story to a friend or relative.

2. Read your story aloud to your classmates.

3. Gather your classmates' stories and scan them to create a digital book of trickster tales. Post the class book on your school's website.

Revise and Edit

- **Guide students** to use the checklist as they work with partners to improve their stories.

- **Remind students** to refer back to trickster tales in the module to be sure their stories teach a lesson or moral.

Present

- **Students can copy** their revised drafts using their best handwriting. For handwriting models, see the resources section in the back of this Teacher's Guide.

- **Students can use** a computer to input their revised drafts. See Literacy Centers Printable **Keyboarding 7.1, 7.2, and 7.3** for keyboarding lessons.

Introduce the Topic

- **Read aloud** the module title, *Food for Thought*.

- **Tell students** that in this module they will be reading and viewing selections on the topic of food.

- **Have students** explain what they know about different types or categories of food.

- Then ask students to discuss the different ways in which the module title can be interpreted. (*Possible responses: It can mean important ideas or information to think about. It can mean thinking about different foods we eat.*)

MODULE

8

Food for Thought

"You are what you eat."

—American saying

Discuss the Quotation

- **Read aloud** the quotation, which is a common American saying.

- **Lead a discussion** in which students discuss whether or not they agree with the saying and why. Explain the meaning of the quote, as needed: *If you eat healthy foods, you'll be healthy. If you eat unhealthy foods, you'll be unhealthy.*

- **Ask students** to give examples of healthy and unhealthy foods. (*Accept reasonable responses.*)

148

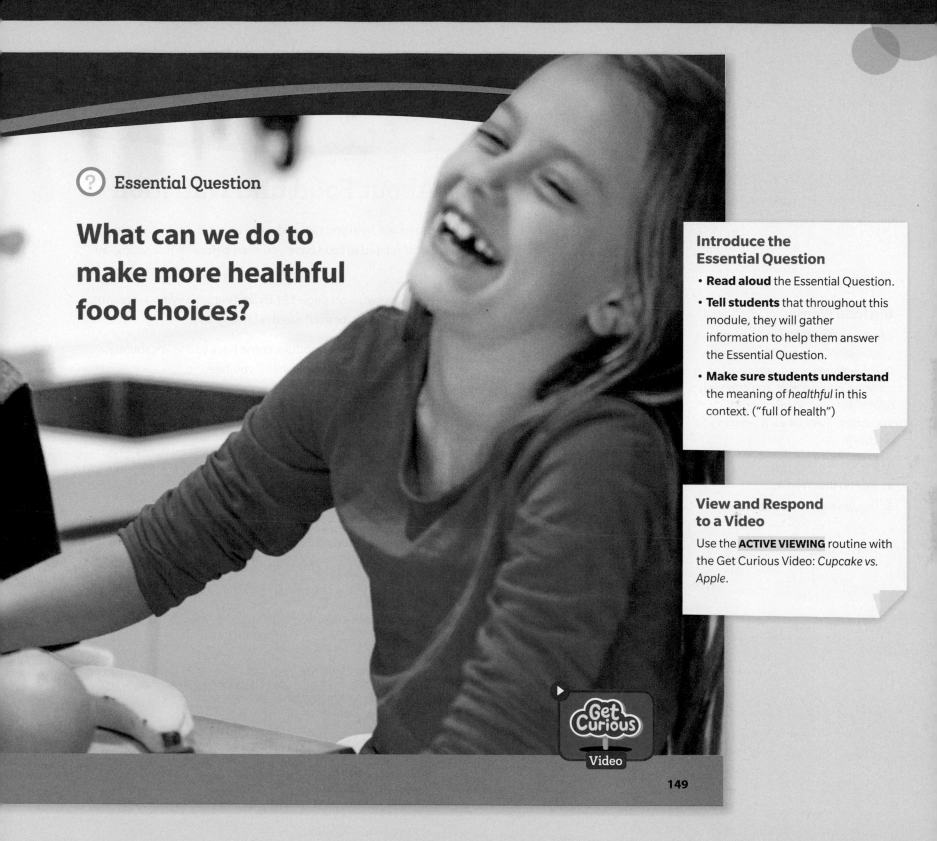

? Essential Question

What can we do to make more healthful food choices?

Introduce the Essential Question

- **Read aloud** the Essential Question.
- **Tell students** that throughout this module, they will gather information to help them answer the Essential Question.
- **Make sure students understand** the meaning of *healthful* in this context. ("full of health")

View and Respond to a Video

Use the **ACTIVE VIEWING** routine with the Get Curious Video: *Cupcake vs. Apple*.

Get Curious

Video

149

Words About Food and Nutrition

The words in the chart will help you talk and write about the selections in this module. Which words related to food have you seen before? Which words are new to you?

Add to the Vocabulary Network on page 151 by writing synonyms, antonyms, and related words and phrases for each word related to food.

After you read each selection in this module, come back to the Vocabulary Network and keep building it. Add more ovals if you need to.

WORD	MEANING	CONTEXT SENTENCE
digest (verb)	When you digest food, it moves through your body to your stomach.	Some foods, like meats and cheese, take longer to digest than others.
sustainable (adjective)	If you use a natural resource that is sustainable, it is able to stay at a certain level and not cause harm to the environment.	Farmers are trying to grow food in a sustainable way.
compost (noun)	Compost is decayed plant waste that can be used to fertilize soil.	The compost we make will be used in our vegetable garden.
nutrition (noun)	If you have good nutrition, you eat the right foods to help you stay healthy and grow.	Good nutrition includes eating fresh fruits, vegetables, and lean protein.

150

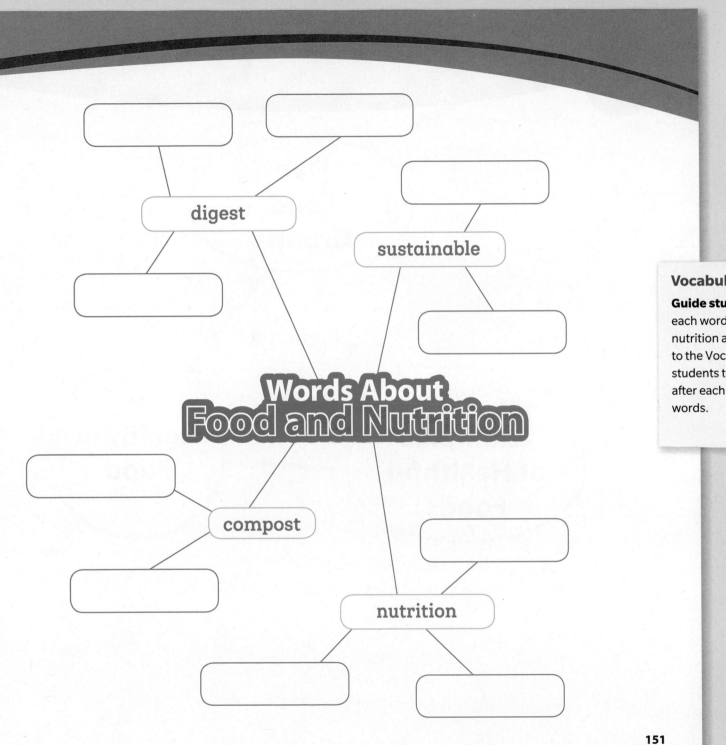

digest

sustainable

Words About
Food and Nutrition

compost

nutrition

151

Knowledge Map

- **Review the categories** on the knowledge map with students. Explain that these categories name the concepts students will learn about in the module.

- **Have students** add information and illustrations to the knowledge map at the end of each week during Make Connections. Remind students to review the texts and video to add details to the map.

- At the end of the module, have students work in pairs or small groups to compare and contrast the information they added to their knowledge maps.

Five
Food
Groups

Examples
of Healthful
Foods

Healthful
Food

Eco-friendly Foods

153

READ FOR UNDERSTANDING

Introduce the Text

- **Read aloud** the title. Tell students that this is an informational text. Discuss with students what they know about informational texts. *(They present facts to inform readers about a topic.)*

- **Guide students** to set a purpose for reading.

- **Point out** the highlighted Big Idea Words.

- **Have students** read the text.

 READ FOR UNDERSTANDING

Text and Graphic Features

- **What kind of text feature is "Serve It Up"?** *(a heading)* **Why does the author use headings?** *(to help identify the main, or central, ideas of each section)*

- **What is the main, or central, idea of "Serve It Up"?** *(There are five main food groups that the USDA recommends we eat from each day.)*

ANNOTATION TIP: Have students underline the main or central idea.

- **What does the diagram in this section show?** *(the daily amount of each food group that kids between the ages of 9 and 13 should eat)*

DOK 2

154

 myNotes

Short Read

To Your Health!

1 Good nutrition is one of the keys to good health. When you eat right, your body digests, or breaks down, vitamins, minerals, and other nutrients that help you grow strong and stay well.

Healthy You, Healthy Planet

2 Eating well can help the planet as well as your body. When you shop with your family, look for sustainable foods, which are often natural, locally-grown foods such as fruits and vegetables.

3 Some people compost bits of unused fruits, vegetables, and other natural waste. The compost can be used in their home gardens. Many cities also collect food waste to create compost. That's good news!

ChooseMyPlate.gov

Serve It Up

9 There are five food groups: protein, grains, vegetables, fruit, and dairy. According to the United States Department of Agriculture (USDA), we should aim to eat from each group every day. Here's what the USDA recommends daily for kids between ages 9 and 13.

10 **Fruits** and **vegetables** keep your heart healthy and protect you from diseases.

Daily Serving:
1½ cups of fruit and 2 to 2½ cups of vegetables

11 **Oils** are not a food group, but they provide important nutrients.

Daily Serving:
The USDA does not recommend more than 5 teaspoons of oil a day

4 Nutrition labels help you make good food choices, but they can seem mysterious. In fact, reading them can be a downright tricky. This diagram tries to take out the mystery.

5 The list of numbers on the right shows what percentage of the USDA recommended daily allowance for adults one serving contains. How many servings of this food would get you a full-day's worth of the recommended fat?

Nutrition Facts

8 servings per container

Serving size	1 cup (68g)

Amount per serving	
Calories	**370**

	% Daily Value*
Total Fat 5g	**7%**
Saturated Fat 1g	**5%**
Trans Fat 0g	
Cholesterol 0mg	**0%**
Sodium 150mg	**6%**
Total Carbohydrate 48g	**15%**
Dietary Fiber 5g	**14%**
Total Sugars 13g	
Includes 10g Added Sugars	**20%**
Protein 12g	
Vitamin A 10mcg	**20%**
Vitamin C 1mg	**100%**
Vitamin D 1mcg	**50%**
Vitamin E 2mcg	**100%**
Riboflavin 5mcg	**75%**
Folic Acid 200mcg	**60%**
Thiamin 2mcg	**35%**
Vitamin B12 5mcg	**100%**
Zinc 7mg	**50%**
Biotin 300mcg	**100%**
Calcium 50mcg	**25%**
Phosphorus 90mcg	**90%**
Magnesium 400mcg	**100%**
Chromium 75mcg	**80%**
Potassium 5g	**100%**

* The % Daily Value (DV) tells you how much a nutrient in a serving of food contributes to a daily diet. 2,000 calories a day is used for general nutrition advice.

6 Calories measure the energy food provides. Here, the label is telling you that 1 cup contains 370 calories.

7 Your body doesn't need added sugar, so look for foods with lower amounts.

8 Your body needs these nutrients. Look for food with high amounts. This food provides 25 percent of the calcium you need each day. How many servings of it would give you a full-day's worth?

 READ FOR UNDERSTANDING

Text and Graphic Features

• **Why does the author include an image of a nutrition label in this section of the text?** *(The text says knowing how to read nutrition labels helps us choose foods that are good for us. This gives students an opportunity to learn how to read nutrition labels.)*

ANNOTATION TIP: Have students underline the details that explain about nutrition labels.

DOK 2

 READ FOR UNDERSTANDING

Text and Graphic Features

• **How does the author use the nutrition label callouts to support the main, or central, idea?** *(The callouts help readers understand how to read a nutrition label and determine if the food contains things a healthy body needs.)*

DOK 3

12 **Protein** is found in meat, fish, beans, eggs, nuts, and seeds. Protein helps build healthy bones, muscles, skin, and blood.

Daily Serving:
5 ounces of protein each day (1 ounce equals ¼ cup of ground meat, one egg, or a tablespoon of peanut butter.)

13 **Dairy**, such as milk, cheese, and yogurt, contains calcium and other minerals. These nutrients support strong teeth and bones.

Daily Serving:
3 cups of dairy each day (1 cup is equivalent to 1½ ounces of cheese or an 8-ounce container of yogurt.)

14 **Whole grains**, such as whole-wheat flour, oatmeal, and brown rice, help your body create energy and supply it with certain vitamins and nutrients.

Daily Serving:
5 to 6 ounces of grains each day (1 ounce equals one slice of bread or ½ cup of cooked rice, pasta, or cereal.)

155

READ FOR UNDERSTANDING

Introduce the Text

- **Read aloud** and discuss the genre information. Point out these examples of each text feature:
  - » problem and solution (page 158)
  - » diagrams (page 163)
  - » directions (page 163)
- Use Display and Engage **Build Background 8.2**.
- **Tell students** to look for the Critical Vocabulary as they read and to think about the words' meanings.

ANNOTATION TIP: Have students use the box to note what they want to learn from the selection.

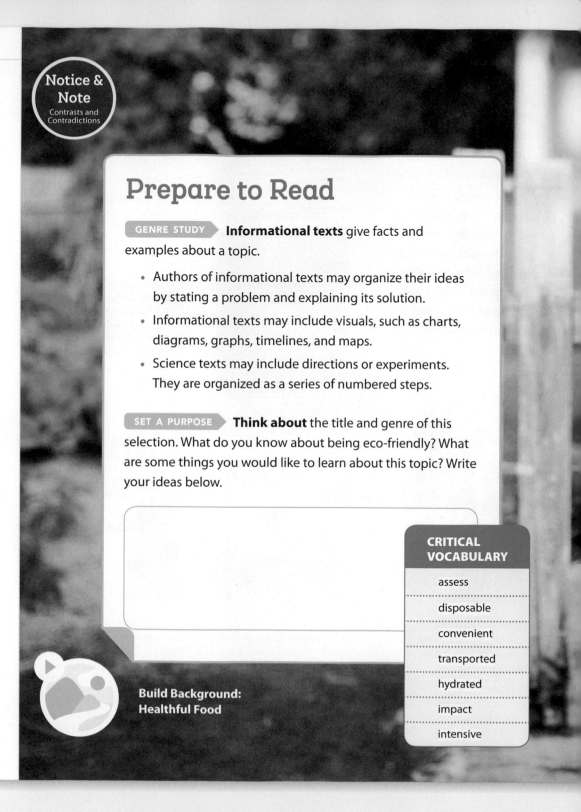

Prepare to Read

GENRE STUDY **Informational texts** give facts and examples about a topic.

- Authors of informational texts may organize their ideas by stating a problem and explaining its solution.
- Informational texts may include visuals, such as charts, diagrams, graphs, timelines, and maps.
- Science texts may include directions or experiments. They are organized as a series of numbered steps.

SET A PURPOSE **Think about** the title and genre of this selection. What do you know about being eco-friendly? What are some things you would like to learn about this topic? Write your ideas below.

Build Background:
Healthful Food

CRITICAL VOCABULARY

assess

disposable

convenient

transported

hydrated

impact

intensive

Eco-Friendly Food by Cath Senker

157

Monitor and Clarify

MODEL MONITORING AND CLARIFYING

🔍 **THINK ALOUD** *As I read, I can pause to think about what I am reading and make sure I understand what I have read. If I don't understand something, I can reread the text, read on to get more information, and look for clues in the graphic features. I know that the word wasteful means to create unnecessary trash, but I am not sure what waste-aware means. I read on to find out how to pack a lunch using fewer disposable items. Now I understand that waste-aware means knowing how to decrease the amount of trash you create.*

DOK 2

 READ FOR UNDERSTANDING

What is the list in the first box? *(a list of disposable items people use to pack their lunch)*

What does the author want readers to understand? *(The author wants readers to understand that it is wasteful to use so many containers to pack one lunch.)*

ANNOTATION TIP: Have students underline all the examples of disposable items in the list.

DOK 2   **158**

 myNotes

Are You
Wasteful
or
Waste-aware?

1 What fast and simple changes can you make so your food and drinks are more eco-friendly, cheaper, and better for you? First, **assess** yourself! Are you wasteful or waste-aware? Check this list of **disposable** items to see how your packed lunch measures up:

- sandwich in a cardboard or plastic box
- salad in a plastic box
- chips, bars, or cookies in plastic packaging

- containers of yogurt
- carton or bottle of a drink
- plastic cutlery
- plastic bags

2 If you have lots of disposable items in your lunch, consider the ideas below. Or if you're having pasta or rice for dinner, why not make a little extra to keep for lunch the next day?

1. Pick a carbohydrate (bread, pasta, rice).
2. Choose fresh vegetables in season or canned vegetables.
3. Add protein (prepared meat, canned fish, cheese, cooked beans).

4. Pack or chop fruit into natural yogurt (from a large carton).
5. Put your meal and yogurt into food containers.
6. Pour juice or water into a drink bottle (strong plastic or metal).

assess   If you assess something, you think about it carefully and judge it.
disposable   If something is disposable, it is meant to be thrown away once it has been used.

TARGETED CLOSE READ

Author's Purpose

Have students reread the box at the bottom of page 158.

Who do you think the author's intended audience is? *(parents, children, and people who pack their own lunch)*

What does the author want readers to do? Use evidence for support. *(The author wants readers to find ways to be less wasteful. The author gives examples of ways to use fewer disposable containers, combine foods, and use reusable containers.)*

DOK 3

159

Monitor and Clarify

What does the word *compost* mean? How can you clarify your understanding of this word?
(Compost is something you put in a garden to make plants grow. I look for text clues that help me figure out the word's meaning.)

If students have difficulty clarifying the meaning of the word *compost*, use this model:

Q THINK ALOUD *When I read an unknown word, I look for text clues. The text says that leftover food is part of compost which fertilizes the garden. These clues help me understand what compost is.*

DOK 2

 myNotes

TARGETED CLOSE READ

Ideas and Support

Have students reread paragraphs 5–6.

What is the claim about these foods? *(They are better for the environment.)*

What evidence does the author use to support this claim? *(The ingredients are chemical-free.)*

What evidence is used to argue against this claim? *(It takes lots of energy to produce, package, and transport the food.)*

DOK 2

Eco Snacks

3   Of course, it can be hard to be organized enough to prepare food every day. At Ithaca Creek State Primary School, in Australia, workers at an on-site snack bar prepare sandwiches and salads with fresh ingredients—some of the produce comes from the school garden. They minimize food waste by making meals or sandwiches when they are ordered. Any leftover food goes in the compost along with fruit and vegetable peelings. The liquid from the compost fertilizes the garden, and the whole cycle begins again!

Processed Organic Foods

4   Pre-packaged organic meals and snacks are convenient, but are they better for the environment?

Pros	Cons
5 The ingredients are products of organic farming, which does not use chemical fertilizers that can harm wildlife.	6 Processing food requires a large amount of energy. Once produced, processed foods are packaged, transported, and often chilled in a refrigerator just like non-organic foods.

convenient   If something is convenient, it is handy and useful.
transported   If something is transported, it is taken from one place to another.

Think
About Your
Drink

7   There is nothing wrong with buying a soda or fruit drink every now and then when you're out. However, although some bottled drinks are healthy, many contain a large amount of sugar and additives, and they are not cheap. Also, packaging, transporting, and refrigerating the beverages come at a cost to the environment.

8   So, how can you cut down on costs and waste but stay hydrated and healthy? If you live in an economically developed country such as the United States, your home will have a fresh water supply—and it is probably cleaner and safer than bottled water. In some areas, the water is safe but does not taste good. You could talk to your family about buying a water filter to make tap water taste better.

hydrated   Something that is hydrated has taken in plenty of water.
impact   Impact is the effect that one thing has on something else.

Eco Impact

myNotes

9   A U.S. report in 2010 showed that:

◊ About 50 percent of bottled water is actually tap water in a plastic bottle.

TAP

◊ About 75 percent of the bottles are thrown away, not recycled.

◊ The plastic in some bottles leaches (leaks) a substance called phthalate into the water. Some studies have linked this chemical with hormonal problems in people.

◊ Bottled water goes through fewer safety tests than tap water.

◊ Bottled water costs 100 times as much as tap water! Bottled water typically costs just over $1 for 1 gallon (3.8 liters) and much more when you buy smaller bottles. Tap water costs about 1 cent per gallon.

16 [1]

Notice & Note
Contrasts and Contradictions

• **Remind students** that when an author compares or contrasts things, it is important to ask why te comparison is important.

• **Have students** explain why the author contrasts bottled water to tap water. (*She wants to share that tap water is likely cleaner, safer, and cheaper than bottled water.*)

ANNOTATION TIP: Have students underline the differences between tap water and bottled water.

• **Have students** reflect on the Anchor Question: *What does this make me wonder about?* and add to their notes.

DOK 2

🔍 TARGETED CLOSE READ
Text and Graphic Features

Have students reread the sidebar information.

How does the information in the sidebar support the author's claim? (*Most bottles are not recycled; some plastic bottles give off harmful substances; bottled water is more expensive than tap water.*)

DOK 3

Monitor and Clarify

Remind students that as they read, it is important to monitor their understanding of the text. Have students use clues in the text and graphic features to explain what a cylinder garden is. *(A cylinder garden is a garden made out of seeds that are planted in a bucket that is placed on top of soil or concrete.)*

DOK 2

🔍 **TARGETED CLOSE READ**

Ideas and Support

Have students reread paragraph 10.

What is the author's claim in the paragraph? *(There is a cheap and easy way to grow your own food.)*

What is one reason the author gives to support this claim? *(Food can be grown in cylinder gardens that can be placed anywhere; you do not need gardening experience; preparation is simple.)*

Who is the intended audience? *(children at school)*

ANNOTATION TIP: Have students underline the author's claim and evidence that supports it.

DOK 2

 myNotes

Growing Food

10   There is a cheap and easy way to grow food at school—even if there are no flower beds! Cylinder gardening uses containers that can be placed almost anywhere. You don't need any gardening experience, and the preparation is simple. Why not give it a try?

Make a Cylinder Garden

11   **You will need:**

- At least one 5-gallon (23-liter) bucket of the type used to transport food (you could ask a local restaurant to supply clean buckets)

- Potting soil

- Vegetable seeds

- Fertilizer

162

Directions

12

1. Figure out where to place your cylinder garden. You can position it on top of soil or on a human-made surface, such as concrete. Try to find an area that will receive at least six to eight hours of sunlight and is close to a source of water.

2. Research vegetables that will grow during the season you are in. If you are gardening at school, look for varieties that you can harvest within a school quarter or semester—30 to 90 days. Search for compact varieties that can grow in a small space. The vegetables that are suitable for cylinder gardening are beans, carrots, parsley, peas, or tomatoes.

3. Cut off the bottom of the bucket and discard it. Then cut the rest of the bucket in half. You will need to ask an adult to help you. Now you have two cylinders. (Note: If you are placing the bucket on concrete, it is better not to cut it, but ask an adult to drill drainage holes in the bottom.)

4. Put the cylinders in position.

5. Fill them with potting soil and mix in some fertilizer.

6. Plant your seeds, following the instructions on the package for spacing, and water gently.

7. Monitor the seedlings as they grow, keeping them moist with water and adding fertilizer regularly. Thin out the seedlings if they are crushed together.

🔍 **TARGETED CLOSE READ**

Text and Graphic Features

Have students reread page 163.

Why is the text on page 163 numbered? *(It is a list of directions for making a cylinder garden. The steps are numbered to show the order in which they are to be done.)*

What do the diagrams show? *(They show how to cut the bucket and plant the seeds.)*

Why do you think the author includes these visuals? *(to help readers easily understand what to do in steps 3 and 5)*

ANNOTATION TIP: Have students underline the text that describes what each diagram shows.

DOK 3

TARGETED CLOSE READ

Author's Purpose

What is the purpose of the text on page 164? *(The author reminds readers how to make eco-friendly food and drink choices.)*

What do you think the author wants readers to do after they read this selection? *(to think about ways they can be less wasteful; to grow and eat foods that are good for them and the environment)*

DOK 3

 READ FOR UNDERSTANDING

Wrap-Up

Revisit the purpose students set before they read the text. Have students explain what they learned from the text and cite text evidence.

DOK 2

Food Miles

13 Growing your own vegetables reduces food miles. The principle behind food miles is that the farther away your food is produced, the worse for the environment. However, keep in mind that beans that are produced locally using oil-based fertilizers and plowed by diesel tractors could be worse than beans grown by less energy-intensive methods in another country. Storing local food for a long time to be eaten out of season can also use up a lot of energy.

Being Green: Summing Up

14 • **Make eco-friendly packed meals and snacks.**

• **Stay hydrated by drinking tap water.**

• **Grow your own food.**

intensive Something that is intensive uses a lot of effort to complete a task.

164

Collaborative Discussion

Look back at what you wrote on page 156. Tell a partner two things you learned from this text. Then work with a group to discuss the questions below. Support your ideas with information and details from *Eco-Friendly Food*. Take notes for your responses. When you speak, use your notes.

1 Review page 158. Which of the ideas that the author lists are wasteful? Which are waste-aware?

2 Reread page 162. What reasons does the author give for making a cylinder garden?

3 What are some ways that growing food at a school garden can be useful?

 Listening Tip

As you listen to each speaker's ideas, think about how you can connect your own ideas to them.

 Speaking Tip

Make sure you use eye contact when you state your ideas and supported opinions.

Academic Discussion

Use the **COLLABORATIVE DISCUSSION** routine. Have students write notes to answer the questions. Then have groups apply the Listening and Speaking Tips as they discuss their responses.

Possible responses:

1. *It is wasteful to pack a lunch with many disposable items and have each item in a separate package. It is waste-aware to combine foods and use reusable packaging.* DOK 1

2. *The author says that a cylinder garden does not require gardening experience and it is simple to prepare.* DOK 2

3. *Growing food at a school garden can be useful because it provides healthy foods and shows children how they can cheaply and easily grow foods at their own homes.* DOK 2

Write Instructions

PROMPT

In *Eco-Friendly Food*, you read instructions for how to make a cylinder garden. The selection included diagrams to help explain the instructions.

Imagine that your class is creating a how-to manual for your school about growing and preparing food. Think of something you know how to grow or make. Write instructions to contribute to the manual. Start with a paragraph introducing what is being made, a list of ingredients and materials, and the steps for growing or making your food. Include a diagram or illustration of the materials and the finished product. Don't forget to use some of the Critical Vocabulary words in your writing.

PLAN

Make notes about the graphic features the author uses. Note words, phrases, or sentences that you think make the instructions easy to follow.

Now write your instructions to tell how to grow or prepare food.

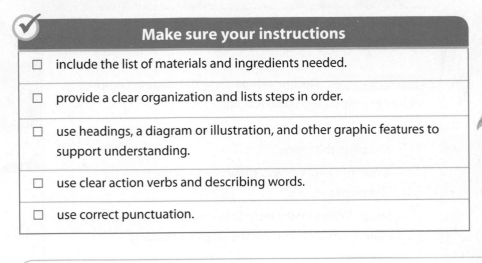

✓	**Make sure your instructions**
☐	include the list of materials and ingredients needed.
☐	provide a clear organization and lists steps in order.
☐	use headings, a diagram or illustration, and other graphic features to support understanding.
☐	use clear action verbs and describing words.
☐	use correct punctuation.

Write About Reading

- **Review with students** the directions and checklist in the Write section.

- **Encourage students** to organize and write their instructions in a way that is easy to follow and makes sense.

VIEW FOR UNDERSTANDING

Introduce the Video

- **Read aloud** and discuss the genre information. Tell students that a recipe video uses a visual and audio format to present the steps to complete a recipe. A narrator introduces the ingredients and explains the steps taken to make the recipe. A recipe video may also contain text.

- Use Display and Engage **Build Background 8.6**.

- **Call attention** to the Critical Vocabulary. Tell students to listen for these words as they watch the video.

ANNOTATION TIP: Have students use the box to note what they want to learn from this video.

 VIEW FOR UNDERSTANDING

Set a Purpose

- **Have students** look at the photograph on this page and think about what the recipe might be and who might appear in the video.

- **Guide students** to set a purpose for viewing.

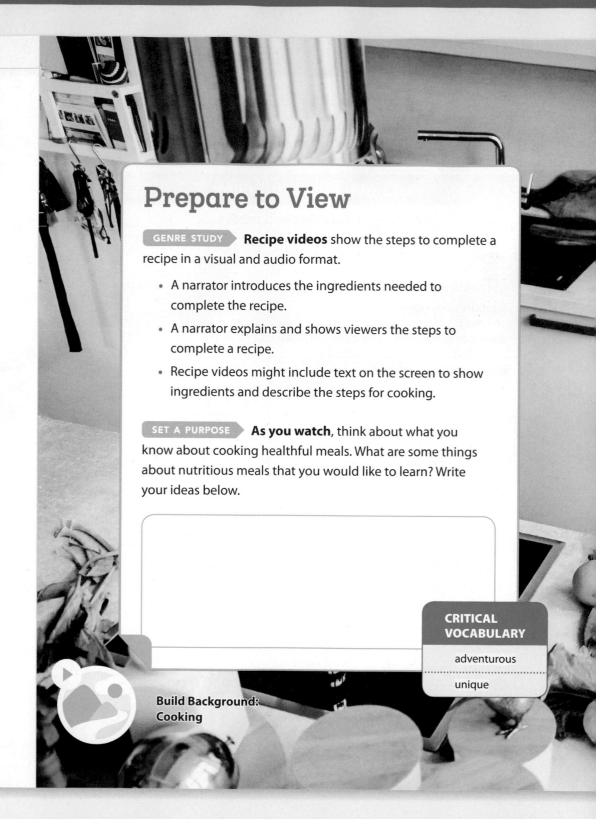

Prepare to View

GENRE STUDY **Recipe videos** show the steps to complete a recipe in a visual and audio format.

- A narrator introduces the ingredients needed to complete the recipe.

- A narrator explains and shows viewers the steps to complete a recipe.

- Recipe videos might include text on the screen to show ingredients and describe the steps for cooking.

SET A PURPOSE **As you watch**, think about what you know about cooking healthful meals. What are some things about nutritious meals that you would like to learn? Write your ideas below.

Build Background: Cooking

CRITICAL VOCABULARY

adventurous

unique

168

Kids Rock Nutrition in the Kitchen

from Nutrition.gov

VIEW FOR UNDERSTANDING

Ask and Answer Questions

MODEL ASKING AND ANSWERING QUESTIONS

🗨 **THINK ALOUD** *To better understand the video, I can ask myself questions. I will ask myself about the purpose of a recipe video. How will this video help me when I could just use a printed recipe? After I watch the video, I realize that watching a chef explain the steps makes the recipe easier to follow. It;s helpful to see the ingredients and the food preparation in action, too.*

VIEW FOR UNDERSTANDING

What recipes are being prepared in the video? *(chicken packets, fish packets, and fruit parfaits)*

TARGETED CLOSE READ

Media Techniques

Have students view the video again and pay special attention to the visual elements.

Identify the adult cook in the video. Is this person an expert in food preparation? Explain. *(Lorraine Butler; She is an expert because she is a chef and a registered dietitian. This information is provided in a text box in the video.)*

Why do you think the video includes close-up views of a variety of vegetables? *(The close-ups support the chef's suggestion to be adventurous and try different vegetables when you want a change.)*

If chicken takes longer to bake than fish, why can both packets be in the oven together and be done baking at the same time? Cite information from the video to support your answer. *(Chicken bakes for about 20 minutes at 165°F and fish for about 10 minutes at 145°F. The fish packets can be put in the oven after the chicken has baked for about 10 minutes, so both will be done at the same time.)*

As you watch *Kids Rock Nutrition in the Kitchen*, think about what you need to know to follow a recipe. What important ideas do you need to remember? Pay attention to how the people, images, and text in the video work together to share important steps and ideas. Do the people, images, and text make the main ideas clear and easy to follow? Why or why not? Take notes in the space below.

Listen for the Critical Vocabulary words *adventurous* and *unique*. Listen for clues to the meaning of each word.

adventurous	Someone who is adventurous tries to do new things.
unique	Something that is unique is different or one of a kind.

Collaborative Discussion

Look back on what you wrote on page 168. Tell a partner two things you learned from this video. Then discuss the questions below. Refer to the details in the video to support your ideas. Take notes for your responses. When you speak, use your notes.

1 What does the dietitian suggest about how to prepare a fish or chicken packet?

2 What do the students learn about the steps for making a fruit parfait?

3 Review the video segment from 01:00 to 01:15. What key points about chicken and fish does the dietitian share?

 Listening Tip

Show you are paying attention by looking at your partner as he or she shares their ideas. Make note of any ideas you want to know more about.

 Speaking Tip

After you speak, ask your partner to share his or her questions or comments about what you have said.

Academic Discussion

Use the **COLLABORATIVE DISCUSSION** routine. Have students write notes to answer the questions. Then have groups apply the Listening and Speaking Tips as they discuss their responses.

Possible responses:

1. *Vary vegetables for color and taste and try different ingredients at different times. Wash hands before making packets. Have a grown-up around for safety when working with knives. Write names on the foil before baking to identify each packet.* DOK 1

2. *First, prepare parfaits while the fish or chicken packets are in oven. The way you make a fruit parfait is up to you. Then, choose the ingredients. Use strawberries, grapes, bananas, blueberries, or any desired fruit that is in season. Use whole-grain granola and some pecans, or use oats, brown rice, whole-grain barley, or whole wheat instead of granola. At least half should be whole grains. Use low-fat yogurt. Next, put either yogurt or granola in parfait bowl, alternating layers. Lastly, add the toppings.* DOK 2

3. *Key points: (1) Although there are some differences in cooking, fish takes less time in the oven. (2) Fish, such as salmon or trout, has important oils in it that are healthy for you. (3) Both chicken and fish are excellent sources of protein.* DOK 3

Write a Blog Post

PROMPT

In *Kids Rock Nutrition in the Kitchen,* you learned about how to make a tasty and nutritious meal. The dietitian in the video is an expert on healthful foods.

Imagine that your community has a food blog in which people share their experiences with food or cooking. Write a paragraph about an interesting food-related experience. You may include a cooking experience that turned out great, a cooking experience that went terribly wrong, or the first time you tried a new or unusual food. Don't forget to use some of the Critical Vocabulary words in your writing.

PLAN

Identify the audience and purpose of *Kids Rock Nutrition in the Kitchen*. Then take notes about details that the video includes to meet the needs of the audience and its purpose.

Write About Reading

- **Read aloud** the prompt with students.

- **Lead a discussion** in which students share their ideas about experiences with food or cooking. Tell students to use the video to help them develop ideas and details to include in their writing.

- **Then read aloud** the Plan section. Have students use ideas from the discussion in their notes.

Now write your blog post.

✓ Make sure your blog post

☐ begins by introducing your food-related experience.

☐ describes events in the order in which they happened.

☐ uses words and phrases to help show the sequence of events.

☐ uses correct punctuation.

☐ ends with a concluding sentence.

Write About Reading

- **Review with students** the directions and checklist in the Write section.

- **Encourage students** to use their own words as they describe their food-related experience.

READ FOR UNDERSTANDING

Introduce the Text

- **Read aloud** and discuss the genre information. Point out that informational texts give facts and examples about a topic. Authors may organize their ideas by using:
  - » comparing, or telling how things are alike, and contrasting, or telling how things are different
  - » headings to introduce the topic of the next section of text
  - » bold print or italics to call attention to certain words in a text
  - » captions to explain what is shown in an illustration or photo
- Use Display and Engage **Build Background 8.8**.
- **Tell students** to look for the Critical Vocabulary as they read and to think about the words' meanings.

ANNOTATION TIP: Have students use the box to note what they want to learn from this selection.

Notice & Note
Contrasts and Contradictions

Prepare to Read

GENRE STUDY **Informational texts** give facts and examples about a topic.

- Authors of informational texts may organize their ideas using headings and subheadings.
- Authors of informational texts may also organize ideas by comparing and contrasting.
- Informational texts may include text features, such as bold print, captions, and italics.

SET A PURPOSE **Think about** the title and genre of this text. What do you know about the unusual foods people in other countries eat? What would you like to learn? Write your ideas below.

Build Background: Unusual Foods

CRITICAL VOCABULARY

pests

edible

forbidden

attitudes

BUG BITES

📖 **READ FOR UNDERSTANDING**

Set a Purpose

- **Have students** read the title and look at the illustration on this page. Then have students look at the next few pages to note headings and view additional illustrations.

- **Guide students** to set a purpose for reading. Discuss with them what they think they will learn from this selection.

DOK 2

175

READ FOR UNDERSTANDING

Using paragraphs 2 and 3, what main ideas are expressed in favor of eating bugs? *(Lots of people in other countries eat them; bugs are nutritious, tasty, and safe to eat.)*

ANNOTATION TIP: Have students underline the names of countries where people eat bugs.

DOK 2

Notice & Note

Contrasts and Contradictions

- **Remind students** that when an author presents two ideas that contrast or contradict one another, you should stop and ask yourself why these differences are important.

- **Have students** identify the contrasting ideas in paragraphs 1-3. Why does the joke matter? *(The author shows a contrast between people who eat bugs and people who wouldn't think of doing so. The joke matters because it introduces the topic by showing the contrast in attitudes.)*

- **Have students** reflect on the Anchor Question: *What does this make me wonder about?* and add to their notes.

DOK 3   **176**

 my Notes

1   *Have you heard the one about the customer who finds a fly in his soup? Outraged, he points it out to the waiter, who says, "Keep your voice down, or everybody'll want one!" OK, so it's an old joke. But the funny part is what the waiter says. Who on earth would want to eat a bug?*

2   Well, would it surprise you if we said lots of people would? It's true. In Australia, South America, Africa, and Asia, eating bugs is no joke. Bugs aren't just pests. They're lunch or dinner or a nice afterschool snack.

3   To those of us who've never crunched a cricket or slurped a worm, the idea of eating bugs sounds pretty gross. We wouldn't eat those creepy-crawlies even if someone dared us! Yet lots of bugs are nutritious, tasty, and perfectly safe to eat.

pests   Pests are insects or small animals that harm crops or annoy people.

EAT UP! WE'RE OUTNUMBERED

4 Eating bugs is an old habit. Ten thousand years ago, before they learned to farm, our ancestors found food by hunting and gathering. Bugs were considered part of the daily diet. It made sense for ancient people to eat a source of nutrition that was right under their noses—or buzzing by their ears.

5 As you've probably noticed, bugs are everywhere. One out of every three animals is a bug, and scientists estimate that there are 200 million of the little critters for every person on the planet. No wonder more than half the people on earth still eat bugs daily. Of the million or so types of bug that scientists have named so far, more than 1,500 are somebody's favorite snack.

6 The most popular bugs to eat are crickets and termites, which are said to taste a bit like pineapple, but lots of other bugs are edible, too. Restaurants in Mexico sell ant tacos. Cans of baby bees line supermarket shelves in Japan. In Thailand, outdoor markets offer silkworm larvae. And in Mozambique, in eastern Africa, people call grasshoppers "flying shrimp."

edible If something is edible, it is safe for people to eat.

myNotes

In the United States, a candy company sells bug-filled lollipops. ▼

This clay pan is filled with dried grasshopper snacks. You can find these snacks all over Mexico. ▼

177

Central Idea

Have students reread the section, "Bugs Do a Body Good," to analyze the text for the connection between the central, or main, idea and supporting details.

What is the central, or main, idea of this section? *(Cooked grasshoppers are more nutritious and better for your body than a hamburger.)*

What are two details that support the central, or main, idea? *(a pound of grasshoppers has less fat than a pound of beef; the insects are higher in calcium and iron)*

How does the author organize details in this section? How does it support the central, or main, idea? *(comparison and contrast; The author compares cooked grasshoppers to a hamburger and gives details that contrast the nutritional values of grasshoppers and beef.)*

DOK 3

📖 **READ FOR UNDERSTANDING**

Ask and Answer Questions

Have students ask themselves a "bug-related" question and answer it using facts from the text. *(Responses will vary.)*

If students have difficulty asking a question, use this model:

💬 **THINK ALOUD** *I will ask myself which foods are bug-related. I read in paragraph 10 that bug-related foods are honey from bees, as well as shrimp, crayfish, crabs, and lobsters.*

DOK 2

✏️ myNotes

Which is more nutritious—
ground beef or grasshoppers?
▼

At this market in Thailand, people can buy a variety of fried insects.
▼

BUGS DO A BODY GOOD

7 Dinner is served: on one plate, a big, juicy hamburger, and on the other, a heaping pile of cooked grasshoppers. Ground beef or bugs? Which one do you think is better for your body?

8 Both have lots of protein, which is what your body uses to build muscle. But in other ways, grasshoppers clearly come out ahead. A pound of grasshoppers has less fat than a pound of beef, and the insects are higher in calcium and iron. Other bugs are good for you, too. Says biologist David George Gordon, author of the Eat-a-Bug Cookbook, "I tell kids, if your bones are still growing, eat more crickets and termites."

9 Still wouldn't pick the grasshoppers? Gordon says they also taste delicious, a lot like green peppers.

A MATTER OF TASTE

10 In North America and Europe, the idea of eating bugs is downright disgusting to most people. But even though we don't think of crickets and termites as food, lots of things we do eat are bug-related. Honey is made by bees. Shrimp, crayfish, crabs, and lobsters are all arthropods, which is what scientists call the bug group of animals. In fact, lobsters have only recently made the transition from bug to edible treat. The first American colonists ate lobsters only when they didn't have anything else. In Massachusetts, servants who were tired of getting the "cockroaches of the sea" for dinner wrote into their contracts that they'd eat lobster only three times a week.

178

They may look scary, but these fried scorpion kebabs are a popular snack in China.

Other parts of the world also have forbidden foods. Lots of people would never eat lobsters and the other sea-dwelling "bugs" we consider delicacies. Many people don't eat pork. Even among people who eat insects, tastes differ. South Africans might munch termites for lunch, but they'd never eat scorpions, which are raised for food in China. In Bali, Indonesia, dragonflies are a treat, but in the Indonesian province of Irian Jaya, no one would think of eating a dragonfly. Cicadas are on the menu instead.

So when it comes to eating, people mostly stick with food they're used to. What's food and what's not is a matter of taste—and what you've been taught.

forbidden If something is forbidden, it is not allowed or accepted.

 myNotes

Notice & Note

Contrasts and Contradictions

- **Remind students** that when they are reading and notice that the author shows a contrast between things, they should ask themselves why these differences are important.
- **Have students** reread paragraphs 11 and 12. Ask students why the author might describe contrasting tastes in food. (*The author wants to support the claim that people have different tastes in different places.*)

ANNOTATION TIP: Have students highlight each place and the insect eaten there, using a different color for each place-insect pair.

- **Have students** reflect on the Anchor Question: *What does this make me wonder about?* and add to their notes.

DOK 3

 READ FOR UNDERSTANDING

Why do you think people in different places eat certain types of bugs and not other types?
(*Paragraph 12 says that people eat mostly what they're used to, so they must be eating the types of bugs that are found in their particular area or that were brought into their area many years ago.*)

DOK 3

Ideas and Support

Have students reread the "Future Food" section to distinguish fact from opinion and to identify the audience.

How does the author support his opinion? *(The author writes about bug appreciation programs and using bugs during space travel.)*

What readers do you think the author had in mind when writing this text? Why do you think so? *(Readers are most likely kids because the "Future Food" section mentions "kids today" and "school lunches;" the illustration shows a kid eating a larvae sandwich.)*

DOK 2

Wrap-Up

Revisit the purpose students set before they read the text. Have students explain what they learned from the text and cite text evidence.

DOK 2

180

FUTURE FOOD

13 Could our tastes change? Could school lunches ever include grasshopper kabobs and caterpillar fritters?

14   Attitudes about bugs are already changing. Thanks to bug-appreciation programs at schools and science centers, kids today are less squeamish about insects. If we can get over the "Gross!" factor, bugs could one day become part of our daily diet. Bugs are even considered a perfect food for long space journeys, because astronauts could breed them in outer space.

15   Still wondering who on earth would want to eat a bug? Better to ask, who wouldn't?

attitudes   Your attitudes are the ways you think and feel about something.

This fried insect burger may look unusual, but it's a popular meal in some countries.

Collaborative Discussion

Look back at what you wrote on page 174. Tell a partner two things you learned from this text. Work with a group to discuss the questions below. Support your ideas with details from *Bug Bites*. Take notes for your responses. When you speak, use your notes.

1 Review page 176. Which words reveal the author's point of view about eating bugs?

2 Reread pages 177–178. What examples does the author provide to support the popularity of eating bugs?

3 How does the author use humor to make the ideas in the selection convincing?

Listening Tip

Be an active listener! Focus on what each person is saying. Try jotting down a few notes to help you remember important points.

Speaking Tip

Be sure to use the correct rate and volume when you state and support your opinions. Be sure to speak clearly.

Academic Discussion

Use the **COLLABORATIVE DISCUSSION** routine. Have students write notes to answer the questions. Then have groups apply the Listening and Speaking Tips as they discuss their responses.

Possible responses:

1. *The author states that "bugs aren't just pests" and "they're lunch or dinner or a nice afterschool snack." The author also points out that "lots of bugs are nutritious, tasty, and perfectly safe to eat" (paragraph 3).* **DOK 2**

2. *Some examples of popular bugs are crickets and termites, ants in tacos sold in Mexico, baby bees canned for sale in Japan, silkworm larvae sold in Thailand markets, and grasshoppers called "flying shrimp" by people in Mozambique in eastern Africa.* **DOK 2**

3. *The author introduces the text with a joke about a customer who finds a fly in his soup and a waiter who says everybody will want one. Certain words and phrases add a touch of humor, such as "crunched a cricket," "slurped a worm," and "creepy-crawlies" in paragraph 3; and "grasshopper kabobs" and "caterpillar fritters" in paragraph 13. Humorous section titles include "Eat Up! We're Outnumbered" and "Bugs Do A Body Good." The illustrations of mouths open to bite down on bugs is humorous.* **DOK 3**

18

Cite Text Evidence

Write an Advertisement

PROMPT

In *Bug Bites,* you learned about some of the bugs that people around the world like to eat. The author explained why people all over the world eat bugs as part of their diet.

Imagine that you have been asked to write a script for a television advertisement encouraging people to eat some of the bugs you read about. Provide strong reasons why people should eat bugs, supported with evidence from *Bug Bites.* Don't forget to use some of the Critical Vocabulary words in your writing.

PLAN

Think of at least two reasons that people should try bugs. Then, write down facts and other details from the text to support each of these reasons.

Write About Reading

- **Read aloud** the prompt with students.

- **Lead a discussion** in which students share their ideas about the reasons people should be encouraged to eat bugs. Tell students to use text evidence to support their ideas.

- **Then read aloud** the Plan section. Have students use ideas from the discussion in their notes.

Now write the script for your advertisement.

Make sure your advertisement
☐ clearly states the claim that people should eat bugs.
☐ provides reasons for the claim.
☐ includes facts, details, and examples from the text to support each reason.
☐ uses series commas correctly.
☐ ends with a concluding statement.

Write About Reading

- **Review with students** the directions and checklist in the Write section.
- **Encourage students** to use their own words as they compose an advertisement about the claim that people should eat bugs.

183

Introduce the Text

- **Read aloud** and discuss the genre information. Point out that realistic fiction includes characters who think, act, and speak like real people. Realistic fiction includes dialogue between characters and may be told through third-person point of view.

- Use Display and Engage **Meet the Author 8.11**.

- **Tell students** to look for the Critical Vocabulary as they read and think about the words' meanings.

ANNOTATION TIP: Have students use the box to note what they think the girl is getting ready to do.

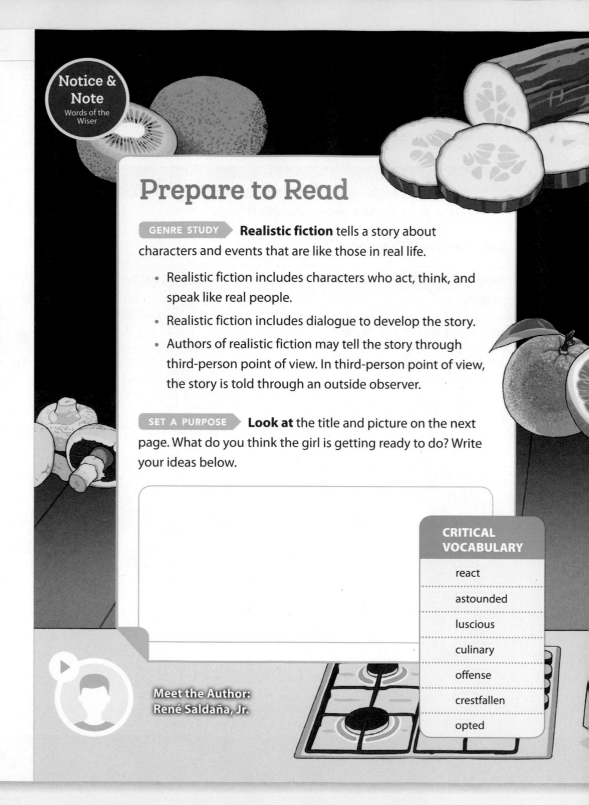

Notice & Note
Words of the Wiser

Prepare to Read

GENRE STUDY **Realistic fiction** tells a story about characters and events that are like those in real life.

- Realistic fiction includes characters who act, think, and speak like real people.

- Realistic fiction includes dialogue to develop the story.

- Authors of realistic fiction may tell the story through third-person point of view. In third-person point of view, the story is told through an outside observer.

SET A PURPOSE **Look at** the title and picture on the next page. What do you think the girl is getting ready to do? Write your ideas below.

Meet the Author:
René Saldaña, Jr.

CRITICAL VOCABULARY

react

astounded

luscious

culinary

offense

crestfallen

opted

184

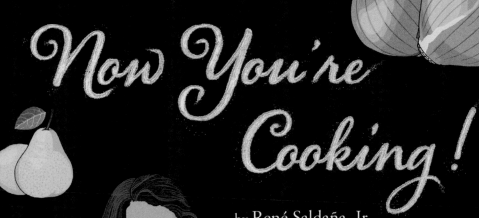

Now You're Cooking!

by René Saldaña, Jr.

illustrated by Jonathan Allardyce

 READ FOR UNDERSTANDING

Set a Purpose

- **Have students** look at the title and the illustration.
- **Guide students** to set a purpose for reading. Discuss with them what they think this selection will be about.

DOK 2

185

READ FOR UNDERSTANDING

Make and Confirm Predictions

MODEL MAKING AND CONFIRMING PREDICTIONS

THINK ALOUD *Before I read, I will look at the illustrations and make a prediction about the characters. Then, as I read, I will look for clues that tell me whether my predictions are correct. I think one girl is nervous about having to cook, but the other girl is excited for her. After I read page 187, I know my prediction is correct. The author says Martina is nervous about being a finalist in a cooking contest, and her friend Avani hugs her and excitedly says, "Now you're cooking!"*

DOK 2

186

1   Martina Deanda couldn't have been more nervous. A few moments ago she had heard her name announced on the school intercom. She was one of two finalists in the Spring Cook-Off, an annual event sponsored by the school district and the local farmers market. She couldn't believe that she'd made it this far. Before she'd entered the contest, her experience in the kitchen had been limited to pouring milk on her cereal for breakfast. Otherwise, her cooking skills were nonexistent. She was an avid viewer of television cooking shows, though.

2   Her best friend, Avani, came up to her smiling, hugged her, and said, "Now you're cooking!" Avani chuckled at her own pun. When Martina didn't react, Avani said, "Get it? You're in a cooking competition and you're moving on to the final cook-off, so now you're cooking? Right?"

react   When you react to something, you act in a way that shows you are aware of it.

🔍 **TARGETED CLOSE READ**

Point of View

Have students reread paragraph 1 to determine the point of view from which the story is told.

From which point of view is paragraph 1 being told? *(third person)*

Why does an author write a story in the third-person? *(The author wants to let the reader know about different characters. Each character can then contribute to the plot differently.)*

ANNOTATION TIP: Have students underline the pronouns in paragraph 1 that show the reader the story is written in third-person point of view.

DOK 3

🔍 **TARGETED CLOSE READ**

Idioms

Have students reread paragraph 2 to find the idiom.

What does Avani mean when she uses the idiom, "Now you're cooking!"? *(It means Marina has finally arrived because she is a finalist in the cooking contest.)*

DOK 3

187

READ FOR UNDERSTANDING

How does Martina's cooking experience compare to Joey's cooking experience? *(Joey has more real-life experience. Martina gets her inspiration from cooking shows, while Joey is learning how to cook from the chef in his family's restaurant.)*

DOK 2

🔍 **TARGETED CLOSE READ**

Idioms

Have students reread paragraph 4 to find the idiom.

What does the idiom "my goose is cooked" mean? *(that Martina is going to have a difficult time winning the contest)*

What clues in the text help you understand the idiom? *(The competitor that Martina is facing works in his family's restaurant, which is the best Mexican restaurant in town. He is learning to cook from the chef.)*

ANNOTATION TIP: Underline the idiom.

DOK 3

188

3   It wasn't that she didn't get it. Martina was just astounded that she'd made it to the finals. She was competing with her classmate Joey Cardenas, whose mother owned the best Mexican restaurant in town, La Tampiqueña. On weekends, Joey helped in the restaurant bussing tables, sweeping the floors, and learning to cook from the chef on Saturdays between lunch and dinner service. He was sure to win.

4   Martina wished she could share in Avani's excitement. "More like my goose is cooked," she told her friend.

5   "You won't win with that kind of attitude," said Avani. "You should be more positive."

6   "Why? I mean, Joey knows how to cook. Me? I only have my cooking shows for inspiration."

7   Avani put her hands on Martina's shoulders. "You're just looking at this all wrong. You don't know as much about cooking as Joey does, but look how far you've gotten today. There were ten contestants. First, you baked some luscious breakfast empanadas and then you made that roasted vegetable panini that the judges described as "mouth-watering." Now the competition is down to the two best cooks—you and Joey. That should tell you *some*thing."

> **astounded**   If you are astounded by something, you are completely surprised by it.
> **luscious**   A food that is luscious is tasty and often juicy.

LA TAMPIQUE

8   "I guess you're right. I'm just nervous."

9   Avani smiled. "I think most people are nervous when they compete. It means what you are doing is really important to you."

10 "It really is," Martina said. "Thanks, Avani."

11 Moments later, a voice on the intercom asked for everyone but the two contestants to leave the stage. "Contestants, it's time for you to show off your **culinary** skills," announced emcee and local television news anchor Jack Jackson. Joey Cardenas's mom whispered some last-second advice in his ear and left the stage.

12 Joey looked confident as he walked up to the girls. "You ready, Freddy?" he asked.

13 "Hey, Joey," said Avani, "Martina is more than ready." As she turned to go Avani looked over her shoulder and said, "She's so on fire today that the thermometer's going to explode!"

> **culinary**   Something that is culinary is connected to cooking.

— myNotes

READ FOR UNDERSTANDING

Why does Joey look confident as he approaches the girls? *(He knows he has a lot of experience, and he is sure he is going to win.)*

DOK 2

Notice & Note

Words of the Wiser

- **Remind students** that authors may have a character that is removed from the problem and may be able to offer insight or advice to the main character. When students find an example of this, they should consider why a character's insight is significant to the story.

- **Have students** identify an example of Words of the Wiser and explain why it is significant. *(Avani reminds Martina of the delicious food she cooked in the competition and the judges' description of the food. She also tells Martina that most people are nervous when they compete because it means they are doing something really important to them. Avani's words are significant because they make Martina feel better about competing against Joey.)*

- **Have students** reflect on the Anchor Question: *What is the life lesson and how might it affect the character?* and add to their notes.

DOK 3

189

myNotes

 TARGETED CLOSE READ

Idioms

Have students reread paragraphs 16 and 17 to find the idiom.

What does the idiom "cook circles around you" mean? *(It means Martina will cook better than Joey.)*

What does this idiom demonstrate in regards to how Martina is feeling about competing? *(Martina is feeling very confident.)*

DOK 3

14   Joey chuckled for a moment, but then his expression became serious. "You ready for this?" he asked Martina.

15   "As much as I'll ever be. You?"

16   "Well, you know, cooking's in my genes," he said. "No offense."

17   "None taken," she responded. "But don't be surprised if I cook circles around you."

18   "If you say so. May the best cook win!" With that, the two took their places.

19   Mr. Jackson joined them at the table where two paper bags from the farmers market awaited them. The audience became quiet. Mr. Jackson looked out over the crowd and said, "We have come to my favorite part of this competition, the finale." In addition to being the emcee, Mr. Jackson had served as one of the judges for the very first Spring Cook-Off ever. Mrs. Cardenas, Joey's mom, had won that one.

> **offense**   An offense is something that makes you feel hurt, annoyed, or insulted.

190

myNotes

20   Martina looked over at Joey, who, for the first time since the start of the competition, looked nervous. He kept fidgeting with the strings on his apron. Martina imagined that the Cardenas family reputation was on the line.

21   Martina looked out at the audience and saw her own parents, both beaming with pride. Avani was sitting next to them, pumping a fist in the air and mouthing the words, "Go, Martina!"

22   Mr. Jackson asked the contestants to empty their bags. "Carefully, though. You don't want to crack those eggs. Your challenge is this: using part or all of every ingredient in the bag, plus a dash of this or a pinch of that, make a delicious, healthful meal."

23   In each bag there were three eggs, a red and a yellow bell pepper, a tomato, strawberries, and a peach. A rack of spices, seasonings, and other ingredients stood next to the table. Martina looked over at Joey, who was now smiling, rubbing his hands together. She could almost see the gears turning in his brain. He knew what he was making. She had no clue.

📖 **READ FOR UNDERSTANDING**

Make and Confirm Predictions

After reading paragraphs 20-23, predict who will win the Spring Cook-Off. (*Students may respond with either Joey or Martina.*)

What evidence from the text helps you make that prediction? (*Joey is smiling and knows immediately what he wants to make and Martina has no clue. Martina has the support of her parents and Avani, and Joey might get nervous again with the pressure to win and make his family happy.*)

If students have difficulty making a prediction, use this model:

💬 **THINK ALOUD** *I predict Martina will win the contest because she is feeling more confident and has her family and friend cheering her on. I will continue to read to see if my prediction is correct.*

DOK 2

191

TARGETED CLOSE READ

Text and Graphic Features

Have students analyze the illustrations on page 192.

What facial expression does each character have? *(Martina is smiling and Joey's face is serious.)*

How do the illustrations add to your understanding of the story?
(I can tell that Martina is feeling happy because she is using a special family memory as inspiration. I also understand that Joey is feeling determined.)

DOK 3

READ FOR UNDERSTANDING

What did Martina learn about herself as a cook? *(She has more to inspire her than just cooking shows. She also has memories of her grandfather teaching her how to make his favorite breakfast.)*

ANNOTATION TIP: Underline the ingredients Martina uses in her meal.

DOK 2

24   "You'll have 20 minutes," said Mr. Jackson. "Cooks, are you ready?" The two nodded. Joey was anxious to get to work. Martina was still thinking, but wasn't coming up with anything. *Oh, no,* she thought, *Joey's going to win this competition!*

25   "Cook!" cried Mr. Jackson and started the timer.

26   Martina ran over to the rack to see if looking at all the spices and other ingredients would inspire her. She saw a basket of bread. Sitting on top were two *bolillos* (boh-LEE-yohz), a kind of bread that reminded her of early mornings visiting her grandparents in Mexico—warm, toasty mornings.

27   Then it struck her. She had more than just the cooking shows to inspire her! She also had memories of her abuelito Servando teaching her to fix his favorite breakfast. Martina took the two pieces of bread, a sprig of cilantro, and some butter, and then she got cooking.

* * *

192

28   In the end, Martina didn't win the cook-off, but she wasn't crestfallen. She noticed that the judges had finished all of her dish, while Joey's was left half-eaten. Mr. Jackson reminded her that the instructions called for a healthful meal, and though she had used the peppers, tomato, strawberries, and peach, she still could've separated the egg whites from the yolks and opted for olive oil instead of butter. "But I'll tell you what, Ms. Deanda," he said, "that was one delicious meal."

29   Martina walked up to Joey, who held the trophy over his head. "Congratulations, Joey," she said. "You cooked a better meal than mine."

30   "It looks that way," he said. But he glanced at the judges' plates. "There's always next year, though."

31   *Yes,* she thought. *There's always next year.* And there would be many more visits to her grandparents' home between now and then. She couldn't wait for her next visit! Maybe she'd give them a telephone call that night and tell them about the competition.

> **crestfallen** If you are crestfallen, you are sad and discouraged.
> **opted** If you opted for something, you chose it.

myNotes

Make and Confirm Predictions

How did you confirm or revise your prediction about who would win the contest? (*Responses will vary.*)

DOK 2

Notice & Note

Words of the Wiser

- **Remind students** that authors may have a character that is removed from the problem and may be able to offer insight or advice to the main character. When students find an example of this, they should consider why a character's insight is significant to the story.

- **Have students** identify an example of Words of the Wiser in paragraph 28 and explain why it is significant. (*Mr. Jackson reminds Martina of the contest instructions and suggests ingredient changes. His words are significant because they help Martina understand why she lost the contest and how she can improve herself for next year's competition.*)

DOK 3

🔍 TARGETED CLOSE READ

Point of View

How do the characters add to the plot of the story? (*The characters have different points of view, and the author can show their different emotions as well as interactions between the characters.*)

DOK 3

Bolillo Boats

Ingredients

- 2 bolillos or other soft white rolls
- 1 tablespoon butter, melted
- 2 eggs
- 1 tablespoon butter or olive oil (for cooking the eggs)
- ¼ cup shredded Monterey Jack cheese
- 2 slices of tomato
- 2 slices of red, yellow, or orange bell pepper
- a few sprigs of cilantro

Instructions

Have an adult help you when using the stove and oven.

1. Preheat oven to 350º.

2. Gently pinch out the middle of the bolillos. They should look like little bread boats.

3. Brush the melted butter onto each bolillo, inside and out.

4. Place bolillos on a baking sheet and bake for 5 minutes. Once lightly toasted, remove from oven.

5. While bread is baking, fry the two eggs and slices of pepper in butter or olive oil. Try cracking the egg inside the slice of pepper.

6. Spoon a fried egg and a slice of pepper into each of the bread boats and top with a slice of tomato. Sprinkle cheese evenly onto the bread boats, and bake for another 5–10 minutes or until cheese has melted.

7. Ask an adult to remove the baking sheet from the hot oven. Garnish with a sprig of cilantro. Serve with sliced peaches and strawberries on the side.

194

Collaborative Discussion

Look back at what you wrote on page 184. Tell a partner two things you learned about the main character, Martina. Then work with a group to discuss the questions below. Find support for your answers in *Now You're Cooking!* During the discussion, ask questions to find out more about others' ideas.

1 Review pages 187–188. What details in the text show how Martina feels about being in the finals?

2 Review page 193. How does Martina feel about the results of the cook-off? How do you know?

3 What parts of the story are presented in a realistic way? Explain your thinking.

 Listening Tip

Listen carefully to identify each speaker's key ideas. What questions can you ask to find out about these ideas?

Speaking Tip

Speak in complete sentences and use correct grammar to clearly express your ideas and supported opinions.

Academic Discussion

Use the **COLLABORATIVE DISCUSSION** routine. Have students write notes to answer the questions. Then have groups apply the Listening and Speaking Tips as they discuss their responses.

Possible responses:

1. *Martina is nervous. She doesn't feel as if she has enough experience to win the contest.* DOK 2

2. *Martina is happy she did her best, and she is gracious enough to congratulate Joey. She is also looking forward to next year's competition and calling her grandparents to tell them about the recipe she used in the contest.* DOK 2

3. *The contest is portrayed realistically with details such as judges and an emcee, the participants feeling nervous and competitive, and a trophy being presented to the winner at the end.* DOK 3

Write a Newspaper Article

PROMPT

In *Now You're Cooking!*, you read a story about a cooking competition.

Imagine that you are a local reporter assigned to cover a cook-off. Write an article for your newspaper about the contestants, what they cooked, and the outcome. Don't forget to use some of the Critical Vocabulary words in your writing.

PLAN

Write the names of each of the contestants and how he or she felt at the end of the competition. Then, write something interesting that the contestant might have said to a reporter.

Now write your newspaper article about the cook-off.

Make sure your article
☐ introduces the topic and the people involved.
☐ tells events in the order in which they happened.
☐ includes concrete details, quotations, and other information related to the topic.
☐ correctly uses commas and quotation marks.
☐ provides a concluding statement related to the topic.

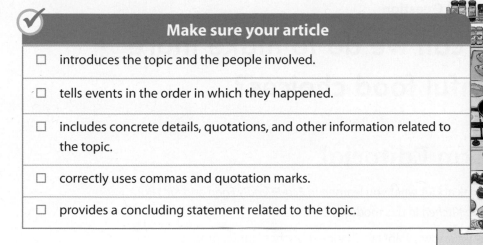

Write About Reading

- **Review with students** the directions and checklist in the Write section.

- **Encourage students** to use their own words as they write their newspaper article.

? **Essential Question**

What can we do to make more healthful food choices?

Write an Editorial

PROMPT Think about what you learned in *Eco-Friendly Food* and *Kids Rock Nutrition in the Kitchen* in this module.

Imagine that your town wants to change the school lunch program. Some people believe school lunches should include more healthful foods and be served in ways that do the least harm to the environment. Write an editorial for your local newspaper to explain your opinion about this topic. Use evidence from the texts to support your opinion.

I will write about _____.

✓ Make sure your editorial
☐ states your opinion clearly in an introduction.
☐ is organized into paragraphs that give reasons that support your opinion.
☐ includes evidence from the text, video, and your own experiences.
☐ uses persuasive language.
☐ ends with a conclusion that will leave readers with something to think about.

198

What evidence from the text and the video support your argument for changing the school lunch program? Look back at your notes, and revisit the texts and video as necessary.

As you plan, use the chart below to record details about healthful food choices and how to make choices that are better for the environment. Use the details to write an opinion statement.

My opinion statement: _____

Details from *Eco-Friendly Food*	Details from *Kids Rock Nutrition*

Plan

- **As needed, guide students** to think of the opinion they want to express in their editorial.

- **Encourage them** to use details from the text and the video to support their opinion.

- **Encourage students** to include Big Idea Words and Critical Vocabulary in their editorials, as appropriate.

DOK2

199

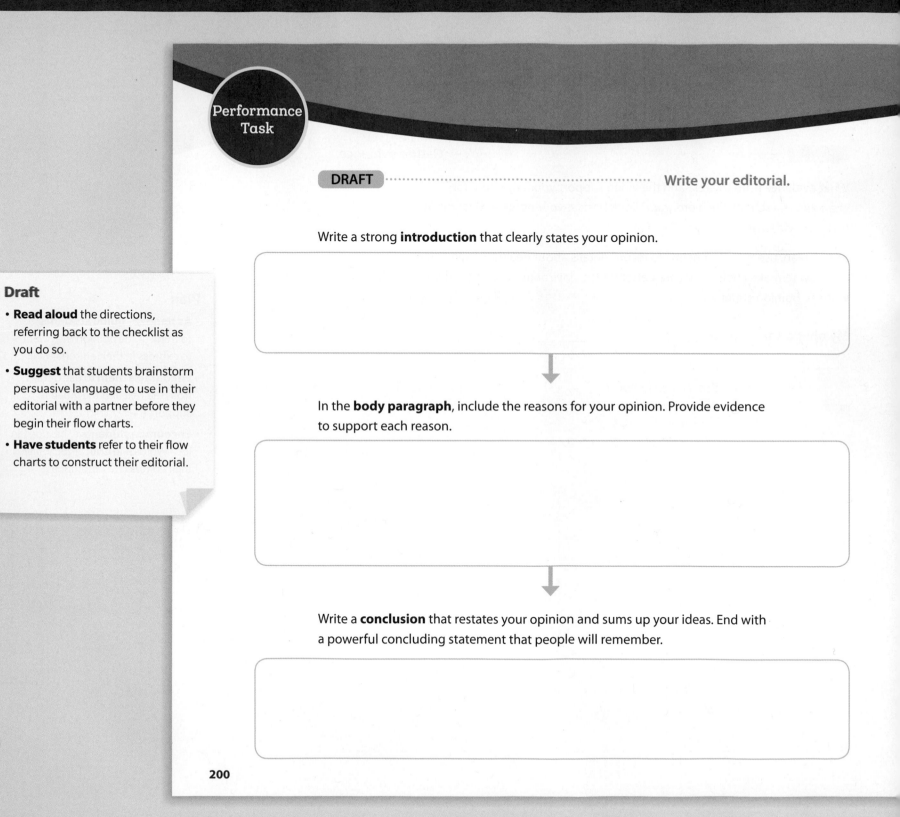

DRAFT .... Write your editorial.

Write a strong **introduction** that clearly states your opinion.

In the **body paragraph**, include the reasons for your opinion. Provide evidence to support each reason.

Write a **conclusion** that restates your opinion and sums up your ideas. End with a powerful concluding statement that people will remember.

Draft

- **Read aloud** the directions, referring back to the checklist as you do so.
- **Suggest** that students brainstorm persuasive language to use in their editorial with a partner before they begin their flow charts.
- **Have students** refer to their flow charts to construct their editorial.

200

REVISE AND EDIT   ··············   Review your draft.

The revision and editing steps give you a chance to look carefully at your draft and make changes. Work with a partner to determine whether you have explained your ideas clearly. Use these questions to help you evaluate and improve your editorial.

PURPOSE/ FOCUS	ORGANIZATION	EVIDENCE	LANGUAGE/ VOCABULARY	CONVENTIONS
☐ Have I clearly stated my opinion? ☐ Have I supported my opinion with reasons?	☐ Does my editorial have a clear introduction? ☐ Have I provided a strong conclusion?	☐ Have I supported each of my reasons with facts and details from the article and video?	☐ Did I use clear, vivid language that will persuade my readers to share my opinion?	☐ Are all of my sentences punctuated correctly? ☐ Did I use pronouns correctly? ☐ Have I spelled all the words correctly?

PUBLISH   ··············   Share your work.

Create a Finished Copy Make a final copy of your editorial. Add a headline that communicates your opinion and will capture the attention of readers. Consider these options to share your writing:

1. Create a digital copy of your editorial and upload it to a school or class website.

2. Present your editorial as a speech to your class. Practice ahead of time so that you can deliver your speech clearly and confidently.

3. Participate in a debate or panel discussion with classmates on both sides of the issue.

Revise and Edit

- **Guide students** to use the checklist as they work with partners to improve their editorials.

- **Remind students** to refer back to the texts in the module to be sure they use appropriate details to support their opinion.

Present

- **Students can copy** their revised drafts using their best handwriting. For handwriting models, see the resources section in the back of this Teacher's Guide.

- **Students can use** a computer to input their revised drafts. See Literacy Centers Printable **Keyboarding 8.1, 8.2, and 8.3** for keyboarding lessons.

Introduce the Topic

- **Read aloud** the module title, *Global Guardians.*

- **Tell students** that in this module they will be reading and viewing selections on the topic of caring for the planet.

- **Have students** explain what they know about environmental problems and what people are doing to solve them.

- Then ask students to discuss the different ways in which the module title can be interpreted. *(Possible responses: Guardians take care of or watch over something or someone. "Global Guardians" may mean watching over the planet by taking care of the environment.)*

Discuss the Quotation

- **Read aloud** the quotation by Lady Bird Johnson.

- **Lead a discussion** in which students discuss whether or not they agree with Johnson's statement, and why. Explain the meaning of the quote, as needed: *The environment is one common thread shared by all people on Earth.*

- **Give examples** of global guardianship as it relates to the environment. *(Accept reasonable responses.)*

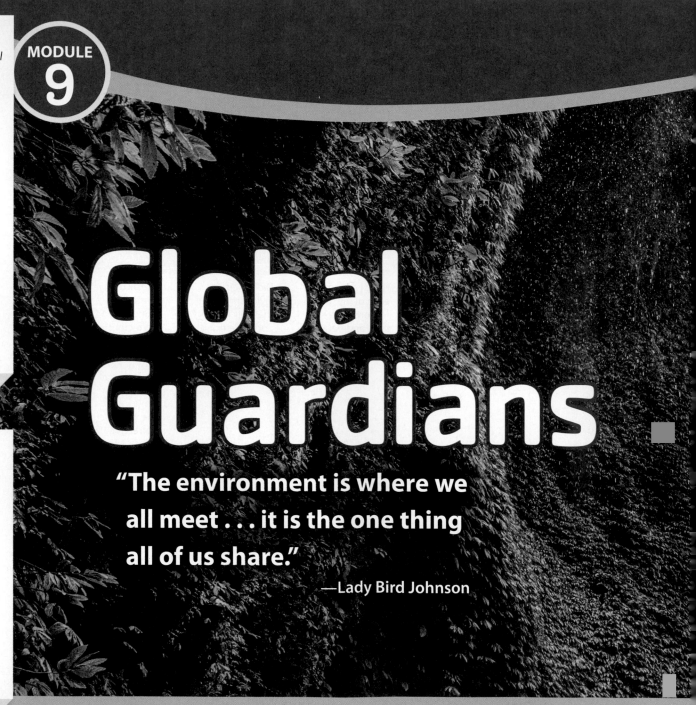

MODULE

9

Global Guardians

"The environment is where we all meet . . . it is the one thing all of us share."

—Lady Bird Johnson

202

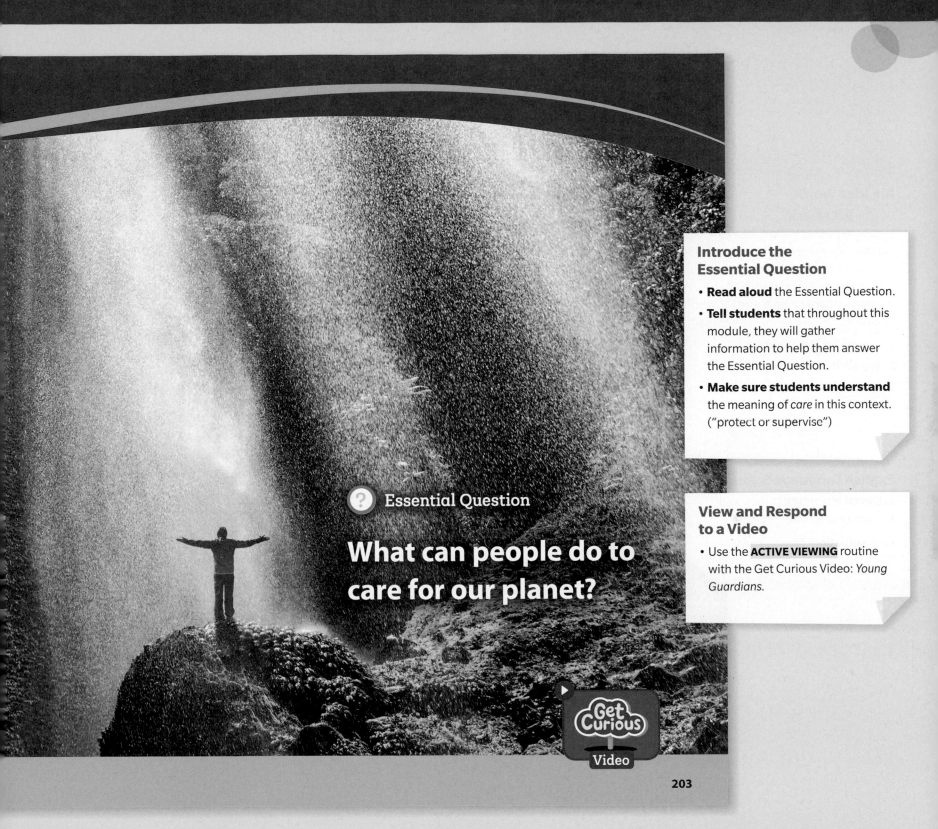

❓ Essential Question

What can people do to care for our planet?

Introduce the Essential Question

- **Read aloud** the Essential Question.
- **Tell students** that throughout this module, they will gather information to help them answer the Essential Question.
- **Make sure students understand** the meaning of *care* in this context. ("protect or supervise")

View and Respond to a Video

- Use the **ACTIVE VIEWING** routine with the Get Curious Video: *Young Guardians.*

203

Big Idea Words

Use the **VOCABULARY** routine and the Vocabulary Cards to introduce the Big Idea Words *ecology, recycle, conservation,* and *sanctuary*. You may wish to display the corresponding Vocabulary Card for each word as you discuss it.

1. Say the Big Idea Word.

2. Explain the meaning.

3. Discuss the context sentence.

English Language Support

ALL PROFICIENCIES Display and discuss these Spanish cognates.

• **conservation** *conservación*

Words About Protecting Our Planet

The words in the chart will help you talk and write about the selections in this module. Which words about protecting our planet have you seen before? Which words are new to you?

Add to the Vocabulary Network on page 205 by writing synonyms, antonyms, and related words and phrases for each word about protecting our planet.

After you read each selection in this module, come back to the Vocabulary Network and keep building it. Add more ovals if you need to.

WORD	MEANING	CONTEXT SENTENCE
ecology (noun)	Ecology is the relationship between the living things in their environment.	I wrote about the ecology of the rainforest for my science project.
recycle (verb)	If you recycle something, you put it through a process so that it can be reused.	Remember to recycle the newspaper after you read it.
conservation (noun)	Conservation is the act of saving and protecting the environment.	People are working hard for the conservation of wildlife in this area.
sanctuary (noun)	A sanctuary is where people or animals go to be safe from danger.	The elephants are safe living in the animal sanctuary.

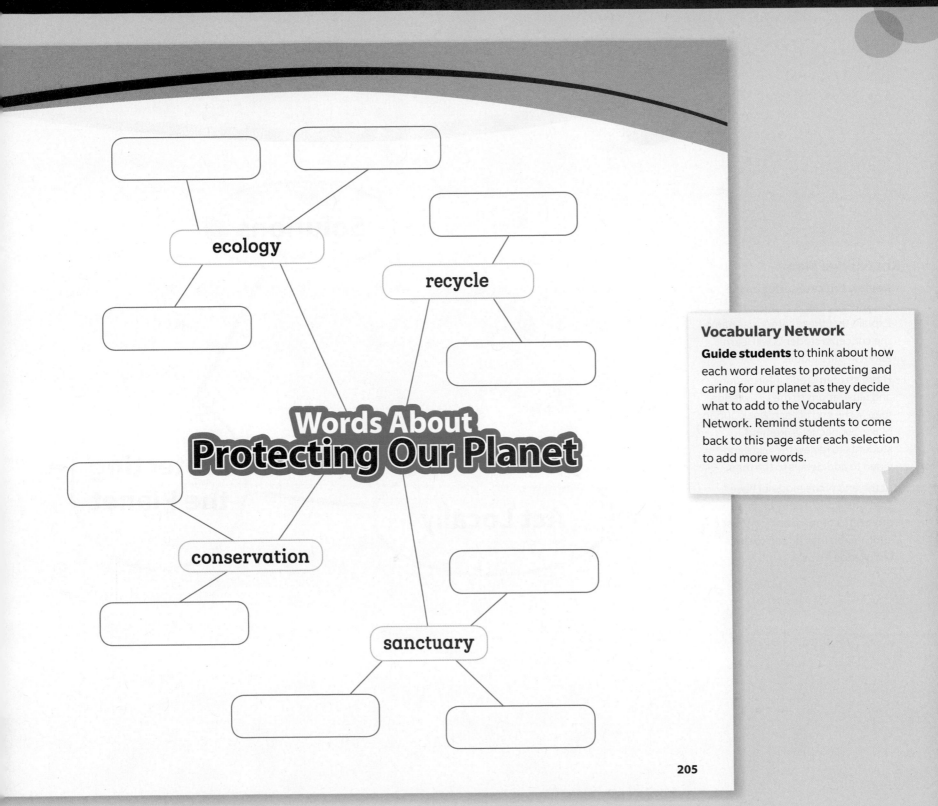

ecology

recycle

conservation

sanctuary

Words About
Protecting Our Planet

Vocabulary Network

Guide students to think about how each word relates to protecting and caring for our planet as they decide what to add to the Vocabulary Network. Remind students to come back to this page after each selection to add more words.

205

Solutions

Knowledge Map

- **Review the categories** on the knowledge map with students. Explain that these categories name the concepts students will learn about in the module.

- **Have students** add information and illustrations to the knowledge map at the end of each week during Make Connections. Remind students to review the texts and video to add details to the map.

- At the end of the module, have students work in pairs or small groups to compare and contrast the information they added to their knowledge maps.

Act Locally

Protecting the Planet

206

**Protect
Animals**

207

Introduce the Text

- **Read aloud** the title. Tell students that these are letters. Discuss with students some reasons to write a letter. *(to make a request, to send an invitation, to conduct business, to keep up with a friend)*

- **Guide students** to set a purpose for reading.

- **Point out** the highlighted Big Idea Words.

- **Have students** read both letters.

 READ FOR UNDERSTANDING

Ideas and Support

- **Who is writing the first letter?** *(the Eco Guardians)* **To whom is it addressed?** *(to Ms. Garcia, an expert on environmental issues)*

- **What is the purpose of the first letter?** *(to get advice on ways to help the environment)*

- **What opinion do the Eco Guardians have about how to use the vacant land?** *(They think it should be a sanctuary for birds and animals.)*

ANNOTATION TIP: Have students underline the words or phrases that tell how the Eco Guardians want to use the land.

DOK 2

208

 myNotes

Short Read

November 19

Emelia Garcia
Vice President, Global Solutions
Active Environmental
500 Main Street
Waco, TX 76633

Dear Ms. Garcia:

1 We are the Eco Guardians, a group of students who are passionate about ecology and conservation. Our faculty adviser, Catherine Leominster, suggested we contact you since you're an expert on environmental issues. Plus, you were her college roommate!

2 We would appreciate your advice on ways to help the environment. One of our ideas is to host an annual environmental awareness day in our town, in which residents could pick up trash in conservation areas and educate others about recycling, biking, and other ways to help the environment. Can you recommend other activities?

3 We have another idea, too. Our city has several acres of vacant land, and some people want to develop it and put up buildings. However, we think the land should become a sanctuary for birds and animals. It has a lot of trees, a pond, and some marshland, so it seems ideal for this purpose. Do you have any thoughts on how we can help make this happen?

4 We look forward to hearing from you, and thank you very much for your time!

Sincerely,

Jolena Walker
The Eco Guardians

5 P.S. Please remember to recycle this letter. It's always better to reuse things, even paper!

December 1

Eco Guardians
Peabody Elementary School
70 Ridge Avenue
Dallas, TX 02140

Dear Jolena and the Eco Guardians,

1   I'm responding to your letter about helping the environment.

2   Let me start by saying I'm delighted the Eco Guardians exist! Earth's future is in the hands of young people like yourselves, and your efforts can help make a clean, green world for generations to come.

3   An environmental awareness day sounds terrific! You might consider planting trees or starting a community garden, or both. People love getting their hands dirty. When they see a sapling grow or a seed sprout, it brings them closer to nature and makes them care about protecting it.

4   The sanctuary is also a wonderful idea. It would preserve many animal habitats and provide a place for people to enjoy nature. I suggest asking your parents to start a petition. If many people sign the petition, your town may decide to set aside the land rather than develop it. Make sure the petition describes the land's natural features and some of the animals that live there. The more people know, the more likely they'll be to support you.

5   Thanks so much for writing, and please let me know how your projects go. Also, please say hello to Mrs. Leominster for me. She was the best roommate in the world!

Sincerely,

Emelia Garcia
Vice President, Global Solutions
Active Environmental

6   P.S. I probably don't need to remind you to recycle this letter!

📖 **READ FOR UNDERSTANDING**

Ideas and Support

- **What support does Ms. Garcia give for her opinion that she is glad the Eco Guardians exist?** *(She writes that, "Earth's future is in the hands of young people like yourselves, and your efforts can help make a clean, green world for generations to come.")*

DOK 1

📖 **READ FOR UNDERSTANDING**

Ideas and Support

- **What opinion does Ms. Garcia state at the beginning of the fourth paragraph?** *(She thinks that the sanctuary is "a wonderful idea.")*

- **Why is this statement an opinion?** *(It is what Ms. Garcia thinks personally. It is not a proven fact.)*

ANNOTATION TIP: Have students highlight the facts that support this opinion.

DOK 2

209

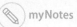
Notice & Note
Tough Questions

Introduce the Text

- **Read aloud** and discuss the genre information. Point out that graphic novels are fictional stories told in comic-strip format through speech bubbles and illustrated panels. They can have realistic characters and are told through a plot.

- Use Display and Engage **Meet the Author 9.2**.

- **Tell students** to look for the Critical Vocabulary as they read, and to think about the words' meanings.

ANNOTATION TIP: Have students use the box to note what they think will happen to Luz and what they want to learn about her.

Prepare to Read

GENRE STUDY   **Graphic novels** are longer fictional stories told in comic-strip format.

- Graphic novels tell stories through speech bubbles and illustrated panels.

- Authors of graphic novels tell the story through the plot—the main events of the story.

- Graphic novels can include characters who act, think, and speak like real people.

SET A PURPOSE   **Think about** the title and topic of this module. What do you think will happen to Luz? What would you like to learn about her? Write your ideas below.

**Meet the Author:
Claudia Dávila**

CRITICAL VOCABULARY
frequent
sufficient
oasis
permission
installing
abandoned

210

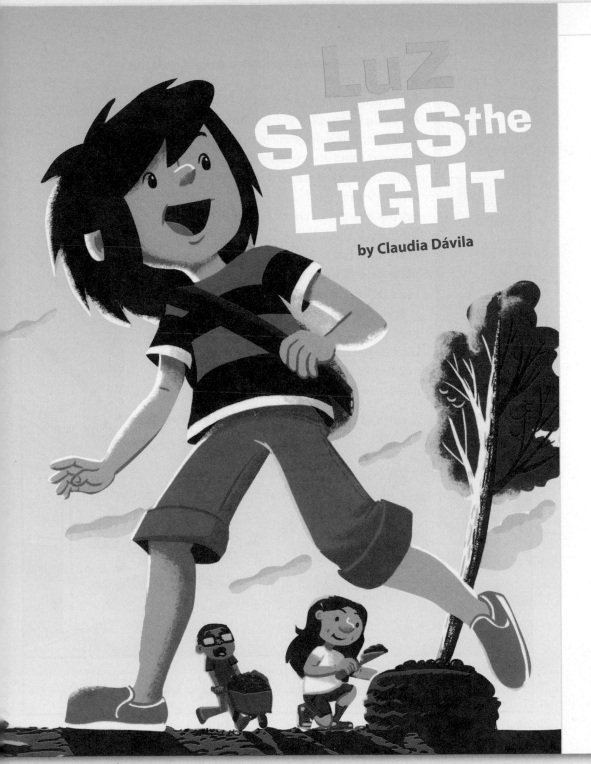

LuZ SEES the LIGHt

by Claudia Dávila

 READ FOR UNDERSTANDING

Set a Purpose

- **Have students** look at the illustration and note the similarities and differences between the characters.

- **Guide students** to set a purpose for reading. Discuss with them what they think this selection will be about.

DOK 2

211

Make Inferences

MODEL MAKING AN INFERENCE

 THINK ALOUD *When I make an inference I discover something that is not directly stated in the text. I read that Luz and her friends enjoy listening to music and going to the mall. Then I read about the blackouts, and both her neighbor's and her mother's comments. I infer that because of these changes Luz is starting to view the world in a more serious way.*

DOK 2

How would you describe where Luz lives, based only on the pictures on pages 212–213? *(The neighborhood where Luz lives is a mixture of private homes and apartments. The fence needs fixing. The grass is overgrown in some places and totally missing in others, and the neighbors seem to get along.)*

What information about the story can you find out only in the text, and not in the pictures? *(Luz likes to go to the mall and listen to music with friends. Blackouts are occurring in the neighborhood. Luz has a friend named Robert and a neighbor named Gord. Her mother talks about the effect of gas prices on Luz's favorite activities.)*

DOK 3   **212**

 myNotes

Luz (pronounced *loose*) and her friends enjoy listening to music and frequent trips to the mall. Then Luz's neighborhood is dimmed by blackouts and she realizes that she can't do some of her favorite activities. While out on a walk with her new friend Robert, her neighbor Gord warns them that they need to prepare for more blackouts by becoming more self-sufficient. Luz thinks Gord's ideas are a bit strange, but when the price of gas goes up, Luz's mother points out that it affects everything from driving to the mall to the cost of groceries and even the new sneakers Luz has been saving for. Luz realizes that maybe it's time to use less energy and be more self-sufficient.

YAWN!

frequent   If something is frequent, it happens often.
sufficient   If something is sufficient, it is just what is needed and no more.

📖 **READ FOR UNDERSTANDING**

What evidence in the images, speech bubbles, and thought balloons shows you that Luz is trying to figure out whether there is a problem? *(First, she scratches her head and thinks about the clues - no TV, no cooking, no air conditioning. She then wonders if there is a problem, that is, a power outage. Her facial expression shows that she is worried.)*

DOK 2

READ FOR UNDERSTANDING

How have Luz's plans changed?
(She does not want to go shopping for sneakers anymore. Instead she will start to work on her community project.)

What do the text and images show about how Luz prepares for what she will do today? (She gets dressed, grabs a notebook and pencil, and grabs a snack. Then she leaves the house.)

DOK 2

📖 **READ FOR UNDERSTANDING**

How do Luz's expressions and position change from frame to frame? *(She is happy, then she is scared, then she is angry.)*

ANNOTATION TIP: Have students circle evidence in the last frame that shows Luz is angry.

DOK 2

myNotes

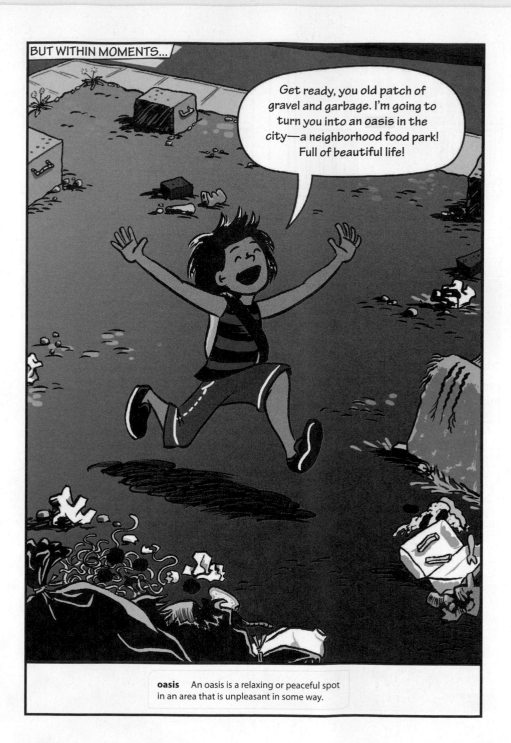

oasis An oasis is a relaxing or peaceful spot in an area that is unpleasant in some way.

 TARGETED CLOSE READ

Theme

Have students read Luz's words and analyze the graphic features on page 216.

How does Luz want to change the empty lot? (*She wants to turn it into a beautiful oasis.*)

What can you infer about the theme of the story from Luz's statement? (*It is possible to change a bad situation into a good situation.*)

DOK 2

READ FOR UNDERSTANDING

How does the illustrator portray Luz on this page? *(Luz is seen in many different poses on the same page. She is telling what she will do in the top-left circle. Then she is shown in many parts of the lot from a bird's-eye view. She is also shown resting in the bottom right-hand box.)*

What is the effect of showing Luz in many different ways? *(It shows that she is very busy and excited about what she is doing.)*

ANNOTATION TIP: Have students number each image of Luz on the page.

DOK 2

217

218

📖 **READ FOR UNDERSTANDING**

What character enters the story?
(her friend named Robert)

What evidence in the images and in the text show that they are friends? *(They are smiling at each other and they appear relaxed. Luz is asking how Robert is after an event they both remember.)*

DOK 2

219

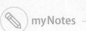

READ FOR UNDERSTANDING

What is Luz's reason for telling Robert her plans for the lot? *(She is excited about her plan. She wants to explain her plan before asking him to help.)*

How does the design of the bottom frame show that Luz and Robert disagree? *(Robert's body is facing away from Luz. The text is between them.)*

DOK 2

220

READ FOR UNDERSTANDING

How does Luz's mood appear to change on this page? *(Luz goes from giving a calm explanation to Robert, to stopping in surprise, to holding her head in frustration.)*

What is the cause for this change? *(Robert miscommunicates Luz's idea by saying she wants the neighborhood to grow their own food to keep from starving.)*

DOK 2

221

READ FOR UNDERSTANDING

How does the bottom frame show that Luz feels alone because of her idea? *(Robert and the girl are standing together, facing each other. Luz is facing away with a defeated look on her face.)*

ANNOTATION TIP: Have students make a list of reasons her friends think her plan is silly.

DOK 2

TARGETED CLOSE READ

Idioms

Have students reread the top left frame on page 223 to find the idiom.

What does the idiom "out to lunch" mean? *(It means not in touch with the real world. Her thinking is strange or crazy.)*

What clues in the text help you understand the idiom? *(Luz asks herself if her idea really is crazy.)*

ANNOTATION TIP: Have students underline the idiom and write its meaning.

DOK 3

Notice & Note

Tough Questions

- **Remind students** that when a character asks a tough question, it often reveals important story information, like the theme.

- **Have students** explain what the questions in the lower left-hand frame reveal about the theme. *(The author points out that changes are taking place and, therefore, people have to change as well.)*

- **Have students** reflect on the Anchor Question: *What does this question make me wonder about?* and add to their notes.

DOK 3

223

TARGETED CLOSE READ

Text and Graphic Features

Have students reread page 224.

Which text on the page is narration? (*"Later that week..."*)

What purpose does this narration serve in the story? (*It shows that time has passed.*)

What purpose do the drawings and speech balloons serve in this part of the story? (*The drawings and speech balloons show that Luz has been home and not working on the garden. She is feeling bored and decides to get back into her project.*)

ANNOTATION TIP: Have students circle the text on the page that is narration.

DOK 3

224

myNotes

READ FOR UNDERSTANDING

How do people react to Luz's idea when she attempts to explain it to them? *(People either think she is selling something or they are not interested.)*

What kind of visual pun does the illustrator use in the lower right-hand frame? *(Luz says, "Oh, what's the point?" and tosses away a pencil, which has a point.)*

DOK 3

READ FOR UNDERSTANDING

What does the narration on this page tell readers about the story? (It tells readers that a short time has passed.)

How is the setting different before and after the narration? (Before the narration, Luz is outside her house. After the narration, Luz is back to work in the empty lot.)

ANNOTATION TIP: Have students circle the text on the page that is narration.

DOK 2

226

227

228

— myNotes

 READ FOR UNDERSTANDING

What does *au contraire* mean? (*It means on the contrary or opposite.*)

What does it mean when Robert says *au contraire* to Luz? (*Luz asks, "Can I help you?" but Robert is implying that he is there to help Luz.*)

DOK 2

READ FOR UNDERSTANDING

Make Inferences

What can you infer about Robert's and Anika's reason for visiting Luz? What evidence supports your thinking? (*Robert and Anika are there to offer their help with Luz's garden. Robert and Anika are excitedly waving their arms and smiling while talking to Luz. Robert says "au contraire" in response to Luz's question about helping her friends. Anika is explaining how Robert told her about the park idea.*)

If students have difficulty making inferences, use this model:

THINK ALOUD *I notice the facial expressions and body language of Robert and Anika. They are running toward Luz while waving and shouting. I also read the words spoken by Robert and Anika. From all these clues, I infer that Robert and Anika finally understand Luz's idea and want to help her.*

DOK 2

229

READ FOR UNDERSTANDING

How have the characters' relationships changed in this part of the story? (*Robert and Anika now agree that Luz's plan for a neighborhood park is a good idea and offer to help her. Luz is no longer upset with her friends.*)

DOK 2

230

Notice & Note

Tough Questions

- **Remind students** that when a character asks a tough or meaningful question, it often reveals important story information.

- **Have students** explain how Robert's question "What are friends for?" adds to the plot. (*The question is the start of real cooperation among Luz, her friends, and other community members. Luz's problem of not being able to transform the empty lot by herself is starting to get solved.*)

- **Have students** reflect on the Anchor Question: *What does this question make me wonder about?* and add to their notes.

DOK 3

READ FOR UNDERSTANDING

How long does it take the volunteers to finish the park?
(two weeks)

List some of the activities necessary for creating the new park. *(notifying the community, picking up trash, laying down grass, planting trees and plants, building a concert area, building a playground)*

ANNOTATION TIP: Have students number the narration boxes to determine how many actions took place during this time period.

DOK 1

BUILDING A CONCERT AREA...

... AND A PLAYGROUND

CAR-FREE SUNDAYS

GORD'S IDEA GETS APPROVED BY THE CITY.

MR. AND MRS. DESOUZA SHARE THEIR PLANTS.

Yay, we're all done!!!

myNotes

🔍 **TARGETED CLOSE READ**

Text and Graphic Features

Have students look at each place on page 233 where text appears.

What are three different ways in which text is used on this page? (narration, speech balloon, signs)

ANNOTATION TIP: Have students underline the text that names Gord's idea. Have students circle the text that shows dialogue.

DOK 3

📖 **READ FOR UNDERSTANDING**

What is the name of the new park? (Friendship Park)

Why do you think that name is chosen for the park? (The name is appropriate for the park because friends come together to create it.)

DOK 2

233

myNotes

234

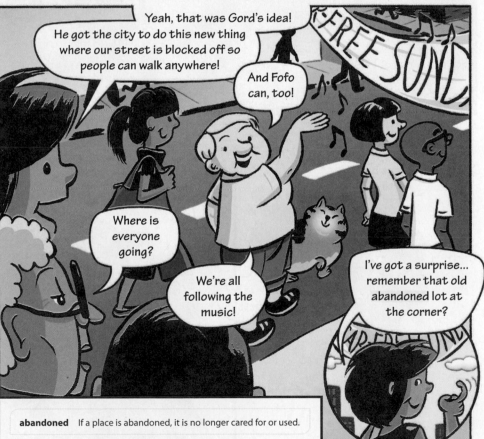

abandoned   If a place is abandoned, it is no longer cared for or used.

📖 **READ FOR UNDERSTANDING**

How has Luz's plan come true? *(All the neighbors are walking in the street because it is a car-free Sunday and people can walk anywhere. Luz is about to surprise her neighbors by showing them the completed park.)*

DOK 2

235

READ FOR UNDERSTANDING

Is the word *oasis* **a good description of this area now? Why or why not?** *(Yes. It is now a place where people can grow food, relax, and enjoy their free time in an earth-friendly way.)*

ANNOTATION TIP: Have students closely study the top frame and number as many earth-friendly activities as they can find.

DOK 2

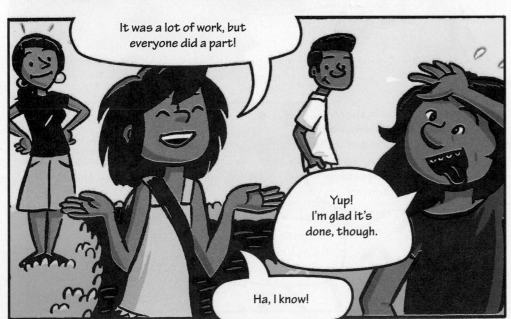

READ·FOR UNDERSTANDING

How is Luz feeling after she shows everyone the park? (Possible responses: relaxed, happy, excited, satisfied)

DOK 2

myNotes

237

TARGETED CLOSE READ

Theme

Have students read Luz's words on page 238.

What story theme can you determine from Luz's words? *(People can work together to make life better.)*

How does knowing the theme help you understand the story events better? *(It helps me understand the purpose for the characters' actions and statements.)*

DOK 3

238

239

myNotes

 READ FOR UNDERSTANDING

How is this pair of sneakers different from the ones Luz wants to buy at the beginning of the story? *(They are one-of-a-kind, made by a friend, and they have Luz's original designs on them.)*

How are the sneakers a symbol of how this experience has affected Luz? *(Luz has shown that she is not like everyone else and she can think on her own. She now has a pair of sneakers that are not like everyone else's.)*

DOK 3

 READ FOR UNDERSTANDING

Wrap-Up

Revisit the purpose students set before they read the text. Have students explain how this story fits the genre of a graphic novel. Have students cite evidence in the text to support their reasoning.

DOK 2

240

Collaborative Discussion

Look back at what you wrote on page 210. Tell a partner two things you learned from this story. Then work with a group to discuss the questions below. Refer to details in *Luz Sees the Light*. Take notes for your responses. When you speak, use your notes.

1 Reread pages 216–217. What does Luz want to do with the empty lot in her neighborhood?

2 Review pages 224–227. Why does Luz feel discouraged when she starts her project?

3 Why does Luz think her project will help the community and the planet?

Listening Tip

As you listen carefully to others, decide whether or not you agree. You can respond by saying, "I agree because . . ." or by suggesting a different point of view.

Speaking Tip

Jot down a few notes from the text that will help you answer each question. Refer to your notes as you speak.

Cite Text Evidence

Write a Journal Entry

PROMPT

In *Luz Sees the Light*, you read about a determined girl who turns an abandoned city lot into a beautiful park. The story is told through illustrations and speech bubbles.

Imagine that you live in Luz's neighborhood and that you go to the party that celebrates the opening of Friendship Park. Write a journal entry about what you experience at the park on its opening day. Don't forget to use some of the Critical Vocabulary words in your writing.

PLAN

Identify text and illustrations used to describe the park on opening day. Write words you would use to describe the event based on the text and illustrations.

Now write your journal entry about the opening of Friendship Park.

✓ Make sure your journal entry

- ☐ begins by introducing the event.
- ☐ uses information from the text to describe opening day.
- ☐ describes events in an order that makes sense.
- ☐ uses correct capitalization.
- ☐ ends with a concluding sentence.

Write About Reading

- **Review with students** the directions and checklist in the Write section.

- **Encourage students** to use their own words as they write their journal entry about the party celebrating the opening of Friendship Park.

READ FOR UNDERSTANDING

Introduce the Text

- **Read aloud** and discuss the genre information. Point out that realistic fiction has characters and events that are like those in real life. Authors use sensory details, figurative language, and dialogue to develop the story. Tell students that informational videos, on the other hand, include real-life visual and audio information.

- Use Display and Engage **Build Background 9.6**.

- **Tell students** to look and listen for the Critical Vocabulary in the text and video, and to think about the words' meanings.

ANNOTATION TIP: Have students use the box to note what they think this realistic fiction text and video will be about.

Prepare to Read and View

GENRE STUDY **Realistic fiction** tells a story about characters and events that are like those in real life.

- Authors of realistic fiction may use figurative language to develop the setting and the characters.

- Realistic fiction includes informal language to make conversations seem real.

Saving the Kemp's
Ridley Sea Turtle

Informational videos present facts and information about a topic in visual and audio form. Videos may include clips of animals in the wild to illustrate the topic.

SET A PURPOSE **Think about** the title and genre of this text and video. What do you think they will be about? Write your ideas below.

Build Background:
Sea Turtles

CRITICAL VOCABULARY

obsessed

disoriented

blunt

recruiting

appointed

stranded

244

On Sea Turtle Patrol

by **Nancy Dawson**
illustrated by **Denise Ortakales**

READ FOR UNDERSTANDING

Set a Purpose

- **Have students** read the titles of the selection and video and look at the illustration and photograph.

- **Guide students** to set a purpose for reading. Discuss with them what they think will happen in this story. Discuss how the informational video will help them better understand the story.

DOK 2

245

myNotes

 READ FOR UNDERSTANDING

Where and when does this story take place? *(It takes place on a beach in Florida. The story's action is happening during the summer in present time.)*

Does the story seem realistic so far? Explain. *(Yes, the characters seem like real people who are at a real beach in Florida.)*

ANNOTATION TIP: Have students underline the text evidence that indicates the setting.

DOK 2

 READ FOR UNDERSTANDING

What does the photograph at the bottom of the page tell you about a sea turtle's route? *(A sea turtle comes out of the ocean to a specific spot on the beach. When the sea turtle is ready to return to the ocean, it goes straight back alongside its original tracks. The turtle does not move away from its tracks or go anywhere else along the beach.)*

DOK 2

1 "**L**ast call, Callie!" Gram jangles her keys as she heads out to the carport.

2 "Coming!" I yell, tossing off the covers. Outside my window the sky is awash with a predawn glow.

3 The trouble with tracking sea turtles is you have to get up early every day. Today is my twenty-fifth day on patrol, which Gram says is probably a record for a twelve-year-old.

4 When Dad dropped me off at Gram's here in Florida two days after school got out, who knew I would morph from a Cincinnati city kid into a turtle-obsessed beach volunteer? If I'm not out on the beach, I'm watching turtle videos or reading turtle books.

5 I pull on cargo shorts and my blue T-shirt, the one with baby turtles scrambling up the front and over the shoulders. I grab a banana off the kitchen counter and rush outside.

> **obsessed** If you are obsessed with something, you think about it all the time.

6 By the time Gram and I get to the beach, the sky glows pale yellow, with the sun peeking up over the edge of the horizon. I breathe in the salty air and lick the tangy taste off my lips. I stuff my flip-flops into my pockets and dig my toes into the white sand.

7 We walk along the water's edge, looking for fresh turtle tracks, which scientists call "crawls." The beachfront is lined with high-rise condos and hotels, but at this early hour no one's out except two joggers running at the edge of the surf. A noisy pack of brown pelicans is fighting over the carcass of a dead fish tangled in seaweed. The only other sound is the *whoosh*, *whoosh* of the waves rolling in and out.

8 "Fresh crawl!" I call out, proud to see turtle tracks before Gram does. The crawl emerges straight out of the ocean, two long lines of depressions in the sand dug out by the turtle's flippers.

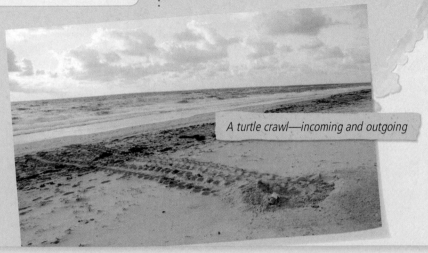

A turtle crawl—incoming and outgoing

9   "What kind of turtle? Which direction?" Gram demands.

10   I study the turtle crawl photos at the back of the clipboard before saying, "Loggerhead, incoming?" Loggerheads are the most common turtle on this stretch of Florida's Gulf Coast. I hold my breath and wait for Gram's verdict.

11   "Good call, Callie," she says. She records the nest location, date, and time on her clipboard. She frowns down at the sand. "Where's the outgoing crawl?"

12   I examine the sand. No outgoing crawl, which should be near the incoming tracks or even on top of them. Turtles can sometimes be disoriented by the bright lights of condos and hotels near the beach. Did this mama turtle lose her way?

> **disoriented** Creatures that are disoriented are confused about where they are.

13   Gram stuffs her clipboard into her backpack. "Come on, Callie, let's follow her tracks."

14   The crawl leads us above the high tide line, where the sand is dry and loose. Seagrass tickles my bare legs as we follow the tracks up the face of a sand dune. We reach the top of the dune, where I see . . .

15   A turtle! She's lying in a slight depression in the sand, motionless. Her eyes are wide open, glassy-brown and rimmed with salt crystals.

16   "Is she OK?" I ask Gram.

17   "I hope so. She's probably resting between bouts of digging out her egg chamber," Gram says. "Keep watching."

Notice & Note

Tough Questions

- **Remind students** that when a character pauses to ask herself or another character a tough question—one that reveals doubt or confusion—the readers get a glimpse at what the character's internal struggle.

- **Have students** identify two questions that Callie asks that reveal her internal struggles. *(Callie asks, "Did this mama turtle lose her way?" and "Is she OK?" Callie reveals that she is worried about the mother sea turtle. Callie might also be worried that she won't be able to help the sea turtle since she is a new volunteer.)*

ANNOTATION TIP: Have students highlight the tough questions.

- **Have students** reflect on the Anchor Question: *What do these questions make me wonder about?* and add to their notes.

DOK 3

📖 READ FOR UNDERSTANDING

Retell/Summarize
MODEL RETELLING

🗨 **THINK ALOUD** *I will retell what has happened. Callie is helping her grandmother track sea turtles. They discover that a mother sea turtle hasn't returned to the sea after coming ashore to dig a nest.*

myNotes

18   I do, but the turtle just lies there. She's about three feet long and has the large head and big, blunt jaws of a loggerhead. Her shell, flippers, and head are covered in a maze of reddish-brown geometric shapes, each outlined by thin white lines. Patches of green algae and gray barnacles cling to her shell.

19   "Gram, look! She's moving her back flippers." The turtle pushes her hind flippers like alternating paddles, scooping out sand from beneath her rear end. She digs and rests, digs and rests.

> **blunt**   Something that is blunt is flat or rounded, rather than sharp.

20   To lay her eggs, she has to dig a nest chamber two feet deep. And she's taking forever! By now the sun is full up. I know the turtle is in a trance, unaware of us or anything happening around her until she is done nesting. But still, we have to keep her safe.

21   "Look! Eggs!" Gram says, pulling my attention back to the turtle. Her stubby tail moves to one side as she pushes out round, white eggs, each the size of a Ping-Pong ball. Clear, gloppy liquid slides off the eggs as they drop down into the nest chamber.

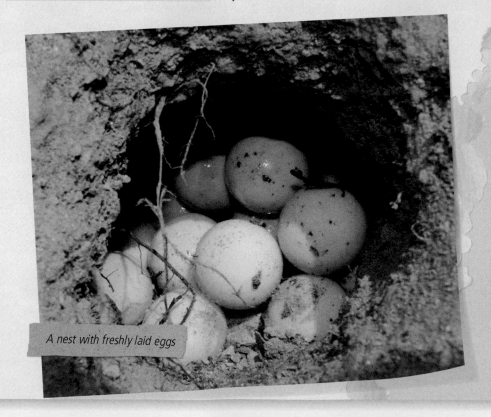

A nest with freshly laid eggs

248

22 "Wow!" I whisper. I feel like I'm starring in a TV nature show. Only the turtle is the real star.

23 "Sea turtles have been coming ashore to lay their eggs for millions of years, all over the earth," Gram says, her voice filled with awe.

24 The turtle is still pushing out eggs, one by one. She'll lay about 120 before she's done. Then she'll return to the sea.

25 *If* she makes it back across the beach. Nighttime is turtle time, but someone forgot to tell this turtle. What if she's confused by the daylight and can't find the ocean? What if she ends up in a hotel parking lot and gets squashed by a car?

26 My stomach knots up and my brain is stuck on terrible turtle troubles. What can we do?

27 Gram's on her phone, recruiting other volunteers to come to our location, quick. "We'll try to help her get back to her ocean home," she says to me. "After that, it's up to her."

recruiting If you are recruiting people, you are asking them to help do something.

28 The turtle's just lying there again. I wonder if she's sick or injured. But then she flips sand into the air and scoots her body around to pack it down over the nest hole. She scatters loose sand on top to hide her nest from marauding raccoons and stray dogs. Then she turns and crawls toward the sea, never looking back.

29 We're on the move, too.

30 "Callie, you patrol the left side, keeping ten feet away and behind her. I'll take the right side. We need to keep people away from her and off her incoming tracks, which she'll follow back to the sea."

31 My side of the beach is empty except for a flock of shorebirds down by the water's edge. They're pecking in the wet sand, hunting for insects and other tasty snacks. Each wave chases them to drier ground. As soon as the wave pulls out, they're back.

Notice & Note

Tough Questions

- **Remind students** to stop and take note when a character asks herself or another character a tough question or one that reveals her inner struggle.

- **Have students** identify the question that reveals what Callie is most worried about and why it worries her. *(In paragraph 26, Callie asks, "What can we do?" She is worried that the mother turtle is in danger and that there is nothing they can do to help her.)*

ANNOTATION TIP: Ask students to highlight the tough question.

- **Have students** reflect on the Anchor Question: *What does this question make me wonder about?* and add to their notes.

DOK 2

249

READ FOR UNDERSTANDING

How does the illustration add to what is happening in the text?
(Possible responses: the illustration shows the location of the characters in relation to the sea turtle; it shows more characteristics of the characters that weren't in the text; it shows the large group of people that are closing in on the turtle in the distance.)

DOK 2

250

32 I turn away from the birds and watch the turtle. One flipper-step at a time, she slowly drags her 300-pound body forward. No wonder female loggerheads come on land only four or five times a summer to lay eggs. They spend the rest of their lives gracefully swimming around in the ocean.

33 Gram points to two men jogging at the edge of the waves. "Stay with the turtle while I go talk to those guys," she says.

34 After she goes I hear a yell down near the water. "Whooo-eee!" From the top of the dune, I spot two guys on bikes doing wheelies in the surf. They're headed straight for the turtle tracks.

35 I start running, but my feet can't get much traction on the loose sand. I'm moving, well, as slow as a turtle. When I get to the wet sand, the running is easier. "Stop!" I yell, flinging my arms out like a traffic cop.

36 "Who appointed you beach police?" a guy with black, spiky hair demands. He's a foot taller than I am, and older, probably in high school. His buddy closes in from the left.

37 I clear my throat and think back to my volunteer training: *Introduce yourself. Turn bystanders into allies.*

38 "I'm Callie. I'm not the beach police, but I am a trained turtle volunteer. We have a stranded sea turtle. Can you help?"

39 "Definitely!" the buddy says. "I'm Eric." He points to the spiky-haired guy. "That's Mateo. Last year in biology we adopted a turtle nest. We got to go dig it up three days after the turtles busted out and we took inventory by counting the number of hatched eggs."

40 I am so jealous, but all I say is, "Great!"

41 Eric scans the beach. "Turtle!" he whoops, pointing.

42 The turtle flops over the top of the sand dune and skids down its steep front. Then she waddles forward, pulling herself with her flippers.

43 A group of adults with three little kids in tow stream out of a condo. They're carrying fold-up chairs and an umbrella and dragging a cooler. I have to stop them before they trample the turtle tracks. I slap on my Save the Turtles visor, hoping it makes me look older and more official.

appointed   If you are appointed to a job, you are assigned to or chosen for it.

stranded   If you are stranded, you are stuck somewhere without a way to leave.

 TARGETED CLOSE READ

Figurative Language

Have students reread paragraph 35 to find examples of figurative language.

What simile describes how Callie feels as she runs? (*"as slow as a turtle"*)

What does the simile mean? (*It means she's moving very slowly because it is difficult to run in sand.*)

ANNOTATION TIP: Have students underline the simile.

DOK 2

TARGETED CLOSE READ

Figurative Language

Have students reread paragraph 36.

Which sensory details describe what the boy on the bike looks like? (*black, spiky hair; a foot taller; older*)

ANNOTATION TIP: Have students highlight the sensory details that describe the boy.

DOK 2

251

READ FOR UNDERSTANDING

Retell/Summarize

Retell what happens after Callie finds the mother sea turtle. *(The turtle lays eggs, and then she begins to make her way back to the ocean. Callie's grandmother and Callie try to keep approaching people away from the turtle and the tracks while they wait for more volunteers to show up. A crowd forms to watch the sea turtle and protect her tracks, and some volunteers arrive.)*

If students have difficulty retelling/summarizing, use this model:

Q **THINK ALOUD** *There are many details that explain how the turtle lays eggs and the interactions with the people, but when I retell, I focus on just the central, or main, idea. The main idea is that the turtle lays her eggs and starts returning to the sea. People begin to get too close to the turtle, and Callie and her grandmother make sure to stop them and enlist their help.*

DOK 2

44 "I'm going to go talk to those people," I tell Eric and Mateo. "You guys please patrol along this side of the tracks. Anyone who comes along, ask them to stay ten feet back from the turtle and off her tracks."

45 I run over to the approaching people and tell them about the sea turtle. They're tourists from Iowa and really excited by the chance to see a turtle. They pile their equipment in a heap and follow me.

46 Eric and Mateo are standing guard beside the crawl, scanning the beach and watching the turtle's slow progress. I spread the Iowa people out in a line next to them.

47 Gram and the joggers are lined up along the other side of the tracks. Some sea turtle volunteers have arrived and are working both sides, all in their official lime green "Sea Turtle Volunteer" T-shirts. I so want one of those T-shirts, but I can't have one until I'm eighteen, old enough to be an official volunteer.

48 A crowd attracts a crowd, that's what Gram always says. Suddenly we have about twenty or thirty people on each side of the tracks. They hold out their phones and take pictures of the turtle, of themselves, of the volunteers, and of me.

🔍 **TARGETED CLOSE READ**

Figurative Language

Have students reread paragraph 52.

What examples of alliteration are in this paragraph? *("wave washes" and "floating free")*

DOK 2

49 A woman stands apart, her eyes focused on the turtle. With her arms, she beckons the turtle forward, as though to say: *Come on, you can do it!*

50 And she can. I think. Only fifteen feet to go before the turtle will meet the edge of the incoming waves. All the official turtle volunteers are down by the water now, so I go there, too.

51 With a final thrust, the turtle meets an incoming wave. Water pours over her body. But then the wave whooshes out, leaving the turtle stranded in the wet sand. I want to run to her and push her forward, but I know not to. The volunteers spread out their arms to keep people back, so I do, too.

52 Another wave washes over the turtle, and then another, and then she is floating free. She glides under the water and is gone.

53 Everyone cheers and claps. A little kid yells, "Bye-bye turtle!" Strangers hug and cry, and I find my own cheeks are wet.

54 Gram puts an arm around my shoulders. "Good job, Callie. I'm proud of you." We stand there, Gram and me, staring out at the infinite ocean.

55 My Best Turtle Patrol Day. Ever!

📖 **READ FOR UNDERSTANDING**

Retell/Summarize

Have students retell the conclusion to the story. *(Callie and the volunteers keep people away from the sea turtle as it returns to the ocean.)*

DOK 2

📖 **READ FOR UNDERSTANDING**

Wrap-Up

Revisit the purpose students set before they read the text. Have students explain how this text fits the genre of realistic fiction. Have students cite evidence in the text to support their reasoning.

DOK 2

253

Saving the Kemp's Ridley Sea Turtle

As you watch *Saving the Kemp's Ridley Sea Turtle,* notice how the narration and the visuals work together to give information. How does the narrator introduce new information about sea turtles? How is this information supported by visuals? How is the information in the video similar to what you learned in *On Sea Turtle Patrol?* Take notes in the space below.

Why have the turtles become endangered? What steps have scientists taken to save the Kemp's Ridley sea turtle? How long did the scientists have to wait to see the results of their efforts? Write your responses in the space below.

Collaborative Discussion

Look back at what you wrote on page 244. Tell a partner two things you learned from the text and video. Then work with a group to discuss the questions. Look for details and examples in *On Sea Turtle Patrol* and *Saving the Kemp's Ridley Sea Turtle*. Choose someone in your group to take notes on your discussion.

1 Reread page 251. Why does Callie ask Eric and Mateo for help?

2 Why do scientists and volunteers look for turtle tracks?

3 How are people helping increase the population of sea turtles?

 Listening Tip

If you are the note-taker, listen carefully to each speaker. When the speaker finishes, jot down the central ideas that he or she shared.

Speaking Tip

After discussing each question, ask the note-taker to read back the group's responses. Decide together if anyone has something more to add.

Academic Discussion

Use the **COLLABORATIVE DISCUSSION** routine. Have students write notes to answer the questions. Then have groups apply the Listening and Speaking Tips as they discuss their responses.

Possible responses:

1. *Callie asks Eric and Mateo for help because there is a sea turtle stranded on the beach.* DOK 2

2. *Scientists and volunteers look for turtle tracks to identify the kind of turtle that made them and to note the direction of the tracks. Also, tracks show where the nests are located, so volunteers can protect the eggs and hatchlings.* DOK 2

3. *People are protecting sea turtle habitats and nests. They have also worked on special projects to move sea turtles to new locations away from danger.* DOK 2

255

Write an Advertisement

PROMPT

In *On Sea Turtle Patrol* and *Saving the Kemp's Ridley Sea Turtle*, you learned about the steps people are taking to protect endangered sea turtles.

Imagine that you are part of a group that goes on turtle patrols. Write an advertisement for your school newspaper or website to recruit more volunteers to help with this work. Don't forget to use some of the Critical Vocabulary words as well as science-related words in your writing.

PLAN

Write two reasons why people might want to protect sea turtles. Then, find details in the text and video to support each of your reasons.

WRITE

Now write your advertisement to encourage others to join the sea turtle patrol.

On Sea Turtle Patrol

by Nancy Dawson
Illustrated by Denise Ortakales

✓ Make sure your advertisement

☐ begins by stating the purpose of the advertisement.
☐ provides reasons to convince people to volunteer.
☐ includes facts, details, and examples from the text to support each reason.
☐ includes science-related words.
☐ ends with a concluding sentence.

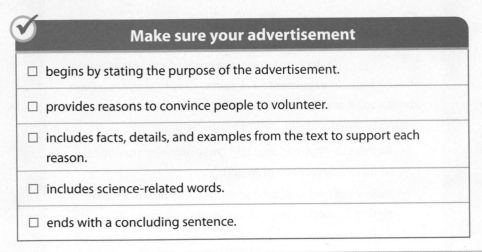

Write About Reading

- **Review with students** the directions and checklist in the Write section.

- **Encourage students** to use persuasive words and details that will help convince the audience to volunteer for the sea turtle patrol.

- **Suggest that students** use Critical Vocabulary and content-area words in their advertisements, where they can.

READ FOR UNDERSTANDING

Introduce the Text

- **Read aloud** and discuss the genre information. Point out these examples of each text feature:
  - headings and subheadings (pages 260–261)
  - facts and examples (page 260)
  - stated problems and solutions (page 271)
- Use Display and Engage **Build Background 9.8**.
- **Tell students** to look for the Critical Vocabulary as they read, and to think about the words' meanings.

ANNOTATION TIP: Have students use the box to note what they want to learn from this selection.

Prepare to Read

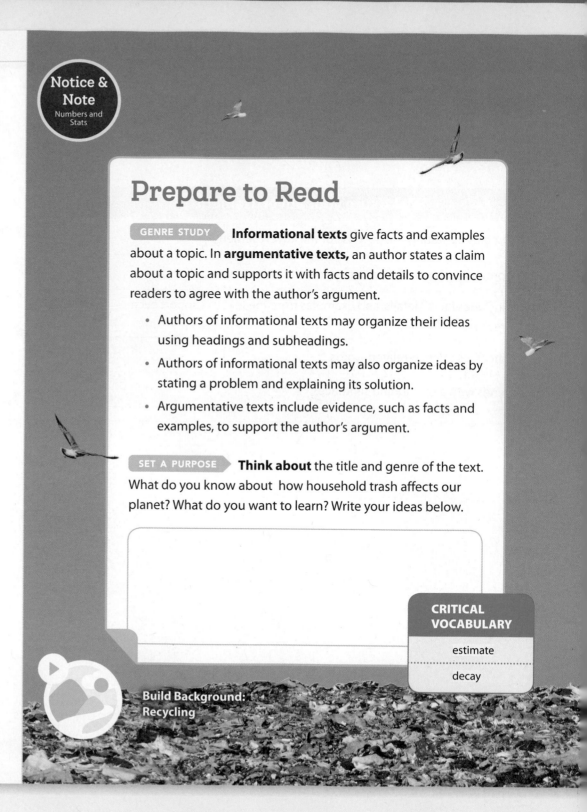

GENRE STUDY   **Informational texts** give facts and examples about a topic. In **argumentative texts,** an author states a claim about a topic and supports it with facts and details to convince readers to agree with the author's argument.

- Authors of informational texts may organize their ideas using headings and subheadings.
- Authors of informational texts may also organize ideas by stating a problem and explaining its solution.
- Argumentative texts include evidence, such as facts and examples, to support the author's argument.

SET A PURPOSE   **Think about** the title and genre of the text. What do you know about how household trash affects our planet? What do you want to learn? Write your ideas below.

CRITICAL VOCABULARY

estimate

decay

Build Background:
Recycling

How Can We Reduce Household Waste?

by Mary K. Pratt

📖 **READ FOR UNDERSTANDING**

Set a Purpose

- **Have students** read the title of the selection and look at the photo.
- **Guide students** to set a purpose for reading. Discuss with them what they think they will learn from this selection.

DOK 2

259

HOUSEHOLD WASTE

1 Household waste includes all the trash created by the things we throw away. And we throw away many things. In the United States, the average person throws away about 4.5 pounds (2 kilograms) of stuff every day. Only 1.5 pounds (0.7 kg) of that gets recycled or composted. The remaining 3 pounds (1.4 kg) is household waste.

2 What happens when you add up all the household waste Americans create? It comes out to about 164 million tons (149 metric tons) each year. But this is only an **estimate** from the US government. No one knows the exact amount of household waste Americans create. In fact, some experts believe it might be up to seven times that amount! In any case, a huge number of unwanted items end up in the garbage. And all of this garbage has serious effects on our environment.

> **estimate** If you give an estimate, you give an amount or size that is not exact.

AMERICAN WASTE
(including recyclables)

yard waste 10.5%
food waste 14.5%
other 3.4%
wood 6.9%
rubber, leather, and fabrics 8.7%
paper products 27.4%
plastics 12.7%
metal 8.9%
4.8%
glass

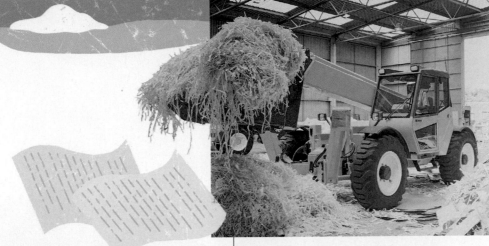

A worker moves shredded paper at a recycling center. Next, water will be added to the paper and it will be turned into pulp.

Types of Household Waste

3 There are four basic categories of household waste. The first category is paper, plastic, metal, and glass. The second category is food waste and yard waste. Cleaning products make up the third category. The fourth category is e-waste, or electronic waste. This includes items such as old cell phones and TVs.

4 Each of these types of waste has different effects on our planet. The good news is that we can fight the effects of every type of household waste. When we recycle and reuse waste, we keep these materials out of landfills. This helps clean the land, air, and water. It also improves our health. Let's explore each type of waste and find out what we can do to reduce its effects.

Plastic bottles decompose slowly in landfills. They should be recycled.

READ FOR UNDERSTANDING

What are the four categories of household waste? (Paper, plastic, metal and glass; food waste and yard waste; cleaning products; electronic waste, or e-waste)

DOK 1

TARGETED CLOSE READ

Text and Graphic Features

Have students look at the top photo on page 261.

What information does the caption add to what is shown in the photograph? (The caption explains what happens to paper in a recycling center. The shredded paper in the photograph will be mixed with water to be turned into pulp.)

ANNOTATION TIP: Have students underline the details in the caption that tell them more about what is happening in the photograph.

DOK 1

261

PAPER, PLASTIC, METAL, AND GLASS

5 Paper makes up more than one-quarter of the materials Americans throw away. Paper trash includes things such as notebooks and magazines. It also includes the cardboard and paper packages on the things we buy.

6 Another quarter of waste comes from plastic, metal, and glass. This includes items such as plastic bags and old toys. It also includes glass jars and metal cans. Soda cans are usually made of a metal called aluminum. Foods such as beans and soup usually come in cans made of steel.

Newspapers are one type of paper trash. What are some others?

myNotes

Americans recycle 71 percent of their steel cans. But they recycle only 50 percent of their aluminum cans.

Effects of Pollution from Paper, Plastic, Metal, and Glass

7 When products are thrown away, they often end up in landfills. These are places where trash is buried in the ground. Other trash items are burned in incinerators.

8 Landfills and incinerators cause problems for our planet. For instance, when paper rots in landfills or burns in incinerators, it sends out greenhouse gases. These gases trap heat in Earth's atmosphere. Greenhouse gases are important because they make our planet warm enough for life. But too much greenhouse gas leads to higher temperatures.

9 Things made of plastic take a long time to decompose, or break down into smaller bits. So these products stay as they are for hundreds of years and take up space in landfills. They often leach, or leak, dangerous chemicals into the environment. When plastic is burned in incinerators, it releases chemicals into the air. Many of these chemicals are harmful to people and plants.

In the United States, more than half of all waste ends up in landfills.

263

Notice & Note

Numbers and Stats

- **Remind students** that when the author uses specific numbers or statistics, they should stop and ask themselves why this information is important.

- **Have students** read the caption at the bottom of page 263 to identify the statistic and explain how it supports the author's argument. *(The statistic states that more than half of our waste ends up in landfills. The author is arguing that a large amount of our waste rots in landfills and ruins the environment.)*

ANNOTATION TIP: Have students highlight the statistic in the caption.

- **Have students** reflect on the Anchor Question: *What does this make me wonder about?* and add to their notes.

DOK 2

 READ FOR UNDERSTANDING

How is plastic waste harmful to the environment? *(Plastic takes a long time to decompose. It sits in landfills and leaks chemicals into the soil. If it is burned, it releases chemicals into the air.)*

DOK 1

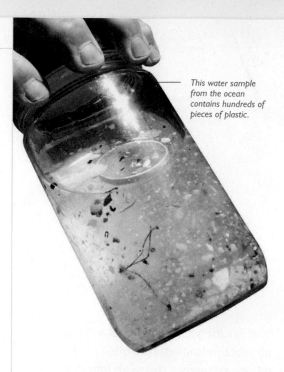

This water sample from the ocean contains hundreds of pieces of plastic.

10   Sometimes trash does not even make it into landfills or incinerators. Many household items end up as litter in parks, forests, rivers, lakes, and oceans. The litter problem is so big that vast sections of the ocean are covered with bits of plastic.

11   All that litter puts toxic chemicals into the land, water, and air. This can make plants and animals, including humans, very sick. Animals can also get trapped in plastic trash and starve. Sometimes animals eat small pieces of trash because they think it is food. These animals often get sick and die as a result.

📖 READ FOR UNDERSTANDING

How do the photographs on this page support the author's idea that waste is harmful to the environment? *(The photographs are shocking. They show how waste collects in our waterways and affects the habitats of animals.)*

DOK 2

264

What Can We Do?

12 You can reduce the amount of trash you create. Start by buying only what you need. When you do buy something, look for items made from recycled materials. Also, look for products that have little or no packaging. One good choice is buying whole fruits and vegetables instead of those in boxes or bags. When shopping, bring reusable bags instead of using disposable plastic bags.

13 When you are ready to get rid of something, look for ways to reuse it. For example, an old shoe box can become a storage bin. If you do not want an item that is in good condition, give it to someone else. If no one wants it, try to recycle it. If you have to throw it out, dispose of it properly so it does not become litter.

myNotes

One way to reuse an old can is to make it into a flowerpot.

Different types of plastic are given different numbers. Numbers 2, 4, and 5 are the least harmful to people and to the environment.

📖 READ FOR UNDERSTANDING

What are three things you can do to reduce trash? *(You can only buy things that you need and will use; buy things made of recycled materials; buy things with little or no packaging.)*

Why do you think the author tells readers about how to throw away trash in a selection about reducing waste? *(The author understands that some things will need to be thrown away. The author wants to give readers the best ways to throw those things away so there is the least amount of damage to the environment.)*

ANNOTATION TIP: Have students highlight ways to reduce trash and underline ways to properly dispose of trash.

DOK 3

265

14 People are also finding ways to make better use of all our trash. For example, some clothing is made from recycled plastic bottles. Scientists are also studying whether a certain fungus can eat a common type of plastic. That would help cut back on all the plastic trash that fills up landfills.

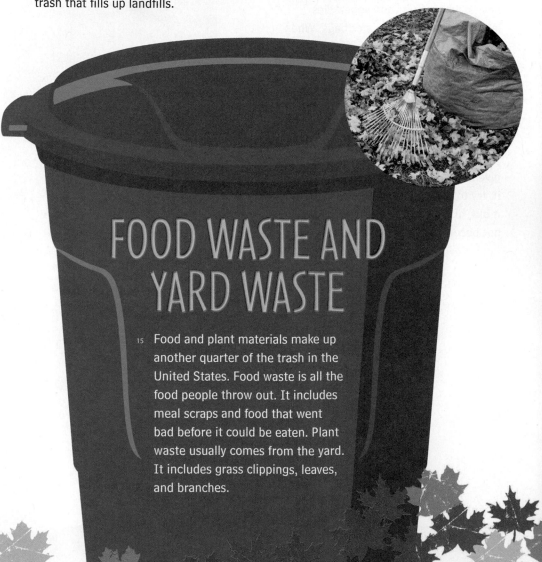

FOOD WASTE AND YARD WASTE

15 Food and plant materials make up another quarter of the trash in the United States. Food waste is all the food people throw out. It includes meal scraps and food that went bad before it could be eaten. Plant waste usually comes from the yard. It includes grass clippings, leaves, and branches.

 READ FOR UNDERSTANDING

What are some examples of food and yard waste? *(meal scraps, rotten food, grass clippings, leaves, branches)*

ANNOTATION TIP: Have students underline examples of food and yard waste in the text.

DOK 1

266

Effects of Food Waste and Yard Waste Pollution

16 In the United States, farmers produce more than 590 billion pounds (268 billion kg) of food every year. But Americans waste between one-quarter and one-half of that food. Farmers sometimes let fruits and vegetables rot in fields. They often do this when the food is not an ideal shape or color, because this makes it harder to sell.

17 Stores throw away a lot of food, too. They want customers to have plenty of choices. So, they stock more food than they plan to sell. They also get rid of many foods that do not look perfect.

18 People waste a lot of food at home as well. Families often fail to use their food before it goes bad. And many people buy more food than they can use. When food and yard waste ends up in landfills, it rots. This creates methane, a powerful greenhouse gas.

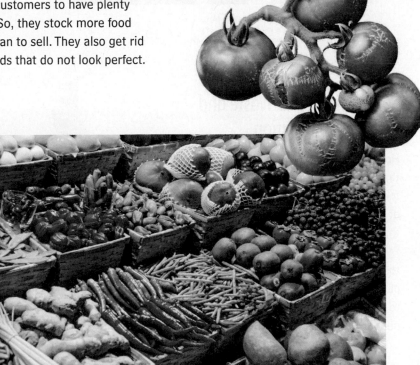

These tomatoes have skin cracks, so the farmer left them in the field.

myNotes

📖 READ FOR UNDERSTANDING

How does food and yard waste affect the environment? *(Food and yard waste rots in landfills and creates methane, a powerful greenhouse gas.)*

DOK 1

Notice & Note

Numbers and Stats

- **Have students** reread paragraph 16 to identify the statistics and explain the author's purpose for including this information. *(Americans waste between one-quarter and one-half of the 590 billion pounds of food produced every year; the author wants to shock the reader by revealing the incredibly large amount of food Americans waste.)*

ANNOTATION TIP: Have students highlight the numbers and statistics in paragraph 16.

- **Have students** reflect on the Anchor Question: *What does this make me wonder about?* and add to their notes.

DOK 2

A woman in Seattle shows her three waste bins.
Waste in the two large bins will be recycled.
Waste in the small black bin will end up in a landfill.

Solutions to Food Waste and Yard Waste Pollution

19 How can you help? Take only the food that you plan to eat. And try not to be too picky. For instance, cut a bruise out of an apple and eat the rest instead of throwing away the whole apple.

20   Governments are getting involved too. The city of Seattle, Washington, passed a law in 2015. It requires people to recycle food waste. The city fines people who do not follow the law.

Mulch can be made from many things, including wood chips, grass clippings, and hay.

21   People can generate less yard waste by keeping leaves and grass clippings on the lawn. These materials provide natural nutrition to the landscape. People can shred leaves and grass clippings to make mulch. Mulch is a layer of material that is spread over the ground. It keeps the soil healthier.

22   You can also turn food and yard waste into dirt. This process is called composting. Some people use special bins for their food scraps and yard waste. Other people simply make a pile out in the open. Over time, these materials will naturally decay and turn into dirt. Then you can use the dirt to plant a garden!

> **decay**   When things decay, they slowly break down and rot.

Composting usually takes two to six months.

269

📖 **READ FOR UNDERSTANDING**

Why might people throw away electronics? *(The electronics may have stopped working. People may also want a new cell phone or computer if the electronics are old, outdated, and don't work as fast or as well as new technology.)*

DOK 2

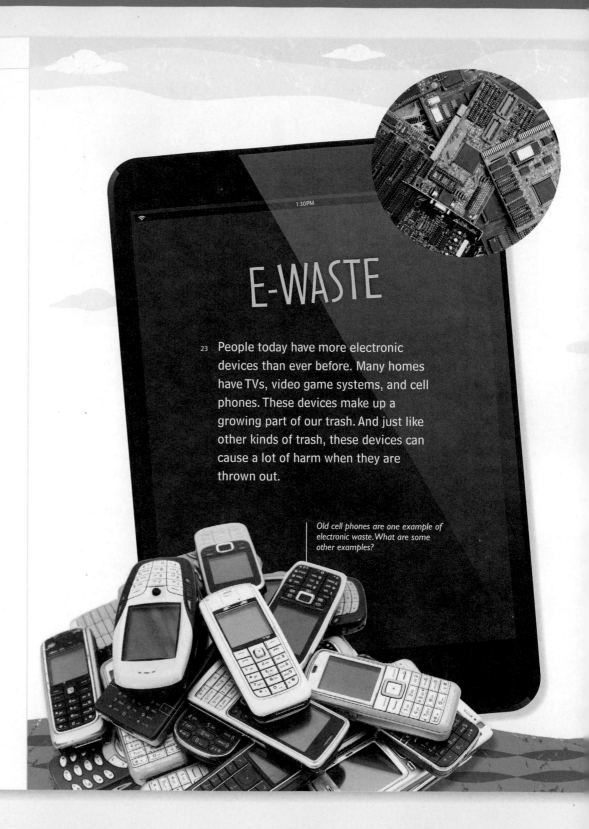

E-WASTE

23 People today have more electronic devices than ever before. Many homes have TVs, video game systems, and cell phones. These devices make up a growing part of our trash. And just like other kinds of trash, these devices can cause a lot of harm when they are thrown out.

Old cell phones are one example of electronic waste. What are some other examples?

270

Take good care of your cell phone so it will last a long time.

Effects of E-Waste Pollution

24 Electronic waste, or e-waste, contains many toxic materials. But less than 15 percent of e-waste is recycled. That means most e-waste ends up in landfills or incinerators. When e-waste is buried or burned, the toxic materials can be released into the land, water, and air.

25 E-waste contains a high amount of lead. If e-waste is not disposed of properly, lead can leach into people's water supplies. When people drink this water, it can damage their kidneys. It also damages their blood and their nervous systems.

Solutions to E-Waste Pollution

26 You can reduce harmful e-waste. First, do not get rid of electronics that still work. Second, when you do get rid of electronics, look for recycling programs at local stores and government offices. These programs should guarantee that the e-waste will be handled responsibly. If your favorite electronics company does not have a recycling program, ask the company to start one.

🔍 **TARGETED CLOSE READ**

Ideas and Support

Have students reread paragraphs 24 and 25 to analyze the text for the connection between the claim and the facts or examples that support it.

What claim does the author make? *(The toxic materials in e-waste are harmful to the environment.)*

What facts or examples does the author provide to support this claim? *(Most e-waste ends up in landfills or incinerators, allowing the toxic materials to be released into the land, water, and air. The high amount of lead in e-waste can leak into people's water supplies and harm their kidneys, blood, and nervous systems.)*

DOK 2

📖 **READ FOR UNDERSTANDING**

What can people do to reduce harmful e-waste? *(not get rid of electronics that still work; recycle electronics instead of throwing them away)*

DOK 1

271

REDUCE, REUSE, RECYCLE

27 You can help stop household waste pollution by following the three Rs: reduce, reuse, and recycle. These Rs are listed in order of importance. That means the most important step is reduce. The less we buy, the less trash we produce.

272

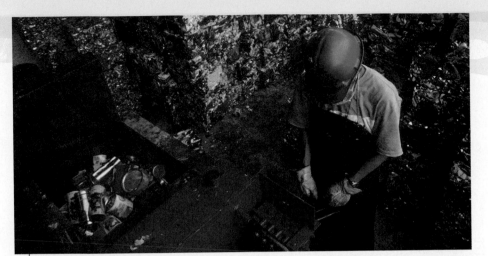

A worker operates a machine at a recycling center.

28   So the next time you are at the store, think about what you really need. If you can live without something, consider leaving it on the shelf.

29   The second most important step is reuse. When you do buy something, try to use it until it wears out. And if you do not need it anymore, give it to someone who will use it. That way, it will not go to a landfill.

30   The third most important step is recycle. When it is time to get rid of something, make every effort to recycle it rather than throwing it in the trash. In most areas, waste disposal companies provide separate recycling bins. So people can easily recycle paper, glass, and some kinds of plastic and metal. Some items, such as paint and batteries, are harder to recycle. But many areas have centers where these items can be brought for recycling.

Do you have old toys that you do not use? Consider giving them to younger kids instead of throwing them away.

273

274

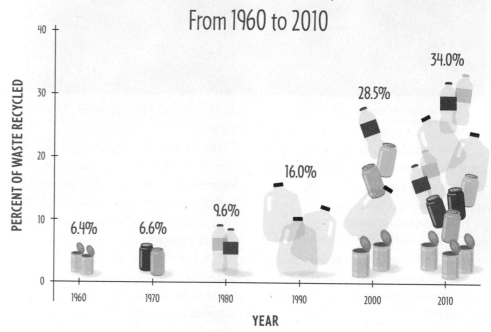

American Recycling Rates
From 1960 to 2010

PERCENT OF WASTE RECYCLED

40

30

20

10

0

6.4% 6.6% 9.6% 16.0% 28.5% 34.0%

1960   1970   1980   1990   2000   2010

YEAR

Working Together to Find Solutions

31 Many places have laws that require people to recycle. The city of Austin, Texas, has set a goal to cut the amount of trash it sends to landfills to nearly zero by the year 2040. The country of Sweden has nearly achieved this goal. It sends only 1 percent of its trash to landfills.

32   Household waste is a major problem. But we have the power to solve it. And the solution begins with making smart choices in our everyday lives.

Collaborative Discussion

Look back at what you wrote on page 258. Tell a partner two things you learned from this text. Then work with a group to discuss the questions below. Refer to details and examples in *How Can We Reduce Household Waste?* to explain your answers. Take notes for your responses. When you speak, use your notes.

1 Review pages 263–264. What are some of the ways that trash harms people, plants, and animals?

2 Reread page 267. What are some reasons that food is wasted in the United States each year?

3 How can people reduce the amount of trash they create?

 Listening Tip

Show others that you are listening and care about what they say. Look at the speaker and smile or nod when you agree with an idea.

Speaking Tip

If someone says something interesting or helpful, tell that person that you like his or her idea. You can also say why you like it.

Academic Discussion

Use the **COLLABORATIVE DISCUSSION** routine. Have students write notes to answer the questions. Then have groups apply the Listening and Speaking Tips as they discuss their responses.

Possible responses:

1. *Trash, like plastics, metals, and paper, can take time to break down and leach chemicals into the soil. If burned, trash can release chemicals into the air and increase greenhouse gases. The chemicals may affect the health of people and animals and the ability for plants to grow. Trash can also clog waterways where animals might eat it or be harmed by it.* DOK 2

2. *Farmers and store owners may waste food that is not perfect enough to sell to customers. Customers may buy too much food and throw away what they don't use.* DOK 2

3. *People can use what they buy and avoid buying what they won't use. They can also reuse items and recycle.* DOK 2

Write a Skit

PROMPT

In *How Can We Reduce Household Waste?*, you learned how the trash that people throw away affects our planet.

Imagine that your class is part of a program to encourage recycling in your school. Write a skit in which characters discuss how and why people should recycle. Include facts and other details from the text to support your idea that recycling is important. Don't forget to include some of the Critical Vocabulary in your writing.

PLAN

Identify key details from the text to include in your skit. Look for facts and ideas that could persuade others to recycle.

WRITE

Now write your skit to encourage people to recycle.

✓ Make sure your skit

- ☐ names the characters.
- ☐ includes stage directions to explain the setting and how the characters should speak.
- ☐ uses dialogue to show how the characters think and feel.
- ☐ uses possessive pronouns correctly.
- ☐ ends with a concluding statement from one of the characters.

Write About Reading

- **Review with students** the directions and checklist in the Write section.
- **Encourage students** to use their own words as they write their skit.

READ FOR UNDERSTANDING

Introduce the Text

- **Read aloud** and discuss the genre information. Point out these features of a biography:
  - third-person point of view
  - sequential order of events
  - literary language and devices to present the events in a person's life
- Use Display and Engage **Meet the Author 9.11**.
- **Tell students** to look for the Critical Vocabulary as they read, and to think about the words' meanings.

ANNOTATION TIP: Have students use the box to note what they would like to learn about the person in the selection.

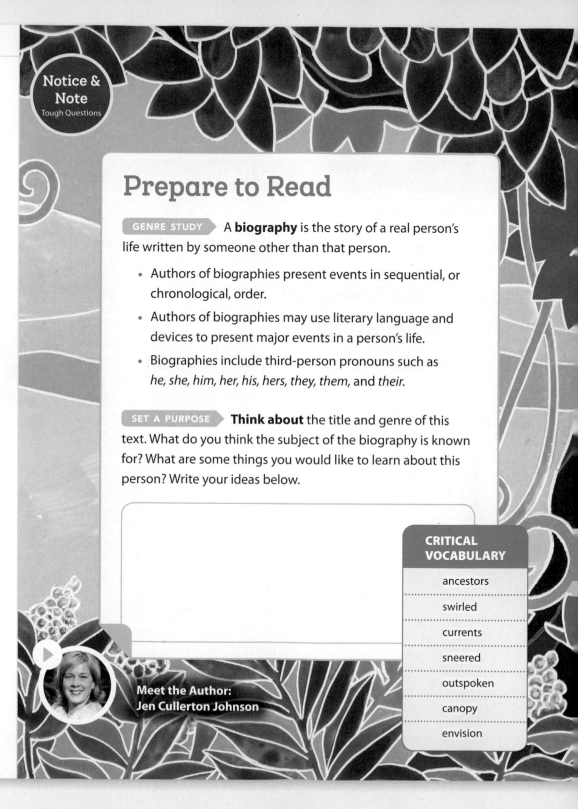

Notice & Note
Tough Questions

Prepare to Read

GENRE STUDY A **biography** is the story of a real person's life written by someone other than that person.

- Authors of biographies present events in sequential, or chronological, order.
- Authors of biographies may use literary language and devices to present major events in a person's life.
- Biographies include third-person pronouns such as *he, she, him, her, his, hers, they, them,* and *their.*

SET A PURPOSE **Think about** the title and genre of this text. What do you think the subject of the biography is known for? What are some things you would like to learn about this person? Write your ideas below.

Meet the Author:
Jen Cullerton Johnson

CRITICAL VOCABULARY

ancestors

swirled

currents

sneered

outspoken

canopy

envision

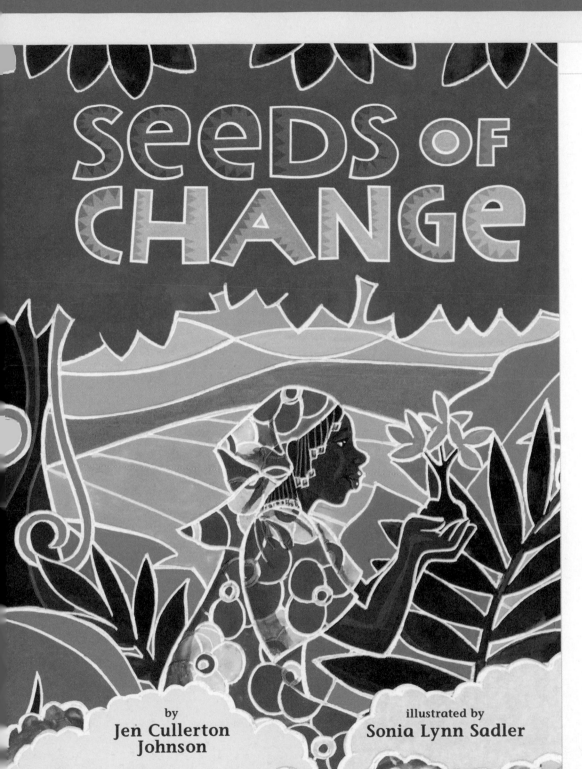

SEEDS OF CHANGE

by
Jen Cullerton Johnson

illustrated by
Sonia Lynn Sadler

myNotes

 READ FOR UNDERSTANDING

Set a Purpose

- **Have students** read the title and look at the illustrations through page 283.

Who do you think this biography will be about? What makes you think so? (*I think the biography will be about the girl shown in the illustrations. She appears in all the illustrations on these pages, so she must be important to the biography.*)

- **Guide students** to set a purpose for reading. Discuss with them what they think this selection will be about.

DOK 2

279

myNotes

🔍 **TARGETED CLOSE READ**

Author's Craft

Have students reread page 280 to analyze the author's use of anecdotes and sensory language.

Why does the author begin the biography with this anecdote about Wangari and her mother?
(The anecdote illustrates the strength of Wangari's ties to her family and culture, and it gives the reader insight into Wangari's motivation to protect the environment.)

How does the author use language to appeal to your senses and to describe actions in a vivid way?
(Tall, wide, green and oval *help the reader see the scene;* smooth *and* rough *help the reader sense how things feel;* delicious *helps the reader know how the wild fig tastes;* snapped *and* chirped *help the reader hear what is happening. The author uses the simile* "wrapped her arms around the trunk as if hugging her great-grandmother's spirit" *to describe the action.)*

ANNOTATION TIP: Have students circle examples of sensory language in the text.

DOK 2

1   "Come," Wangari's mother called. She beckoned her young daughter over to a tall tree with a wide, smooth trunk and a crown of green, oval leaves.

2   "Feel," her mother whispered.

3   Wangari spread her small hands over the tree's trunk. She smoothed her fingers over the rough bark.

4   "This is the *mugumo*," her mother said. "It is home to many. It feeds many too."

5   She snapped off a wild fig from a low branch and gave it to her daughter. Wangari ate the delicious fruit, just as geckos and elephants did. High in the tree, birds chirped in their nests. The branches bounced with jumping monkeys.

6   "Our people, the Kikuyu of Kenya, believe that our ancestors rest in the tree's shade," her mother explained.

7   Wangari wrapped her arms around the trunk as if hugging her great-grandmother's spirit. She promised never to cut down the tree.

---

ancestors   Your ancestors are the people in your family who lived long ago.

280

READ FOR UNDERSTANDING

Where do you think Wangari lives? What evidence supports your thinking? *(She lives in the African countryside. I know because she is dressed in traditional African clothing, and the area appears rural. There are monkeys in the trees, and there aren't any houses or buildings in the illustration. Wangari's mother also said their people were of Kenya, which is in Africa.)*

What do the details in the illustration on page 280 and 281 show you about the value of the mugumo tree? *(It provides food for people, such as Wangari and her mother. They are eating fruit they have gathered from the tree. It also provides food for animals, like the monkey and the elephant. The tree is most likely a home for the monkeys, the gecko and the birds.)*

DOK 2

281

myNotes

 READ FOR UNDERSTANDING

Ask and Answer Questions

MODEL ASKING AND ANSWERING QUESTIONS

⊘ **THINK ALOUD** *I have a question: Why doesn't Wangari go to school like her brother? I'll keep reading to see if I can find the answer. In paragraph 14, I find the answer to my question: It is unusual for girls to get an education.*

ANNOTATION TIP: Have students underline the words on page 284 that help answer the question.

 READ FOR UNDERSTANDING

What does the illustration show you about the characters? *(Nderitu appears to be older than his sister. He is pointing to something in the water, indicating that he is explaining something to Wangari while she listens carefully. The two siblings appear to have a close and respectful relationship.)*

DOK 2

282

8   Each year the mugumo grew, and so did Wangari. As the oldest girl in her family, she had many chores. Every day she fetched water, clear and sweet, from the river. In the rainy season she planted sweet potatoes, millet, and beans. When the sun shone brightly in the dry season, she shooed the chickens into the shade.

9   Sometimes when her brother, Nderitu, returned from school, he and Wangari played among the arrowroot plants by the stream, where thousands of eggs hatched into tadpoles and tadpoles turned into frogs. During those times, Nderitu told Wangari what he had learned in his classes. "Plants give air for people to breathe," he said. "Twenty divided by two is ten. There are seven great seas to sail."

10   Wangari listened as still as a tree, but her mind swirled with curiosity like the currents in the stream. Even though she knew few Kikuyu girls who could read, Wangari dreamed of going to school and learning, just like her brother.

11   "I must go to school," she told him.

12   "You will," he promised.

13   Nderitu talked to their parents. "Why doesn't Wangari go to school?" he asked.

> **swirled**   If something swirled, it moved quickly around in circles.
> **currents**   Currents are flowing movements of water in a lake, river, or ocean.

myNotes

🔍 TARGETED CLOSE READ

Author's Craft

Have students reread the first sentence of paragraph 10.

How does the author's use of similes help you understand Wangari's focus on her brother's teaching? *(The simile "as still as a tree" shows that she is listening intently. The simile "mind swirled with curiosity like the currents in the stream" describes Wangari's strong desire to learn.)*

ANNOTATION TIP: Have students underline the similes.

DOK 3

Notice & Note

Tough Questions

- **Remind students** that when a character pauses to ask himself or another character a tough question—one that reveals doubt or confusion—the readers get a glimpse at the character internal struggle.

- **Have students** explain what Nderitu's question in paragraph 13 reveals about his internal struggle. *(He feels guilty that he goes to school while his sister does not.)*

- **Have students** reflect on the Anchor Question: *What does this question make me wonder about?* and add to their notes.

DOK 2

283

14   Wangari's parents knew she was smart and a hard worker. Although it was unusual for a girl to be educated, they decided to send her to school. They knew she would not disappoint them. After some time to arrange for fees and supplies, Wangari's mother came to her. "You are going to school," she told her daughter.

15   Wangari grinned widely and hugged her mother. "Thank you!" she cried. "I will make you proud."

16   Wangari walked the long road to a one-room schoolhouse with walls made of mud, a floor of dirt, and a roof of tin. In time she learned to copy her letters and trace numbers. Wangari's letters soon made words, and her words made sentences. She learned how numbers could be added and subtracted, multiplied and divided. Animals and plants, she discovered, were like human beings in many ways. They needed air, water, and nourishment too.

17   When Wangari finished elementary school, she was eleven years old. Her mind was like a seed rooted in rich soil, ready to grow. Wangari wanted to continue her education, but to do so she would have to leave her village and move to the capital city of Nairobi. Wangari had never been farther than her valley's ridge. She was scared.

📖 **READ FOR UNDERSTANDING**

What can you tell about the family based on their facial expressions and gestures in the illustration?
(Their facial expressions show love and pride. Wangari's mother wraps her arm around her daughter, showing her affection.)

DOK 2

🔍 **TARGETED CLOSE READ**

Literary Elements

Have students revisit pages 280-285.

Who is this biography written about? *(Wangari)*

Who are the secondary characters introduced so far? *(Wangari's brother and her parents)*

DOK 1

285

READ FOR UNDERSTANDING

What do the illustrations show and the text tell you about the cultural and historical setting of the selection? *(The illustrations show Kenya a long time ago. They show how the people dress and how the countryside looks. The text tells about Wangari getting water from the river and the foods she planted.)*

DOK 1

 READ FOR UNDERSTANDING

What do you notice about Wangari's dress compared with that of the other women and girls in the illustration? *(Her dress does not have the bright colors and patterns that the others' clothing has. It is much simpler.)*

What might this difference represent? *(Wangari is moving to the city, where people probably dress differently than the rural people, like those in Wangari's community. Wangari's dress shows that she is becoming different from the other members of her family and community.)*

DOK 3

286

18   "Go," her mother said. She picked up a handful of earth and placed it gently into her daughter's hand. "Where you go, we go."

19   Wangari was sad to leave, but she knew that what her mother said was true. Wherever Wangari went, so went her family, her village, and her Kikuyu ways. She kissed her family and said good-bye to the mugumo tree, remembering her promise always to protect it.

20   Wangari's new life in the city amazed her. Skyscrapers towered above her head, not trees. People rushed through the streets like river water over stones. At school she lived with other girls like her, all trying to weave their village customs with new city ones. At night when the girls slept, Wangari dreamed of home and the sweet figs of the mugumo tree. Her dreams reminded her to honor her Kikuyu tradition of respecting all living things.

 READ FOR UNDERSTANDING

What does the handful of earth represent to Wangari and her family? *(The handful of earth represents Wangari's home, her family, and her culture.)*

Why does Wangari's mother give it to her? *(Her mother gives her the dirt as a reminder of who Wangari is and where she comes from. It will help Wangari feel as if her family is still with her in the city.)*

DOK 3

287

What problem does Wangari have as she nears graduation? (*She wants to become a biologist, but she knows there are not many native women scientists. She will have to travel halfway around the world to continue her studies.*)

How do Wangari's experiences in America change her ideas about the role of women in science? (*She sees women as leaders. She learns from American women that she can do anything she wants to.*)

DOK 2

Text Structure

Have students reread page 288.

What important events occur in Wangari's life after she starts school in the city? List the events in sequential order. (*Science becomes her favorite subject; she wants to become a biologist; she wins a scholarship and goes to college in Kansas; she studies in Pennsylvania; she returns to Kenya and teaches at the University of Nairobi.*)

Why does the author include all these events? (*The sequence of events shows how Wangari changes into a well-educated scientist who believes women can do anything they want to.*)

DOK 3   **288**

21   Wangari was an excellent student, and science became her favorite subject. She especially loved studying living things. Air, she learned, was made from two molecules of oxygen bonded together. Bodies were made up of cells. Leaves changed color because of photosynthesis.

22   As graduation neared, Wangari told her friends she wanted to become a biologist.

23   "Not many native women become scientists," they told her.

24   "I will," she said.

25   Wangari would have to travel halfway around the world to the United States to study biology. She had never left Kenya and had little money. But with her teachers' help, she won a scholarship to a college in Kansas.

26   America was very different from Kenya. In college, many of Wangari's science professors were women. From them she learned that a woman could do anything she wanted to, even if it hadn't been done before. While Wangari discovered how molecules move under a microscope lens and how cells divide in petri dishes, she also found her strength as a woman scientist.

27   After she graduated from college, Wangari traveled to Pennsylvania to continue her studies. Letters from home told Wangari about changes in Kenya. The people had elected a Kikuyu president, Jomo Kenyatta. Proud of her country and proud to be Kikuyu, Wangari decided to return home to Kenya to help her people.

28   America had changed Wangari. She had discovered a spirit of possibility and freedom that she wanted to share with Kenyan women. She accepted a teaching job at the University of Nairobi. Not many women were professors then, and even fewer taught science. Wangari led the way for other women and girls. She worked for equal rights so that female scientists would be treated with the same respect as male scientists.

— myNotes

289

myNotes

29   Wangari watched sadly as her government sold more and more land to big foreign companies that cut down forests for timber and to clear land for coffee plantations. Native trees such as cedar and acacia vanished. Without trees, birds had no place to nest. Monkeys lost their swings. Tired mothers walked miles for firewood.

30   When Wangari visited her village she saw that the Kikuyu custom of not chopping down the mugumo trees had been lost. No longer held in place by tree roots, the soil streamed into the rivers. The water that had been used to grow maize, bananas, and sweet potatoes turned to mud and dried up. Many families went hungry.

 READ FOR UNDERSTANDING

Ask and Answer Questions

Remind students that as they read, it is important to ask questions about what they would like to know. Have students ask a question about something they would like to know on page 290. (*Responses will vary.*)

ANNOTATION TIP: Have students underline the details that help them ask their question.

DOK 2

31   Wangari could not bear to think of the land being destroyed. Now married and the mother of three children, she worried about what would happen to all the mothers and children who depended on the land.

32   "We must do something," Wangari said.

33   Wangari had an idea as small as a seed but as tall as a tree that reaches for the sky. "*Harabee!* Let's work together!" she said to her countrywomen—mothers like her. Wangari dug deep into the soil, a seedling by her side. "We must plant trees."

34   Many women listened. Many planted seedlings. Some men laughed and sneered. Planting trees was women's work, they said. Others complained that Wangari was too outspoken—with too many opinions and too much education for a woman.

35   Wangari refused to listen to those who criticized her.

sneered   If you sneered, you showed disapproval and lack of respect by the look on your face.
outspoken   If you are outspoken, you say what you think even when others do not agree.

📖 **READ FOR UNDERSTANDING**

What do the men's actions show about attitudes and ways of life in Kenya? *(Many people still hold to old cultural traditions of separate roles for men and women. The men do not like that Wangari is educated and shares her opinions.)*

How does the landscape in this illustration differ from the one shown on pages 280 and 281? *(The landscape shown on pages 280 and 281 is green and lush, with many people and animals enjoying it. The landscape on this page looks brown and torn apart.)*

How has this difference affected the people and animals who live in this place? *(The animals have lost their homes; tired mothers walk miles for firewood; many families are going hungry; the water supply has dried up.)*

DOK 2

291

READ FOR UNDERSTANDING

How will the forest that grows from the trees the women are planting differ from a forest that grows naturally? *(The trees the women are planting will grow in straight rows. Trees in natural forests grow in a more random pattern.)*

DOK 2

292

36   Instead she told them, "Those trees you are cutting down today were not planted by you but by those who came before. You must plant trees that will benefit the community to come, like a seedling with sun, good soil, and abundant rain, the roots of our future will bury themselves in the ground and a canopy of hope will reach the sky."

37   Wangari traveled to villages, towns, and cities with saplings and seeds, shovels and hoes. At each place she went, women planted rows of trees that looked like green belts across the land. Because of this they started calling themselves the Green Belt Movement.

38   "We might not change the big world but we can change the landscape of the forest," she said.

39   One tree turned to ten, ten to one hundred, one hundred to one million, all the way up to thirty million planted trees. Kenya grew green again. Birds nested in new trees. Monkeys swung on branches. Rivers filled with clean water. Wild figs grew heavy in mugumo branches.

> **canopy**   A canopy is a rooflike covering, like the top branches of trees in a forest.

READ FOR UNDERSTANDING

How do Wangari and the Green Belt Movement change Kenya?
(Wangari and the other women plant up to thirty million trees. As a result, the animals have new homes, the rivers are full of clean water, and food grows again for families to eat.)

ANNOTATION TIP: Have students underline the text that shows how Kenya has changed.

DOK 1

293

TARGETED CLOSE READ

Author's Craft

Have students read the anecdote in paragraph 41.

Why does the author include this anecdote? *(This anecdote is like a bookend. The anecdote on page 280 describes Wangari at the beginning of her life. The anecdote on this page tells what happens to Wangari after the narrative ends, at the end of her life.)*

DOK 2

 READ FOR UNDERSTANDING

Wrap-Up

Revisit the purpose students set before they read the text. Have students explain how this story fits the genre of a biography. Have students cite evidence in the text to support their reasoning.

DOK 2

40   Mothers fed their children maize, bananas, and sweet potatoes until they could eat no more.

41   *Wangari continued to fight for her cause, planting trees and helping village women. She traveled to many places to spread her message and to guide people to take care of the land. She earned the nickname "Mama Miti," or "Mother of Trees." In 2004, she won the Nobel Peace Prize for her environmental work and her dedication to women's rights. She continued planting trees until her death in 2011. Today, people all over the world remember her and continue her great work. Because of Wangari, those who carry on her work can envision a clean, safe environment for all.*

envision If you envision something, you picture it in your mind.

Collaborative Discussion

Look back at what you wrote on page 278. Tell a partner two things you learned from this text. Then work with a group to discuss the questions below. Support your answers with details and examples from *Seeds of Change*. Take notes for your responses. When you speak, use your notes.

1 Reread page 283. How is Wangari's life different from her brother's? How does her brother help her?

2 Review page 288. What new ideas does Wangari learn in the United States?

3 What problems does Wangari hope to solve by planting trees?

Listening Tip

Wait for your turn to speak. As you listen, write down any questions you want to ask once the speaker has finished talking.

Speaking Tip

Always make suggestions in a helpful way. Say things like, "Another way to think about it is …" or "I can see why you think that, but …"

Academic Discussion

Use the **COLLABORATIVE DISCUSSION** routine. Have students write notes to answer the questions. Then have groups apply the Listening and Speaking Tips as they discuss their responses.

Possible responses:

1. *Wangari's life is different from her brother's in that he is allowed to go to school, but she has to stay home. Her brother helps her by sharing the things he learns in school with her.* DOK 2

2. *In the United States, Wangari learns that women can hold important positions. She sees examples of professors and scientists who are women. She also expands her knowledge of science through her studies.* DOK 2

3. *By planting trees, Wangari hopes to solve the problems caused by cutting down the trees, such as cleaning up the water to make gardening possible again, bringing back trees that provide food and habitats for animals, and reviving the setting in which she grew up.* DOK 2

295

Write a Speech

PROMPT

In *Seeds of Change*, you read about the life of environmentalist and Nobel Peace Prize winner Wangari Maathai.

Imagine that you have been invited to speak at an Earth Day celebration for younger students at your school. Write a speech to tell them about Wangari's life. Plan to include key events in the order in which they happen. Don't forget to use some of the Critical Vocabulary words in your writing.

PLAN

Identify key details from the text about Wangari. Write events in order or write numbers next to them to show the order you will tell about them in your speech.

Now write your speech about Wangari's life.

✓ ## Make sure your speech

☐ introduces the topic.

☐ summarizes the main events in Wangari's life.

☐ tells events in the order in which they happened.

☐ includes facts, details, and examples from the text.

☐ provides a concluding statement that sums up the information.

Write About Reading

- **Review with students** the directions and checklist in the Write section.

- **Encourage students** to use their own words as they summarize the events in Wangari's life.

Performance
Task

Revisit the Essential Question

• **Read aloud** the Essential Question.

• **Remind students** that the information about the environment that they read and viewed in this module can help them answer the question.

Write a Speech

• **Guide students** to think about what they learned from reading *Luz Sees the Light* and *How Can We Reduce Household Waste?* before selecting a helpful environmental change as the topic for their speech.

• **Review the features** of a speech using the checklist. Tell students to use the checklist as they draft, revise, and edit their speeches.

(?) **Essential Question**

What can people do to care for our planet?

Write a Speech

PROMPT Think about what you learned from reading *Luz Sees the Light* and *How Can We Reduce Household Waste?*

Imagine that you are giving a speech at your school council meeting about a change your school could make to help the environment. Write the speech you would give at the meeting. Use evidence from the texts to support your idea. Don't forget to use some of the Critical Vocabulary in your speech.

The change I will suggest is _____.

✓ Make sure your speech
☐ has an introduction that states your idea.
☐ is organized into paragraphs based on the reasons for your recommendation.
☐ includes facts, examples, and other supporting evidence from the texts.
☐ uses linking words and phrases, such as *also, because,* and *for example*.
☐ sums up your idea in a conclusion.

298

What change will you present? Think about the problems that you and your classmates could solve that would help the environment. Look back at your notes, and revisit the texts and video as necessary.

Use the graphic organizer to plan your writing. Jot down notes about problems and a change or solution for each. Use the Critical Vocabulary words where appropriate.

My change is: _____

Problem	Solution

Plan

- **As needed, guide students** to think about changes their school could make to help the environment.

- **Encourage them** to use information from the texts they read in this module as supporting details.

- **Encourage students** to include Big Idea Words and Critical Vocabulary in their speeches, as appropriate.

299

DRAFT ·· Write your speech.

Write a strong **introduction** that clearly states the change you think your school should make. Think of an interesting way to get your audience's attention.

Draft

- **Read aloud** the directions, referring back to the checklist as you do so.

- **Suggest** that students try rewording the prompt, if they are having trouble generating an introduction.

- **Have students** refer to their problem-solution charts as they construct their body paragraphs.

For each **body paragraph**, write a topic sentence that states one reason for your recommendation and supporting sentences.

In your **conclusion**, restate your idea.

REVISE AND EDIT · Review your draft.

The revision and editing steps give you a chance to look carefully at your draft and make changes. Work with a partner to determine whether you have explained your ideas clearly. Use these questions to help you evaluate and improve your speech.

PURPOSE/ FOCUS	ORGANIZATION	EVIDENCE	LANGUAGE/ VOCABULARY	CONVENTIONS
☐ Have I clearly stated my idea? ☐ Have I stayed on topic?	☐ Will my introduction grab the attention of the audience? ☐ Have I written a conclusion that sums up my main points?	☐ Have I used facts, examples, and details from both texts to support my ideas?	☐ Did I use linking words and phrases to show how my ideas are related? ☐ Did I include some of the Critical Vocabulary in my speech?	☐ Did I use possessive pronouns correctly? ☐ Did I indent each new paragraph? ☐ Have I used capital letters and punctuation marks correctly?

PUBLISH · Share your work.

Create a Finished Copy Make a final copy of your speech. Consider these options to share your writing:

1. Post your speech on your class or school website, or send it to a science magazine for students.

2. Read your speech aloud in a small-group discussion about the environment.

3. Pretend that your class is the school council. Deliver your speech to the council. Use diagrams, illustrations, or other visuals to support your ideas.

Revise and Edit

- **Guide students** to use the checklist as they work with partners to improve their speeches.

- **Remind students** to check the texts in the module to be sure their ideas and details are accurate.

Present

- **Students can copy** their revised drafts using their best handwriting. For handwriting models, see the resources section in the back of this Teacher's Guide.

- **Students can use** a computer to input their revised drafts. See Literacy Centers Printable **Keyboarding 9.1, 9.2, and 9.3** for keyboarding lessons.

Introduce the Topic

- **Read aloud** the module title, *Communication Nation*.

- **Tell students** that in this module they will be reading and viewing selections on the topic of communication.

- **Have students** explain what they know about communication—purposes, types, and history.

- Then ask students to discuss the different ways in which the module title can be interpreted. (*Possible response: It can mean we are a group, or nation, made up of communicators.*)

Discuss the Quotation

- **Read aloud** the quotation by Lawrence Clark Powell.

- **Lead a discussion** in which students discuss whether or not they agree with Powell's statement, and why. Explain the meaning of the quote, as needed: *Writing and speaking both allow us to communicate our ideas and opinions. As readers, we learn information and grow as individuals from that information.*

- **Give examples** of things we can learn through communicating. (*Accept reasonable responses.*)

Communication Nation

"Write to be understood, speak to be heard, read to grow."
—Lawrence Clark Powell

302

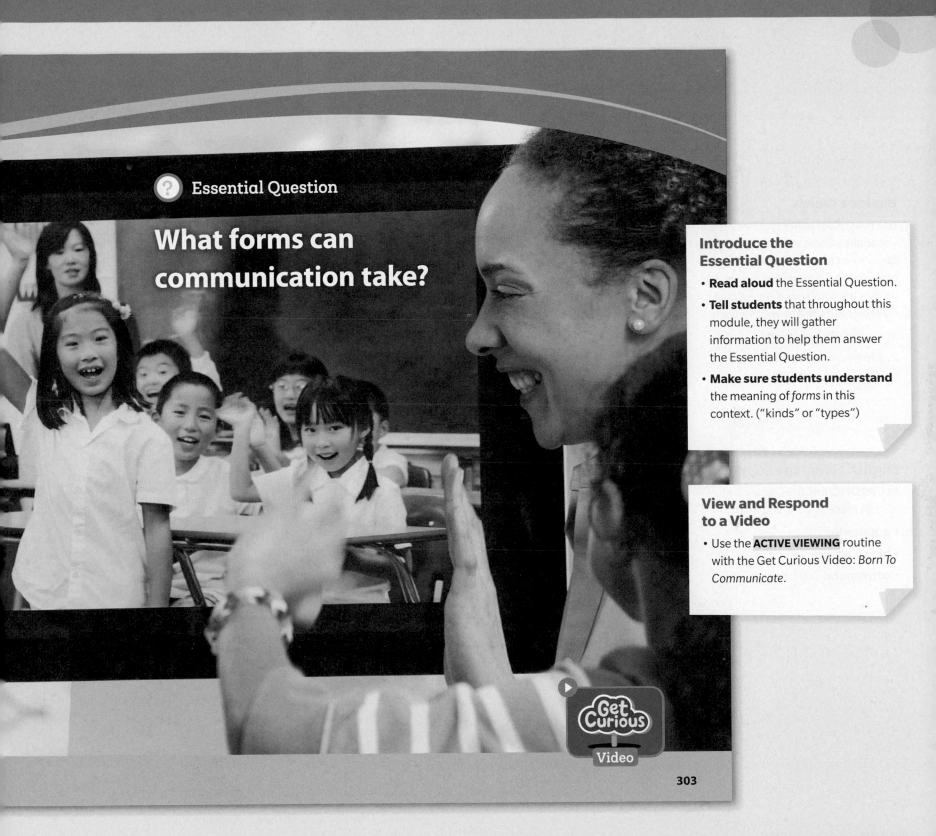

Essential Question

What forms can communication take?

Introduce the Essential Question

- **Read aloud** the Essential Question.
- **Tell students** that throughout this module, they will gather information to help them answer the Essential Question.
- **Make sure students understand** the meaning of *forms* in this context. ("kinds" or "types")

View and Respond to a Video

- Use the **ACTIVE VIEWING** routine with the Get Curious Video: *Born To Communicate*.

Get Curious Video

303

Big Idea Words

Use the **VOCABULARY** routine and the Vocabulary Cards to introduce the Big Idea Words *broadcast, publication, blog,* and *correspond*. You may wish to display the corresponding Vocabulary Card for each word as you discuss it.

1. Say the Big Idea Word.
2. Explain the meaning.
3. Discuss the context sentence.

English Language Support

ALL PROFICIENCIES Display and discuss these Spanish cognates.

- **publication** *publicación*
- **blog** *blog*
- **correspond** *corresponder*

Words About Communication

The words in the chart will help you talk and write about the selections in this module. Which words about communication have you seen before? Which words are new to you?

Add to the Vocabulary Network on page 305 by writing synonyms, antonyms, and related words and phrases for each word about communication.

After you read each selection in this module, come back to the Vocabulary Network and keep building it. Add more ovals if you need to.

WORD	MEANING	CONTEXT SENTENCE
broadcast (noun)	A broadcast is a program or speech on the television or radio.	Robert listened to the radio broadcast of the concert.
publication (noun)	A publication is something that has been printed and made available for sale.	My favorite publication is a newspaper that contains stories from local authors.
blog (noun)	If you write a blog, you are writing regular and informal updates, or entries, on a website.	The students created a blog about how to care for a community garden.
correspond (verb)	When you correspond with someone, you exchange letters or emails with that person.	The class was assigned to correspond with their pen pals for the entire school year.

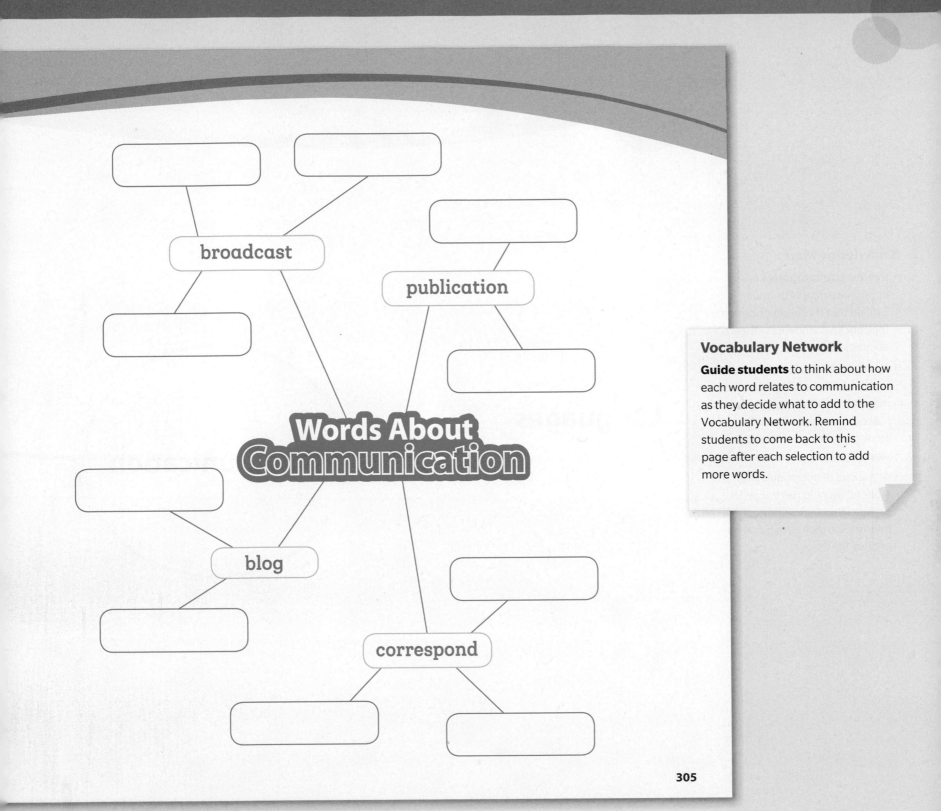

broadcast

publication

Words About
Communication

blog

correspond

Vocabulary Network

Guide students to think about how each word relates to communication as they decide what to add to the Vocabulary Network. Remind students to come back to this page after each selection to add more words.

305

Knowledge Map

- **Review the categories** on the knowledge map with students. Explain that these categories name the concepts students will learn about in the module.

- **Have students** add information and illustrations to the knowledge map at the end of each week during Make Connections. Remind students to review the texts and video to add details to the map.

- At the end of the module, have students work in pairs or small groups to compare and contrast the information they added to their knowledge maps.

Languages

Communication

306

Advances in Technology Throughout History

307

Introduce the Text

- **Read aloud** the title. Tell students that this is an informational text and a timeline that tell about how technology has affected communication through the years. Discuss with students what they know about informational texts and timelines. *(Informational texts contain facts about a topic. Timelines sequence important events across a certain period of time.)*

- **Guide students** to set a purpose for reading.

- **Point out** the highlighted Big Idea Words.

- **Have students** read the text.

 READ FOR UNDERSTANDING

Text and Graphic Features

- **What do the headings tell you about the selection?** *(They tell what each section is about. They describe the central, or main, idea in each section.)*

- **Why are the headings written in bold?** *(To call your attention to them and to separate them from the rest of the text.)*

ANNOTATION TIP: Have students underline the headings in the article.

DOK 2

308

 myNotes

Short Read

How Technology Has Changed Communication

Timeline of Communications Technology

This timeline shows when important communication devices became popular in the United States.

The **telegraph** sent messages long distances over wires. Telegraph operators tapped out messages in Morse code, a system of dots and dashes that stand for letters.

1850s

The **telephone** has been called the greatest invention of the 19th century. People no longer had to be in the same room to talk to one another!

1870s

After **television** was invented, people could see events as they happened. Television brought people together to witness important moments in history.

1950s

1860s

Before the **typewriter**, people wrote letters and other documents by hand. The typewriter made writing a book or other lengthy publication much faster.

1920s

In the 1920s, everyone wanted a **radio** for their living room. Families gathered around it to hear a news or entertainment broadcast.

1 Imagine it's 1866, and your family has just arrived in Houston, Texas, after a long trip by ship. Your grandmother in New York City is anxious to hear from you. So you pull out paper, a pen, and ink. You dip the pen nib in ink and write a letter by hand. You take it to the post office. It will travel on a ship that's leaving for New York City at the end of the week, and about 2,300 miles and weeks later, your letter will reach your grandmother!

2 Fast forward to the present. Your family has just arrived in Houston. You borrow your mom's cell phone and text, "We made it!" to your grandmother in New York City, along with a photo of the Houston skyline. She gets your message almost instantly and texts back, "Have fun! See you next week!"

Personal computers changed the way people work by allowing users to store and share information over computer networks.

When the **World Wide Web** came along, it was like a giant electronic information library. Later it grew to include online stores, cat videos, and just about anything else imaginable

People use **social media** to connect and communicate. Through blogs, websites, and apps, people share photos and information about their lives.

1970s

1990s

2010s

1980s

The first **mobile phones** allowed people to talk on the go. Starting in the 1990s, mobile phones, now known as cell (or cellular) phones, let people text, too.

Email, short for *electronic mail*, is a tool for sending documents and photos from computer to computer. It's a fast, easy way to correspond with people anywhere in the world.

2000s

Smartphones are mini computers that allow users to email, search for information, buy things, listen to music, take photos and videos—and, yes, make phone calls.

309

Notice & Note
3 Big Questions

Prepare to Read

GENRE STUDY **Informational texts** give facts and examples about a topic.

- Authors of informational texts may present their ideas in sequential, or chronological, order.
- Informational texts include visuals, such as charts, diagrams, graphs, timelines, and maps.
- Social studies texts also include words that are specific to the topic. These are words that name things or ideas.

SET A PURPOSE **Think about** the title and genre of this text. What do you know about the history of communication? What are some things you'd like to learn? Write your ideas below.

CRITICAL VOCABULARY

significantly

enabled

patent

peak

transmitted

plucked

proposed

influence

Build Background:
Communication Today

The *History of* Communication

illustrations by Danny Schlitz

311

myNotes

What Is Communication?

1 Communication is the sharing of ideas and information. People can share information through spoken and written words, by making and looking at images, and by making and listening to sounds. People can also communicate through gestures and facial expressions.

2 Over time, people have developed ways to share information with many people at once. Such methods of mass communication have included books, magazines, newspapers, television, radio, and, more recently, the Internet. Communication also takes place through sound recordings, motion pictures, and signs. Taken together, these tools allow people all over the world to communicate with one another.

 READ FOR UNDERSTANDING

Monitor and Clarify

MODEL MONITORING AND CLARIFYING

💬 **THINK ALOUD** *I will monitor and clarify the information in paragraphs 1–3 to make sure I understand what the author is saying. I understand the information in paragraphs 1 and 2 from what I already know about communication, so I can move on. The word "Renaissance" is a new term. I can use context clues in paragraph 3 to help me figure out what it means. I see that it means "rebirth." So, the Renaissance was a period of time in which new ideas were born.*

The **Printing Press**

3 Between 1300 and 1600, a cultural movement called the Renaissance (rebirth) swept across Europe. The Renaissance was a period of great advancement in educational and artistic ideas, and it created a huge demand for books. Hand copying and block printing could not keep up with this demand.

4 In about 1440, a German inventor named Johannes (yoh-HAHN-uhs) Gutenberg developed a printing press that used movable type. Gutenberg made separate pieces of metal type for each letter of the alphabet. He assembled the pieces in a frame to form pages and applied ink to the type. The machine pressed the inked type against paper to print words.

This English engraving shows a steam-driven printing press from 1826.

312

Johannes Gutenberg

Newspapers are printed by the thousands, like these copies of the Houston Chronicle.

myNotes

5   The Gutenberg press could print about 300 copies of a page daily. By 1500, there were more than 1,000 print shops in Europe, and several million books had been produced.

6   Printing quickly became an important communication tool. It significantly increased the production of religious texts. In addition, debates about social problems, religious beliefs, and government matters quickly appeared in print.

7   There were few changes to the printing press from Gutenberg's time until the 1800s. In 1811, a German named Friedrich König invented a steam-powered press that could print about 1,100 sheets per hour. In 1846, Richard Hoe of the United States invented a press that used rotating cylinders (revolving drums) to print 8,000 sheets per hour. Later models turned out as many as 20,000 sheets per hour.

8   The printing press is one of the most important inventions in history. It has enabled millions of people to receive knowledge through books, newspapers, magazines, and other printed formats.

significantly   If something changes significantly, the change is great enough to be noticed or important.

enabled   If you are enabled to do something, you are given a chance to do it.

 READ FOR UNDERSTANDING

How did the Gutenberg press change people's lives? Cite evidence from the text to explain your answer. *(Since "printing quickly became an important communication tool," significantly more religious texts were produced. People learned more quickly about government matters, social problems, and religious beliefs.)*

ANNOTATION TIP: Have students underline the text evidence.

DOK 1

 READ FOR UNDERSTANDING

Why is the printing press one of the most important inventions in history? Cite evidence from the text to explain your answer. *(It has allowed millions of people to receive knowledge through magazines, newspapers, books, and other printed formats.)*

ANNOTATION TIP: Have students highlight the text evidence.

DOK 1

313

The **Telegraph**

9 By the mid-1800s, people could share ideas through books, newspapers, and other written texts. However, there was still no way for people to communicate quickly if they were located in two different places. This would begin to change with the arrival of the electric telegraph, which could send messages by using electric current traveling along wires.

10 In 1820, a Danish scientist named Hans Christian Oersted (UR-stehd) found that an electric current can cause a magnetized needle to move. This discovery led to the invention of the telegraph. In communication by telegraph, an operator would send a message by using a special device to vary the electric current flowing through the wires. When the amount of electricity changed, a device at the receiving end would convert the signals into a specific series of clicks. An operator would then decode these clicks into words, or a telegram.

11 A number of inventors created early telegraphic devices, but the American painter and inventor Samuel F. B. Morse is credited with making the first practical telegraph in 1837. Morse received a U.S. patent for it in 1840.

> **patent** If you have a patent for an invention, you are the only one who is allowed to make or sell the invention.

314

However, Morse's invention built upon years of research and experiments by people who came before him.

12   The telegraph became an important way to send information quickly to different locations. Reporters used the telegraph to send stories to their newspapers. Armies on both sides of the American Civil War (1861–1865) also relied heavily on the invention. The number of telegrams sent in the United States reached its peak in 1929, when more than 200 million were transmitted.

> **peak**   A peak is the highest point of something.
>
> **transmitted**   If something is transmitted, it is sent electronically from one place to another.

Samuel F. B. Morse

13   Samuel F. B. Morse was born on April 27, 1791, in Massachusetts. He received the patent for the first successful electric telegraph in the United States in 1840. He also invented Morse code, a system of sending messages using short and long sounds combined in various ways.

🔍 TARGETED CLOSE READ

Central Idea

Have students reread paragraphs 9–12 to identify the central, or main, idea of this section.

What is the central, or main, idea of the section, "The Telegraph"? *(The telegraph made it possible for people to communicate quickly if they were located in two different places.)*

What details in the text support the central, or main, idea? *(Messages could be sent by using electric current traveling along wires. Reporters sent stories to their newspapers using the telegraph. Civil War armies relied on the telegraph to relay messages.)*

ANNOTATION TIP: Have students highlight details that support the central, or main, idea.

DOK 2

📖 READ FOR UNDERSTANDING

What is Morse code? *("a system of sending messages using short and long sounds combined in various ways")*

ANNOTATION TIP: Have students underline the text evidence that defines Morse code.

DOK 1

315

The **Telephone**

14 For most of the 1800s, there was no way for people at two distant locations to speak to each other directly. They could communicate only by sending letters or telegrams. But in the 1870s, a Scottish-born inventor named Alexander Graham Bell discovered a way to send people's voices across long distances.

15 In 1871, Bell arrived in Boston, Massachusetts, to become a teacher to people who were deaf. He performed experiments at night, working to improve the telegraph by creating a device that could send several telegraph messages over one wire at the same time.

16 On June 2, 1875, while conducting an experiment, Bell had a breakthrough. One of the metal reeds (thin pieces) on his device got stuck. Bell's assistant, Thomas Watson, plucked the reed to loosen it. In the other room, Bell heard the sound in his receiver.

Bell's telephone is shown here in illustrations from an English newspaper in 1877.

plucked If something is plucked, it is pulled away from where it is.

He realized that the vibrating reed had created changes to the electric current that passed through the wire. These changes were then reproduced in the receiver at the other end of the wire.

17   This discovery led to more experiments, and Bell received a patent for the first telephone on March 7, 1876. Three days later, he transmitted human speech over a telephone for the first time. In 1877, the Bell Telephone Company was founded. Within 10 years, there were more than 150,000 people who owned telephones in the United States.

18   Today, most people take the telephone for granted. With a worldwide network of telephone wires, it is easy for people to call someone in a different part of the world.

Alexander Graham Bell

19   Alexander Graham Bell (1847–1922) was born in Edinburgh, Scotland. His mother was a painter, and his father helped teach people who were deaf to speak. Bell also was an educator of deaf students, but he is best known as the inventor of the telephone.

20   Bell and his assistant, Thomas Watson, helped start telephone service in the United States. In 1877, Bell married Mabel Hubbard, one of his students, and they took the invention to England. But Bell did not stay in the telephone business. Instead, he preferred to continue his work with the deaf and to develop other inventions. Bell became a U.S. citizen in 1882.

 TARGETED CLOSE READ

Text and Graphic Features

Have students reread page 317 to note any text or graphic features.

What unique text or graphic feature do you notice on page 317? *(a sidebar)*

What information does it give? *(information about Alexander Graham Bell's personal life)*

ANNOTATION TIP: Have students highlight details that tell about Bell's personal life.

DOK 2

317

myNotes

Radio

21 The telegraph and the telephone enabled people at distant locations to communicate with each other, but only if the locations were connected by wires. This began to change in the late 1800s, when scientists discovered ways to send radio signals through the air. The invention of the radio allowed people to communicate quickly between any two points on land, at sea, and, later, in the sky and in space.

22 The development of the radio began in the 1830s with an idea proposed separately by an American professor named Joseph Henry and a British scientist named Michael Faraday. Both Henry and Faraday proposed that an electric current in one wire could produce an electric current in another wire, even when the wires are not connected.

23 Though many people contributed to the radio's development, Nikola Tesla, an American inventor from Austria Hungary, is credited with its invention. In 1891, he invented the Tesla coil, an extremely important component (part) of radio transmitters.

24 In 1895, an Italian inventor named Guglielmo Marconi (goo-LYEHL-moh mahr-KOH-nee) sent radio signals more than a mile through the air in the form of telegraph code signals. In 1901, Marconi's equipment transmitted signals all the way across the Atlantic Ocean, from England to Canada. In 1906, a Canadian-born scientist named Reginald Fessenden first transmitted voice by radio.

Guglielmo Marconi poses with his wireless radio receiver in 1896.

> **proposed**   If you proposed an idea, you suggested that it was useful or true.

 READ FOR UNDERSTANDING

How were telegraph and telephone signals different from radio signals? *(The telegraph and telephone sent signals through wires. Radio signals were sent through the air.)*

ANNOTATION TIP: Have students highlight details that tell the difference between telegraph and telephone signals and radio signals.

DOK 2

318

my Notes

Families used to gather around the radio to listen to news, sports, and entertainment.

25   Radio broadcasting (programming) began on a large scale during the 1920s. Soon, families could gather in their living rooms to listen to comedies, adventure dramas, live music, variety shows, and other kinds of radio programming.

Nikola Tesla

26   Nikola Tesla (1856–1943) was born in Austria Hungary, in an area that is now part of Croatia. In 1884, Tesla left Europe for the United States. He worked for the inventor Thomas Edison but quit after one year.

27   Tesla became a pioneer in electrical technology, and he received more than 100 patents for a variety of inventions. His Tesla coil is still used in radio and television transmission today. Tesla's other achievements include groundbreaking work with X rays, radar, aircraft design, and neon and fluorescent lighting.

319

TARGETED CLOSE READ

Text and Graphic Features

Have students reread paragraph 25 to analyze the connection between the text and the photograph and caption.

How do the photograph and caption on page 319 connect to the text in paragraph 25? *(They show and explain how, beginning in the 1920s, people were able to listen to a variety of programs in their own homes, thanks to radio broadcasting.)*

How do the photograph and caption add to your understanding of the ideas in the text? *(They show a family gathered around a radio to listen to a radio program.)*

DOK 2

TARGETED CLOSE READ

Text Structure

Have students reread paragraphs 22–25 to analyze the text structure.

What is the structure of this part of the text? How do you know? *(chronological order; The author puts the events of the development of the radio in order from the 1830s to the 1920s.)*

ANNOTATION TIP: Have students underline the words and phrases that signal a chronological text structure.

How does knowing the structure of the text help you understand the central, or main, ideas on this page? *(It helps the reader know what happens first, next, and last.)*

DOK 3

Television

28   By the early 1900s, when operators were first transmitting words by radio, many scientists had begun experimenting with the transmission of pictures. These experiments eventually led to the development of the television—a tremendously popular communication system that is used daily in nearly every corner of the world.

29   Many scientists contributed to the invention of television. Among them was Philo Farnsworth, an American scientist who created an electronic scanning system in 1922. This became a breakthrough in television technology.

<table>
<tr><td>

READ FOR UNDERSTANDING

According to paragraph 28, how are radios and televisions different? (*Radios transmit words and televisions transmit pictures.*)

ANNOTATION TIP: Have students underline details that tell how radios and televisions are different.

DOK 1

</td></tr>
</table>

Ways Television Signals Reach Homes

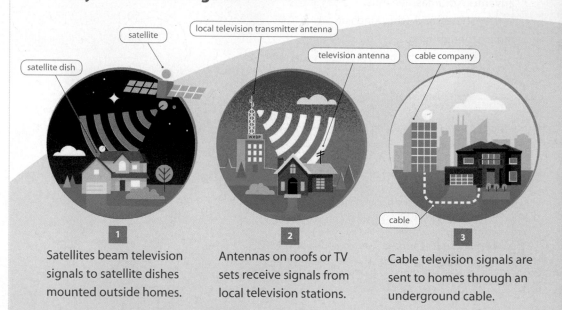

1 Satellites beam television signals to satellite dishes mounted outside homes.

2 Antennas on roofs or TV sets receive signals from local television stations.

3 Cable television signals are sent to homes through an underground cable.

myNotes

30 Television works by changing pictures and sounds into electronic signals, which are then sent through the air. A television set receives these signals and turns them back into pictures and sounds.

31 As more families came to own television sets, TV programming began to influence people's attitudes and beliefs. By watching TV shows, viewers can see the latest fashions and hear the opinions of people with different backgrounds and beliefs. Through advertisements, people are encouraged to buy certain products. Television also plays a major role in how people learn about their government and select their leaders.

> **influence** If you influence people, you use your power or ability to change what they think.

🔍 TARGETED CLOSE READ

Text and Graphic Features

Have students reread paragraph 30 to analyze the connection between the text and the visuals.

How does the diagram on page 320 connect to the text in paragraph 30? *(It shows ways television signals reach homes.)*

How does the diagram add to your understanding of the ideas in the text? *(The diagram shows how a television set receives different types of signals so that it can turn them into pictures and sounds.)*

DOK 2

📖 READ FOR UNDERSTANDING

According to paragraph 31, how has watching TV influenced people's attitudes and beliefs? *(TV viewers hear the opinions of people with different backgrounds and beliefs. They see the latest fashions. Advertisements persuade people to buy certain products. People can also learn about their government and leaders through television.)*

ANNOTATION TIP: Have students highlight details that tell how TV viewers are influenced.

DOK 1

321

Microwave signal

Communications satellite

Microwave signal

Communications satellites act as message relays as they orbit Earth.

Microwave tower

Microwave tower

The **Satellite**

32   A communications satellite is a type of satellite that receives radio, television, and other signals in space and relays (sends) them back to Earth.

33   Interestingly, a British science-fiction writer named Arthur C. Clarke is credited with inventing communications satellites. In an article published in 1945, Clarke described a satellite in orbit that could serve as an information relay station in the sky. This idea would turn out to be one of the greatest advances in modern communication.

34   Because a satellite is high above Earth, it can direct radio waves to any location within a large region. Without satellites, most radio transmissions could not reach far beyond the horizon (the distant, curved line where the land and sky appear to meet). Satellites can send messages to many places at once, and they offer instant service when radio links are needed quickly.

35   Early communications satellites were built to carry long-distance telephone calls. Satellites still perform this task today, providing

322

service in places where it is difficult to install telephone cables. Satellites also send telephone signals across oceans and to people in remote places. A ship's crew at sea, for instance, can talk to people anywhere in the world on mobile satellite phones.

36   Today, communications satellites also play a major role in television broadcasting. Satellites deliver programs to local cable TV companies or directly to homes. Satellite TV subscribers use dish-shaped antennas to receive hundreds of TV channels.

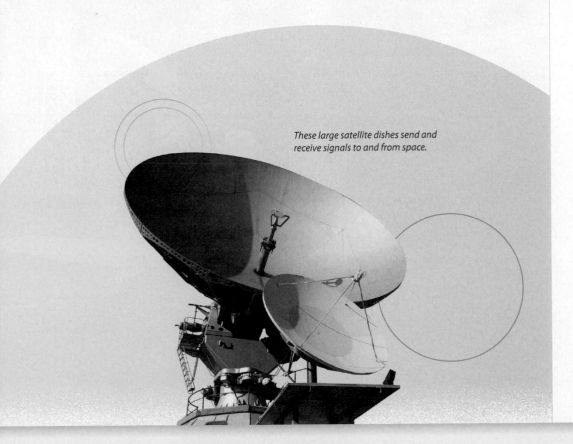

These large satellite dishes send and receive signals to and from space.

READ FOR UNDERSTANDING

How are satellites important today? *(They provide "service in places where it is difficult to install telephone cables." They also send telephone signals to people in remote places and across oceans. In addition, satellites deliver programs directly to homes as well as to cable television companies .)*

ANNOTATION TIP: Have students underline the words or phrases that explain why satellites are important today.

DOK 1

323

myNotes

The **Internet**

37 Computers first came into practical use in the mid-1900s. However, for many years, there was no way to link computers together to allow the sharing of information among them. Over the second half of the 1900s, the emergence of the Internet became one of the most important breakthroughs in the history of communication.

38 In the 1960s, the United States government's Department of Defense developed a network (interconnected system) of military and government computers. The network was intended to protect the information on those computers in case of a war or disaster. Soon, universities, corporations, and other organizations developed their own computer networks. Eventually, these networks joined with the government network to form the Internet. The word *Internet* means an interconnected network of networks.

🔍 **TARGETED CLOSE READ**

Central Idea

Have students reread paragraphs 37–38 to identify the central, or main, idea in this section.

What is the central, or main, idea of the section, "The Internet"?
(One of the most important breakthroughs in the history of communication was the emergence of the Internet.)

ANNOTATION TIP: Have students highlight details that support the central, or main, idea.

DOK 2

324

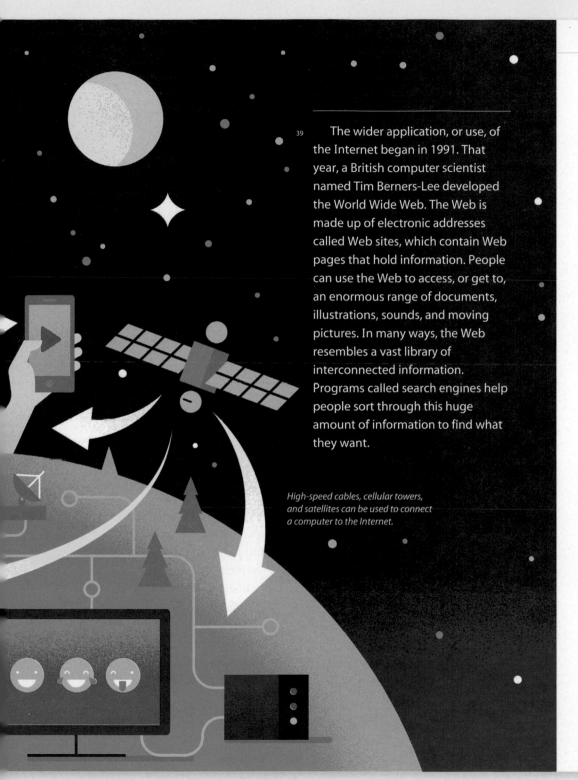

39   The wider application, or use, of the Internet began in 1991. That year, a British computer scientist named Tim Berners-Lee developed the World Wide Web. The Web is made up of electronic addresses called Web sites, which contain Web pages that hold information. People can use the Web to access, or get to, an enormous range of documents, illustrations, sounds, and moving pictures. In many ways, the Web resembles a vast library of interconnected information. Programs called search engines help people sort through this huge amount of information to find what they want.

High-speed cables, cellular towers, and satellites can be used to connect a computer to the Internet.

READ FOR UNDERSTANDING

Monitor and Clarify

Remind students that as they read, it is important to monitor and clarify key information in each paragraph to make sure they understand what the author is saying. Have students monitor and clarify the information presented in paragraph 39.

DOK 2

Notice & Note

3 Big Questions

- **Have students** explain why they might use the 3 big questions strategy on page 325. *(to focus on key information; to confirm what I already know; to identify surprising information)*

ANNOTATION TIP: Have students highlight what the author assumes they already know.

- **Have students** reflect on the Anchor Questions: *What surprised me? What did the author think I already knew? What challenged, changed, or confirmed what I already knew?* and add to their notes.

DOK 2

325

READ FOR UNDERSTANDING

How has the way people communicate changed from before the Renaissance to present day? Cite evidence from the text. *(Before the Renaissance, few people had books. The invention of the printing press made books available to many more people. The inventions of the telegraph and telephone enabled people located far apart to communicate through connected wires. Radio and television enabled people to listen to programming and see pictures. The Internet connects the world.)*

ANNOTATION TIP: Have students highlight important details in each section that tell about each type of communication.

DOK 3

 READ FOR UNDERSTANDING

Wrap-Up

Revisit the purpose students set before they read the text. Have students explain what they learned from the text and cite text evidence.

DOK 2

40   The Internet enables users of computers and similar devices to send and receive messages called e-mail, or electronic mail. Many people communicate over the Internet using instant messaging (IM). This feature enables two people to communicate through text messages that can be seen by both users as the messages are typed.

People can also see and speak to one another through microphones and cameras that are connected to the Internet.

41   New technologies continue to change the way people use the Internet. Handheld computers, cellular telephones, and tablets enable users to access the Internet from almost any location.

326

Collaborative Discussion

Look back at what you wrote on page 310. Tell a partner two things you learned from this text. Then work with a group to discuss the questions below. Refer to details and examples in *The History of Communication* to explain your answers. Take notes for your responses. When you speak, use your notes.

1 Reread pages 312–313. What does the growth of the printing business tell you about people's interests at the time?

2 Review pages 318–319. What features made radio an improvement over the telephone and the telegraph?

3 Which of the inventions are based on an earlier invention?

Listening Tip

Listen carefully as you wait for your turn to speak. Think about questions you may need to ask to better understand what a classmate has said.

Speaking Tip

Make sure that your comments relate to the question the group is discussing. Save your ideas about other topics until another time.

Academic Discussion

Use the **COLLABORATIVE DISCUSSION** routine. Have students write notes to answer the questions. Tell students to use the Critical Vocabulary words and content-area words in their responses, as appropriate. Then have groups apply the Listening and Speaking Tips as they discuss their responses.

Possible responses:

1. *It shows that people were interested in reading and learning about social issues, religious beliefs, and government matters.* DOK 2

2. *Radio is an improvement over the telephone and telegraph because it can be broadcast from wire to wire without the wires being connected.* DOK 2

3. *The steam-powered press is based on the Gutenberg press. Morse's telegraph is based on Hans Christian Oersted's telegraph.* DOK 2

327

Write an Advertisement

PROMPT

In *The History of Communication*, you learned about how inventions over the years made communicating with others faster and more effective.

Imagine that you work for an advertising agency. Choose one of the inventions from *The History of Communication* and create an advertisement to explain how this invention will help people communicate. Include a diagram or drawing to show your ideas. Don't forget to use some of the Critical Vocabulary words in your writing.

PLAN

Make notes about important details about your chosen invention. Then explain how it will help people communicate.

Write About Reading

- **Read aloud** the prompt with students.

- **Lead a discussion** in which students share their ideas about how the new inventions helped people communicate with others faster and more effectively. Tell students to use text evidence to support their ideas.

- **Then read aloud** the Plan section. Have students use ideas from the discussion in their notes.

Now write your advertisement for the invention.

✓ Make sure your advertisement

☐ introduces the topic clearly.

☐ uses facts and details from the text.

☐ uses correct spelling.

☐ ends with a concluding statement.

☐ includes a diagram, drawing, or other visual element that helps readers better understand the invention.

Write About Reading

- **Review with students** the directions and checklist in the Write section.

- **Encourage students** to use their own words as they create their advertisement. Remind them to use appropriate content-area words.

329

READ FOR UNDERSTANDING

Introduce the Text

- **Read aloud** and discuss the genre information. Remind students that narrative nonfiction tells a true story by giving factual information. Point out these examples of features and other components in a narrative nonfiction text:

  » headings (page 332)

  » real people, places, and events presented in chronological order (pages 332–333)

- Use Display and Engage **Build Background 10.6**.

- **Tell students** to look for the Critical Vocabulary as they read, and to think about the words' meanings.

ANNOTATION TIP: Have students use the box to note what they want to learn from this selection.

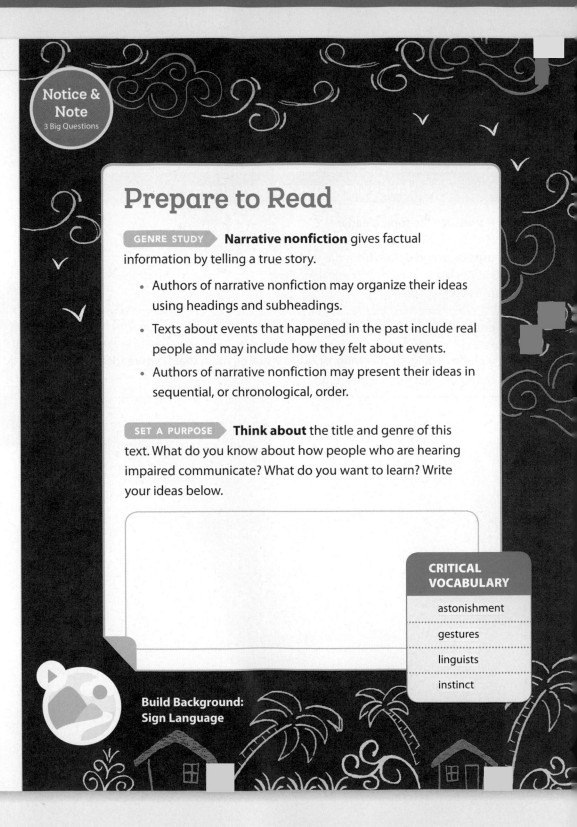

Prepare to Read

GENRE STUDY **Narrative nonfiction** gives factual information by telling a true story.

- Authors of narrative nonfiction may organize their ideas using headings and subheadings.

- Texts about events that happened in the past include real people and may include how they felt about events.

- Authors of narrative nonfiction may present their ideas in sequential, or chronological, order.

SET A PURPOSE **Think about** the title and genre of this text. What do you know about how people who are hearing impaired communicate? What do you want to learn? Write your ideas below.

**Build Background:
Sign Language**

CRITICAL VOCABULARY

astonishment

gestures

linguists

instinct

330

A New Language—Invented by Kids!

by Charnan Simon

331

Ask and Answer Questions

MODEL ASKING AND ANSWERING QUESTIONS

 THINK ALOUD *I will ask and answer a question after I read the first three paragraphs to help me better understand the text. I will ask, "Why did the children start to make signs with their hands?" The text says the children are "silent children" who cannot hear or speak. They feel lonely, but once they are together at a new school, they use their hands to create a new language and communicate with each other.*

🔍 TARGETED CLOSE READ

Text Structure

Have students reread paragraphs 4–5 to analyze text structure.

What text structure does the author use in this part of the text? (problem-solution text structure)

ANNOTATION TIP: Have students underline words and phrases that signal the text structure.

How does knowing the text's structure help you understand the central, or main, idea of these paragraphs? (The text structure helps me understand why the children need to create their own language.)

DOK 3

---

 myNotes

1 It sounds like a fairy tale. Once upon a time, in a faraway country, there lived children who could neither hear nor speak.

2 Their lives were lonely, even in the midst of loving families. But one day an amazing thing happened. The silent children, as they were known, were brought together at a new school. They began to make signs with their hands. Faster and faster their hands flew.

3 As the grownups watched in **astonishment**, a new language was born.

The Silent Children

4 The best part about this fairy tale is that it's true. For many years, children who are deaf in the Latin American country of Nicaragua were kept hidden. They were not taught sign language or lipreading or how to write. They were truly children without language.

5 Then, in 1979, the Nicaraguan government set up two schools for them. When the children arrived, they couldn't understand their teachers.

Instead, the children began to "talk" to each other with their hands. At first they shared just simple **gestures**. But soon they invented more and more signals, until they had their own gesture language.

> **astonishment** If you look at something with astonishment, you feel very surprised by it.
>
> **gestures** If you make gestures, you make movements with your hands or arms to share a message.

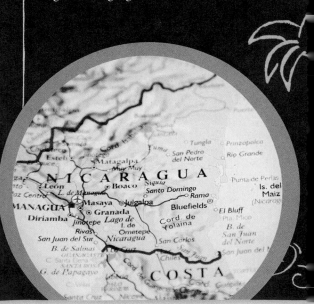

In Our Own Words

6 Their early signing was pretty basic, like baby talk. But as new students arrived at the school, younger children learned from older students and added new signs of their own. The language became richer and more complex. Instead of speaking like two-year-olds and saying, for instance, "I go play," children with more signs could speak fluently—"OK, with Eduardo and Julia, we have enough kids to play soccer. If we hurry, we'll have time for a game before school starts."

7 Can you imagine inventing all the sign language you'd need to say all that?

8 Linguists from around the world were excited about what these Nicaraguan children had done. The children seemed to prove that humans have a natural instinct for language. But unless it is used, this instinct fades away and is eventually lost. For most of us, simply growing up surrounded by people speaking is enough to trigger language learning. For the Nicaraguan children, the trigger seemed to be meeting other children who spoke with hand gestures and who were eager to make friends.

9 Today, Nicaraguan Sign Language is an officially recognized language. It is unlike any other sign language in the world—and it was created entirely by deaf children.

Now that's a happy ending.

> **linguists** Linguists are people who study languages and the way they are put together.
> **instinct** An instinct is something you do or know naturally, without being taught.

myNotes

📖 **READ FOR UNDERSTANDING**

Ask and Answer Questions

Ask and answer a question about paragraphs 6–9. *(Responses may include: How do the children develop their language? They first use simple words and sentences, but as students learn these signs, they continue to add new signs and teach each other.)*

If students have difficulty asking and answering questions, use this model:

💭 **THINK ALOUD** *I will ask and answer questions to help me clarify the details in the text. I can ask a question about how the children develop their language and then look for the answer in the text.*

DOK 2

🔍 **TARGETED CLOSE READ**

Text Structure

Have students reread paragraphs 6–9 to analyze text structure.

How does the author use chronological events to support the central, or main, idea? *(The events show the development of Nicaraguan Sign Language. It grows from being a basic language used by children, to a complex language taught to others, to an officially recognized language.)*

DOK 3

333

Notice & Note

3 Big Questions

- **Remind students** that authors may provide information based on what they believe the readers know or do not yet know.

- **Have students** explain why they might use the strategy when reading page 334. *(Responses may include: I am surprised to learn that there is also a form of written language called SignWriting.)*

ANNOTATION TIP: Have students highlight any information that they read that surprised or challenged them.

- **Have students** reflect on the Anchor Questions: *What surprised me? What did the author think I already knew? What challenged, changed, or confirmed what I already knew?* and add to their notes.

DOK 2

 READ FOR UNDERSTANDING

Wrap-Up

Revisit the purpose students set before they read the text. Have students explain what they learned from the text and cite text evidence.

DOK 2

334

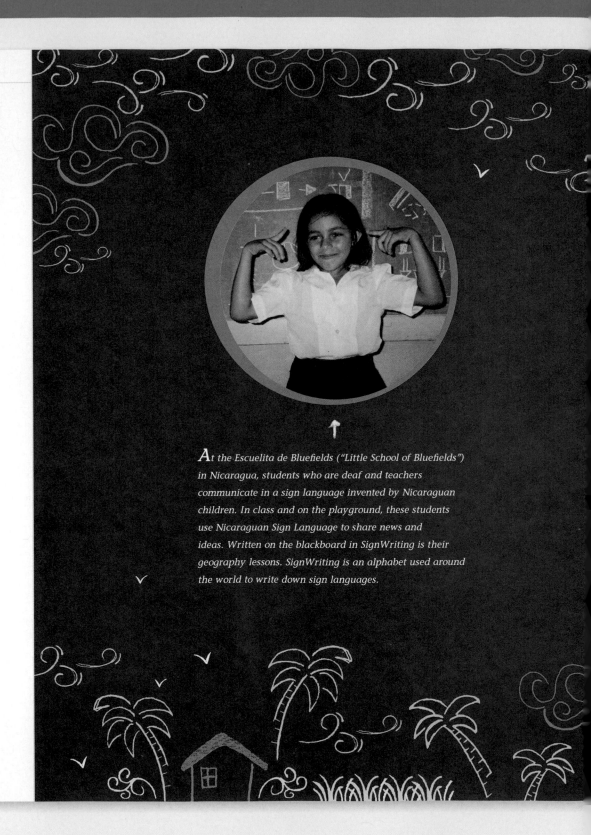

At the Escuelita de Bluefields ("Little School of Bluefields") in Nicaragua, students who are deaf and teachers communicate in a sign language invented by Nicaraguan children. In class and on the playground, these students use Nicaraguan Sign Language to share news and ideas. Written on the blackboard in SignWriting is their geography lessons. SignWriting is an alphabet used around the world to write down sign languages.

Collaborative Discussion

Look back at what you wrote on page 330. Tell a partner two things you learned from this text. Then work with a group to discuss the questions below. Refer to details and examples in *A New Language—Invented by Kids!* to support your ideas. Take notes for your responses. When you speak, use your notes.

1. Reread page 332. Why does the author say that Nicaraguan children who were deaf were "without language"?

2. Review page 333. What did the children do to invent a new language?

3. How did the new language change the lives of the students?

Listening Tip

Listen carefully to what others have to say. Wait until another speaker has finished talking before you add your own ideas.

Speaking Tip

Don't do all the talking! If you've already shared an idea, wait for someone else to speak up before you share again.

Academic Discussion

Use the **COLLABORATIVE DISCUSSION** routine. Have students write notes to answer the questions. Then have groups apply the Listening and Speaking Tips as they discuss their responses.

Possible responses:

1. *They were without language because they could not speak and were not taught any form of communication with other people.* DOK 2

2. *They first started to use signs and gestures for simple words and sentences. Then they made up more signs for additional words and complex ideas.* DOK 2

3. *The students were no longer lonely. They could make friends, play, learn in a school, and communicate their ideas and feelings to other people.* DOK 2

Write a Summary

Write About Reading

- **Read aloud** the prompt with students.

- **Lead a discussion** in which students share their ideas about how to help other students understand what makes the kids in the article so amazing. Tell students to use text evidence to support their ideas.

- **Then read aloud** the Plan section. Have students use ideas from the discussion in their notes.

PROMPT

In *A New Language—Invented by Kids!,* you read about how children who could not hear or speak found a way to communicate. The author explained how the children found a solution to their communication problem.

Imagine that your class is putting together a reading list of stories about amazing kids. You have been asked to write summary of *A New Language— Invented by Kids!* to help other students understand what makes the kids in the article amazing. Don't forget to use some of the Critical Vocabulary words in your writing.

PLAN

Make notes about important details from the text. Then explain why this article should be on a reading list about amazing kids.

WRITE

Now write your summary of *A New Language—Invented by Kids!*

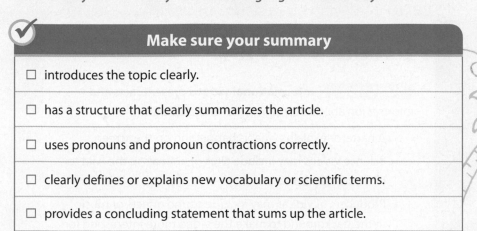

Make sure your summary

- ☐ introduces the topic clearly.

- ☐ has a structure that clearly summarizes the article.

- ☐ uses pronouns and pronoun contractions correctly.

- ☐ clearly defines or explains new vocabulary or scientific terms.

- ☐ provides a concluding statement that sums up the article.

Write About Reading

- **Review with students** the directions and checklist in the Write section.

- **Encourage students** to use their own words as they summarize the kids' amazing abilities.

VIEW FOR UNDERSTANDING

Introduce the Video

- **Read aloud** and discuss the genre information.
- Use Display and Engage <u>Build Background 10.8</u>.
- **Call attention** to the Critical Vocabulary. Tell students to listen for these words as they watch the video.

ANNOTATION TIP: Have students use the box to note what they want to learn from this video.

 VIEW FOR UNDERSTANDING

Set a Purpose

- **Have students** look at the photograph on this page and think about what they'd like to learn about how dolphins communicate with one another.
- **Guide students** to set a purpose for viewing.

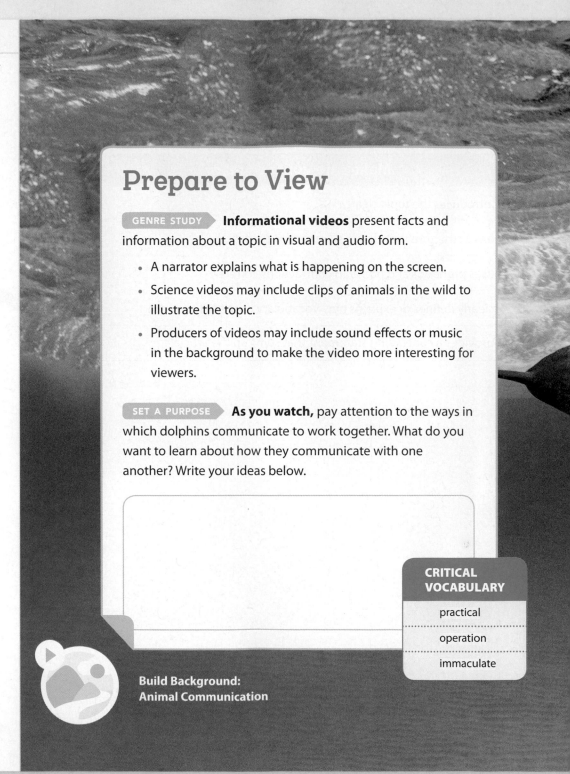

Prepare to View

GENRE STUDY **Informational videos** present facts and information about a topic in visual and audio form.

- A narrator explains what is happening on the screen.
- Science videos may include clips of animals in the wild to illustrate the topic.
- Producers of videos may include sound effects or music in the background to make the video more interesting for viewers.

SET A PURPOSE **As you watch,** pay attention to the ways in which dolphins communicate to work together. What do you want to learn about how they communicate with one another? Write your ideas below.

**Build Background:
Animal Communication**

CRITICAL VOCABULARY

practical

operation

immaculate

Dolphin Dinner

from National Geographic Kids

📖 **VIEW FOR UNDERSTANDING**

Ask and Answer Questions

MODEL ASKING AND ANSWERING QUESTIONS

💬 **THINK ALOUD** *I will ask and answer questions to help me make a prediction about the video and connect to what I will see. I will ask myself, "What does the title mean and what prior knowledge can I use to help me?" I think it must be about the dolphins eating because the title includes the word "dinner." I have knowledge about animal communication, so I think it must be about dolphins communicating with each other about how they might find food.*

339

Ask and Answer Questions

Remind students that as they view, it is important to ask and answer questions. Have students ask and answer a question about the video.

DOK 2

 TARGETED CLOSE READ

Central Idea

What is the video's central, or main, idea ? *(Dusky dolphins work as a team to find and secure their food.)*

What are two supporting details? *(Some dolphins scout for food in teams. They also herd fish in teams.)*

What is the video's text structure, and how does it support the central, or main, idea? *(chronological order; the events explain how dolphins get their food)*

DOK 3

 TARGETED CLOSE READ

Media Techniques

Which media techniques are used? *(sound, voice-over, live action)*

How does the music support the events? *(It changes to match the actions of the dolphins.)*

How do the media techniques support the video's purpose? *(Live action scenes show how dolphins hunt and capture their food.)*

DOK 3

As you watch *Dolphin Dinner*, think about the narrator's main purpose. How does the narrator introduce how dolphins communicate with each other? How is that information supported through the visuals? Do the visuals and music make the video more interesting? Why or why not? Take notes in the space below.

Listen for the Critical Vocabulary words *practical*, *operation*, and *immaculate* for clues to the meaning of each word. Take notes in the space below about how the words were used.

---

practical   If something is practical, it has a useful purpose.

operation   An operation is a set of actions that are carried out to meet a goal.

immaculate   Something that is immaculate has no mistakes or faults.

Collaborative Discussion

Dolphin Dinner

Look back at what you wrote on page 338. Tell a partner something you learned from this video. Then work with a group to discuss the questions below. Support your answers with details and examples from *Dolphin Dinner*. During the discussion, be sure you are sharing your ideas in a way that everyone can understand.

1 How do dusky dolphins use teamwork to get food for their dinner?

2 Why do dolphins send signals to one another? How do they do that?

3 What other animal likes the same kind of food as dolphins?

Listening Tip

Listen closely to what others say about your comments. If they didn't understand something, think of another way to say it, or add details to make your ideas clearer.

Speaking Tip

Use complete sentences and correct grammar when you speak. Include some science words from the video to help your listeners.

Academic Discussion

Use the **COLLABORATIVE DISCUSSION** routine. Have students write notes to answer the questions. Then have groups apply the Listening and Speaking Tips as they discuss their responses.

Possible responses:

1. *They take on different jobs to get food. Groups of dolphins scout out the food and guide fish underwater to the surface. Others jump above the water, creating splashes to herd the fish or to signal for more help.* DOK 2

2. *They might send signals if they need more help securing their food. They can jump very high in the air to notify other dolphins. Their splashes make loud noises underneath the water, too.* DOK 2

3. *Sea lions like the same kind of food as dolphins.* DOK 1

Cite Evidence

Write a Fantasy Story

PROMPT

In *Dolphin Dinner*, you watched a video about how dolphins communicate and work together.

Imagine what dolphins would say if they could speak in English. Use details from the video to write a fantasy story for your class library. Include a problem the dolphins must solve and dialogue to show how they solve the problem. Don't forget to use some of the Critical Vocabulary words in your writing.

PLAN

Make notes describing important details about dolphin communication in the video. Then think about how you could use this information as the basis for a fantasy story.

Now write your fantasy story about dolphins.

✓	**Make sure your fantasy story**
☐	has an introduction that establishes the setting and characters.
☐	includes a problem for the dolphins to solve.
☐	uses dialogue to show what the dolphins say to each other.
☐	uses pronouns correctly.
☐	provides a conclusion that follows logically from the events in your story.

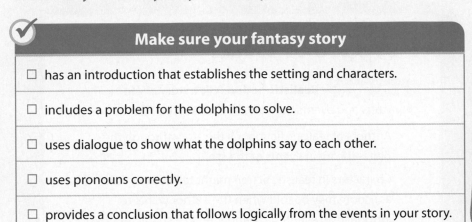

Write About Reading

- **Review with students** the directions and checklist in the Write section.
- **Encourage students** to use lively dialogue that entertains the audience, and also moves the plot along.

Notice & Note
Aha Moment

READ FOR UNDERSTANDING

Introduce the Text

- **Read aloud** and discuss the genre information. Point out that realistic fiction tells a story through a plot that includes a conflict and a resolution. Explain that students should look for anecdotes and a lesson learned by the main character.

- Use Display and Engage **Meet the Author 10.11**.

- **Tell students** to look for the Critical Vocabulary as they read, and to think about the words' meanings.

ANNOTATION TIP: Have students use the box to note what they want to learn about the main character.

Prepare to Read

GENRE STUDY **Realistic fiction** tells a story about characters and events that are like those in real life.

- Authors of realistic fiction tell the story through the plot—the main events of the story.

- Characters in realistic fiction might tell an anecdote. An anecdote may be told when the author wants to introduce an event that happened in a character's past.

- Some realistic fiction includes a theme or lesson learned by the main character.

SET A PURPOSE **Look at** the pictures in this text. What do you notice about the main character? What would you like to learn about him? Write your ideas below.

Meet the Author:
Sun Yung Shin

CRITICAL VOCABULARY

inspect

liveliest

stammered

expectantly

demonstrated

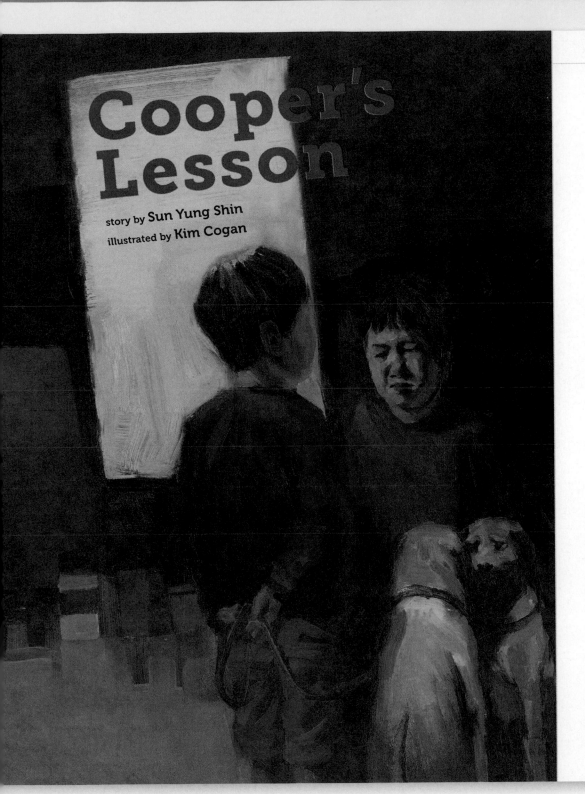

Cooper's Lesson

story by **Sun Yung Shin**
illustrated by **Kim Cogan**

345

TARGETED CLOSE READ

Point of View

Have students reread paragraphs 1–5 to determine the point of view.

What point of view does the author use to tell the story? *(third person)*

How do you know the story is written in third person? *(The author uses the main character's name, Cooper, or* he *instead of* I. *The author also uses* his *instead of* my.*)*

ANNOTATION TIP: Have students highlight the words in the text that show it is told from the third-person point of view.

DOK 2

346

1 **C**ooper's pocket felt heavy with his allowance. He leashed his dog, Catso, and laced his shoes.

2 "Be home by dinnertime!" called Cooper's dad.

3 "Cooper!" exclaimed his mom. "Could you pick up some ginger at Mr. Lee's store? *Kamsahamnida!*"

4 Cooper sighed. His mom always insisted on speaking only Korean to Mr. Lee, even though Cooper could barely follow along. Once, Mr. Lee had scolded him—in Korean—for not speaking Korean. Since then, Cooper felt funny every time he walked past the old man's store.

5 "Sure, Mom!" Cooper called over his shoulder, as he and Catso began their walk through the neighborhood.

6 A poster hung in the window of Mr. Lee's grocery store for a new Tae Kwon Do gym in the neighborhood. Both kids on the poster had black hair and yellow-brown skin.

7 Cooper studied his reflection in the window. Brown hair and some freckles. Grandmother Park always said, "Such white skin!" and Grandmother Daly always said, "What brown skin!" One cousin always teased him about being "half and half."

8 Cooper frowned. In the window, the stacked packages of powdered *insam* and bars of soap wrapped in red-and-white paper made a perfect miniature skyline.

9 He tied Catso's leash to a No Parking sign and went inside.

10 Inside, families filled the aisles, laughing and smiling. Mothers picked up vegetables to carefully inspect their leaves and roots, or gently squeezed round, sweet melons. Fathers examined the fish in the tank, searching out the largest and liveliest.

inspect   If you inspect something, you look at it carefully to judge its quality.

liveliest   The liveliest person or animal is the one that is the most active or full of energy.

 READ FOR UNDERSTANDING

Make Inferences

MODEL MAKING INFERENCES

Q THINK ALOUD   *I read that Cooper's grandmothers talk about the color of his skin, his cousin teases him about being "half and half," and Cooper frowns when he thinks about this. I can infer that Cooper must be only part Korean, and he is unhappy when people comment about it to him.*

347

11   Cooper's ears were buzzing. He realized he had never been inside without his mother. *Everyone seems to belong here,* he thought.

12   One woman with a small, sleeping boy in her arms smiled at Cooper and said, "*An yong.*"

13   "Hello," Cooper stammered, blushing.

14   "*An yong ha se oh,*" he added quietly, but she was already out the door.

15   Cooper wandered past the boxes of green tea and packages of shrimp crackers, and stopped at a display of hairbrushes and barrettes.

16   Cooper remembered. The week before, he had gone outside to brush Catso. He had grabbed the first brush he could find—his mother's—and spent the next half-hour brushing Catso's coat to a glossy shine.

> **stammered**   If you stammered, you spoke with many pauses and repeated words.

---

17   The next morning, when Cooper left for school, his mother found her brush on the table in the hallway, full of Catso's brown and white fur.

18   "Cooper! My brush! Ruined!" cried his mom.

19   *I know—I'll buy her a new one with my allowance!* Cooper smiled to himself.

20   But Cooper's heart sank—even the smallest brush on display cost more than the three dollars in his pocket.

21   Mr. Lee called out to him from the register, but Mr. Lee's Korean was too quick for Cooper to catch.

22   Mr. Lee walked over to Cooper. *Is he laughing at me?* Cooper wondered. He wanted to answer back in Korean, English, anything, but his tongue lay as heavy and still in his mouth as a dead fish.

23   He was sorry that he had paid so little attention when his mother had tried to teach him Korean. Mr. Lee watched him expectantly.

> **expectantly**   If you do something expectantly, you are excited that something good is about to happen.

myNotes

---

myNotes

 READ FOR UNDERSTANDING

Why does Cooper steal the hairbrush? *(He is frustrated that his allowance is not enough to pay for it. He is also upset because he does not speak Korean well and Mr. Lee will not speak to him in English. Cooper acts quickly out of anger and steals the brush.)*

ANNOTATION TIP: Underline the words or phrases in the text that help you understand why Cooper steals the brush.

DOK 2

24   "Uh . . . is this all you have?" Cooper finally squeaked out.

25   Mr. Lee frowned and said, "*Ye. Mullon imnida?*" When Cooper didn't answer, Mr. Lee shook his head and walked away.

26   The Korean writing on the cans and boxes seemed to dance off the labels. The aisles were closing in on him from all sides.

27   Cooper felt the money in his pocket. *Dumb, small allowance!*

28   He looked at Mr. Lee and thought to himself, *Why don't you speak English to me?* Cooper felt hot prickles under his skin.

29   Suddenly, Cooper's hand reached out and grabbed the biggest brush from the rack. As though in a dream, he turned and moved toward the door.

30   He was halfway outside when a firm hand gripped his shoulder.

31   "What do you have there?"

32   "Nothing," stammered Cooper, his eyes open wide. Since when could Mr. Lee speak English?

33   Mr. Lee took the brush from Cooper's hand.

34   "It—it was for my mother!"

35   Mr. Lee bent down to look at Cooper. "Would your mother want you to steal for her? Is that what she teaches you?"

36   "No . . . " said Cooper, blushing red to his ears.

37   "Any other 'nothings' in your pocket?" asked Mr. Lee. Cooper pulled his allowance from his pocket. Mr. Lee shook his head in disbelief. "Come with me," he sighed.

350

350 Module 10

READ FOR UNDERSTANDING

What does Mr. Lee do after he catches Cooper stealing? *(He hands Cooper a broom and has him sweep the floor of the store. He tells Cooper to return to the store tomorrow.)*

DOK 1

38   Mr. Lee handed Cooper a broom. "Do you know how to use one of these?" he asked. Cooper nodded, his voice nowhere to be found. He had never felt so ashamed in his entire life.

39   So Cooper swept. And swept. And swept some more.

40   After sweeping the day's dust into the trash bin, Cooper went and stood in front of Mr. Lee, unsure of what to say or do.

41   "Come back tomorrow, same time," said Mr. Lee, with a look that told Cooper he'd better return.

42   Cooper's stomach hurt as he thought about what to tell his mother. Would Mr. Lee call her before he got home?

43   Cooper closed the front door quietly behind him, but not quietly enough.

44   "Oh good, you're back! Cooper, we need that ginger, quick!" his mom called from the kitchen.

351

45   Visions of the afternoon—his too-small allowance, the hairbrush, the broom—flashed before him. "Oh no," he groaned, his chin dropping to his chest.

46   "You forgot? *Aigo!* What were you doing all this time?" asked his mom. Cooper wanted to apologize, but she had gone back to cooking. Once again, his tongue failed him. He would tell her about Mr. Lee and the hairbrush tomorrow.

47   The next day after school, Cooper dragged his feet to Mr. Lee's store.

48   Mr. Lee demonstrated how to place cans on the shelves so that the labels lined up perfectly. He spoke to Cooper first in Korean and then in English. Cooper tried it. Mr. Lee nodded silently, then walked away.

49   After he had placed the last can on the shelf, Cooper watched Mr. Lee chat with his customers at the register. Cooper realized suddenly that sometimes, if he paid very close attention, he could understand what they said.

50   On his way home, Cooper passed a leafy oak tree. *Namu.* The Korean word for *tree* rose in his mind, surprising him, like a fish breaking the surface of a calm pond.

> **demonstrated**   If you demonstrated something, you showed how it is used or done.

352

Notice & Note

Aha Moment

- **Remind students** that there are points in a story plot where characters suddenly realize something that changes the way they sees themselves or others around them. This is an aha moment. When students see this in a story, they should take note of it as being significant.

- **Have students** explain why they might use this strategy when reading page 353. *(Cooper suddenly realizes that if he pays close attention, he can understand Korean. The Korean word for* tree *also comes to Cooper's mind without him even trying to think of it.)*

ANNOTATION TIP: Have students highlight Cooper's aha moment in the text.

- **Have students** reflect on the Anchor Question: *How might this change things?* and add to their notes.

DOK 2

353

TARGETED CLOSE READ

Plot

Have students reread paragraphs 51–55 to analyze the plot.

What is the setting of the story? (*a Korean grocery store in present day*)

How does the setting contribute to the development of the plot? (*In the beginning of the story, the Korean store makes Cooper feel uncomfortable and angry. As the story continues, it becomes a place where he happily goes to work and to practice speaking Korean.*)

DOK 3

354

51   By the end of the week, Cooper's feet no longer dragged as he walked to Mr. Lee's. He even caught himself whistling as he swept.

52   Mr. Lee approached. His tired face was gentle. He bent down to look Cooper in the eye and said, "So. Are you ready to tell me why you stole from me?"

53   "I don't know!" Cooper said, although then he felt that perhaps he did know. "I'm sorry. I thought you were laughing at me because I couldn't speak Korean. I got mad."

54   "I know how that feels, believe it or not," said Mr. Lee, "but stealing is still wrong."

55   "I know," said Cooper, his voice small.

56   "Oh good," said Mr. Lee. "Maybe there's hope for you yet."

57   Suddenly Mr. Lee motioned for Cooper to follow him to the register. He pulled a slim photo album from beneath the counter and opened it to a photo of a young man in a white coat next to a modern-looking building. The sign over the door was in bold Korean lettering.

58   Cooper's eyes widened. "Is that you?"

59   Mr. Lee nodded. "When I was a chemist in Korea, I had the neatest lab in the company."

 READ FOR UNDERSTANDING

Make Inferences

Remind students that as they read, it is important to make inferences throughout their reading of the selection. Have students make an inference regarding how Cooper feels about working in Mr. Lee's store.

DOK 2

355

60   "You were a chemist?"

61   "Yes. But when I came here, I had to start over with a new language."

62   "But English is easy!" Cooper blurted.

63   Mr. Lee laughed. "Yes . . . About as easy as Korean." Cooper blushed.

64   "Anyway, now I speak both. And now that I'm a citizen, I'm Korean and American, both."

65   "I guess I'm both too, but people ask me where I'm from all the time," said Cooper.

66   "What do you tell them?" asked Mr. Lee.

67   "That I'm from right here. But then they say, *No, where are your parents from?* Sometimes I feel like I can't really say I'm Korean if I can't speak the language. But they look at me funny if I say I'm American, even though I am." Cooper glanced back at the photo album. He wondered if people looked at Mr. Lee funny for saying he was Korean and American, too.

68   "People like things to be simple, easy to put in a box," sighed Mr. Lee.

356

69   "Sometimes I wish I were just one thing or another. It *would* be simpler," Cooper said.

70   "Oh? You want to be the same as everyone else, like the cans on this shelf, or those rows of frozen fish?"

71   Cooper wrinkled his nose. The bell on the door jingled. "There you are!" said a voice from behind Cooper.

72   "Mom! I was . . . here to get the ginger. I mean, *saenggang*," said Cooper, choosing a thick piece and fishing in his pocket for a dollar bill.

73   Cooper's mother looked surprised. Then she smiled and said, "Well, better late than never."

Notice & Note

Aha Moment

- **Have students** explain why they might use the aha moment strategy on page 357. *(Cooper suddenly realizes he does not want to be "just one thing or another" like everyone else. The text says "Cooper wrinkled his nose" after Mr. Lee asked him if he wanted to be the same as everyone else. Mr. Lee helps Cooper see that he is special and unique and should be proud of who he is.)*

ANNOTATION TIP: Have students highlight Cooper's aha moment in the text.

- **Have students** reflect on the Anchor Question: *How might this change things?* and add to their notes.

DOK 2

 TARGETED CLOSE READ

Plot

How does Mr. Lee's character contribute to the plot? *(Mr. Lee encourages Cooper to learn Korean. Mr. Lee's experiences of being Korean and American help Cooper solve his problem of feeling uncomfortable about being part Korean. Also, he now knows that he is not alone.)*

DOK 3

357

74   Cooper's mother turned to Mr. Lee and spoke in Korean.

75   Mr. Lee began to close the store. In English, he replied, "Thank you, I would be honored to join you for dinner. And perhaps on the way home Cooper can tell you why he's been here so much lately. Right, Cooper?" said Mr. Lee.

76   Cooper looked at his mom's curious face. He suddenly felt more grown-up than he ever had before.

77   They left the store and Cooper began, *"Igosul Hanguk-o-ro mworago malhamnikka?"—How do you say this in Korean?* Cooper's Korean felt awkward and funny in his own ears, but he worked hard to say exactly what he meant.

78   His mom looked at him, even more surprised. "Well, tell me what it is and we'll figure it out together," she said. Mr. Lee nodded.

79   The sun dipped behind them as they walked along, the soft sound of their languages mingling in the gentle evening air.

READ FOR UNDERSTANDING

How does Cooper change from the beginning of the story to the end?
(Responses may include: he is no longer scared of Mr. Lee; he feels better about being Korean and American; he is interested in learning to speak Korean better)

DOK 2

READ FOR UNDERSTANDING

Wrap-Up

Revisit the purpose students set before they read the text. Have students explain how this story fits the genre of realistic fiction. Have students cite evidence from the text to support their reasoning.

DOK 2

358

Collaborative Discussion

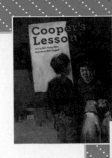

Look back at what you wrote on page 344. Tell a partner two things you learned about Cooper. Then work with a group to discuss the questions below. Use details and examples from *Cooper's Lesson* when you explain your answers. Take notes for your responses. When you speak, use your notes.

1 Review pages 347–348. Why does Cooper feel out of place in Mr. Lee's store?

2 Reread pages 349–350. What details in the text show why Cooper decided to take the hair brush?

3 What does Cooper learn from Mr. Lee?

 Listening Tip

Pay close attention to what each speaker says. Then try to think of new details on the same topic that come from the text.

Speaking Tip

Link the ideas that you share with the comments already made by other group members.

Academic Discussion

Use the **COLLABORATIVE DISCUSSION** routine. Have students write notes to answer the questions. Then have groups apply the Listening and Speaking Tips as they discuss their responses.

Possible Responses:

1. *Cooper cannot usually understand what people are saying when they speak Korean. He also looks different from the other people in the store.* DOK 2

2. *"even the smallest brush on the display cost more than the $3 in his pocket"; "He looked at Mr. Lee and thought to himself, 'Why don't you speak English to me?'"; "Cooper felt hot prickles under his skin."* DOK 2

3. *Cooper learns he is not alone. Mr. Lee is also Korean and American. Cooper learns to appreciate that he is not just one thing like everyone else.* DOK 2

359

Write a Sequel

PROMPT

In *Cooper's Lesson*, you read about a boy who makes a mistake but then makes a new friend and learns a lesson.

Imagine that the author has asked readers to offer ideas for what might happen next in Cooper's life. What might he do as a result of what he learned? Continue the story by telling what Cooper does in the days or weeks after *Cooper's Lesson* ends. Don't forget to use some of the Critical Vocabulary words in your writing.

PLAN

Make notes describing key characteristics of Cooper and the lesson he learns. Then make notes predicting what you think might happen in the days or weeks to come.

Write About Reading

- **Read aloud** the prompt with students.

- **Lead a discussion** in which students share their ideas about how the lesson Cooper learns might affect his actions in the days and weeks that follow. Tell students to use text evidence to support their ideas.

- **Then read aloud** the Plan section. Have students use ideas from the discussion in their notes.

Now write your sequel describing what happens to Cooper next.

Make sure your sequel

☐ builds on characters and details from *Cooper's Lesson*.

☐ tells events in an order that makes sense.

☐ uses dialogue and descriptions so readers can understand the story.

☐ uses commas in sentences correctly.

☐ provides a conclusion that follows logically from the events.

Write About Reading

- **Review with students** the directions and checklist in the Write section.

- **Encourage students** to stay true to the character as they write their sequel.

Revisit the Essential Question

- **Read aloud** the Essential Question.

- **Remind students** that the information about communication that they read and viewed in this module can help them answer the question.

Write an Informative Article

- **Guide students** to think about what they learned about communication from the narrative nonfiction text and the video before selecting a form of communication as the topic for their article.

- **Review the features** of an informative article using the checklist. Tell students to use the checklist as they draft, revise, and edit their articles.

? Essential Question

What forms can communication take?

Write an Informative Article

PROMPT Think about what you learned from reading *A New Language— Invented by Kids!* and *Dolphin Dinner* in this module.

Imagine that your local library is hosting an exhibit on communication. Write an article about an unusual or unexpected form of communication for the exhibit. Use facts and examples from the text and the video to support your ideas.

I will write about _____.

✓ Make sure your article
☐ states your topic clearly.
☐ has a new paragraph for each central idea and supporting details.
☐ uses evidence from the text and the video.
☐ uses words related to the topic.
☐ provides a clear summary at the end.

What ideas will you present? Look back at your notes, and revisit the text and the video as necessary.

Use the web below to record the type of communication in the center oval and facts, details, and text evidence in the surrounding ovals. Use Critical Vocabulary and words related to the topic where appropriate.

My Topic: _____

Details

Details

Details

Details

Plan

- **As needed, guide students** to think of the central, or main, idea for their article.
- **Encourage them** to use information from the text and the video as supporting details.
- **Encourage students** to include Big Idea Words and Critical Vocabulary in their articles, as appropriate.

363

DRAFT ·· Write your article.

Write a strong **introduction** that clearly states the topic and lets readers know what your article will be about.

> [ ]

For the **body paragraph**, present a central idea, or the type of communication you will write about, with supporting sentences.

> [ ]

In your **conclusion**, restate your central idea.

> [ ]

Draft

- **Read aloud** the directions, referring back to the checklist as you do so.
- **Suggest** that students try rewording the second sentence of the prompt, if they are having trouble generating an introduction.
- **Have students** refer to their webs to construct their central, or main, idea and details sentences.

REVISE AND EDIT
········· Review your draft.

The revision and editing steps give you a chance to look carefully at your draft and make changes. Work with a partner to determine whether you have explained your ideas clearly. Use these questions to help you evaluate and improve your article.

PURPOSE/ FOCUS	ORGANIZATION	EVIDENCE	LANGUAGE/ VOCABULARY	CONVENTIONS
☐ Have I clearly stated the topic? ☐ Have I stayed on topic?	☐ Does each paragraph tell about one central idea and its supporting details? ☐ Have I written a conclusion that sums up my main points?	☐ Have I used facts, examples, and details from the text and video to support my ideas?	☐ Did I use linking words and phrases to show how my ideas are related? ☐ Did I use words related to the topic?	☐ Have I used pronouns correctly? ☐ Did I indent each new paragraph? ☐ Have I used proper spelling?

PUBLISH
········· Share your work.

Create a Finished Copy Make a final copy of your article. Consider these options to share your writing:

1. Collect the articles of your classmates and bind them in a school newsletter.

2. Scan or create a digital copy of your article and upload it to the school or library website.

3. Read your article aloud at a library event. Invite questions at the end, and be prepared to answer them.

Revise and Edit
- **Guide students** to use the checklist as they work with partners to improve their articles.
- **Remind students** to check the texts in the module to be sure their central, or main, ideas and details are accurate.

Present
- **Students can copy** their revised drafts using their best handwriting. For handwriting models, see the resources section in the back of this Teacher's Guide.
- **Students can use** a computer to input their revised drafts. See Literacy Centers Printable **Keyboarding 10.1, 10.2, and 10.3** for keyboarding lessons.

365

Glossary

This glossary contains meanings and pronunciations for some of the words in this book. The Full Pronunciation Key shows how to pronounce each consonant and vowel in a special spelling. At the bottom of the glossary pages is a shortened form of the full key.

Full Pronunciation Key

CONSONANT SOUNDS

b	**bib**, ca**bb**age	r	**r**oa**r**, **rh**yme
ch	**ch**ur**ch**, sti**tch**	s	mi**ss**, **s**auce,
d	**d**ee**d**, maile**d**,		**sc**ene, **s**ee
	pu**dd**le	sh	**di**sh, **sh**ip, **s**ugar,
f	**f**ast, **f**i**f**e, o**ff**,		ti**ss**ue
	phrase, rou**gh**	t	**t**igh**t**, stopp**ed**
g	**g**ag, **g**et, fin**g**er	th	ba**th**, **th**in
h	**h**at, **wh**o	*th*	ba**th**e, **th**is
hw	**wh**ich, **wh**ere	v	ca**v**e, **v**al**v**e, **v**ine
j	**j**u**dg**e, **g**em	w	**w**ith, **w**olf
k	**c**at, **k**i**ck**, s**ch**ool	y	**y**es, **y**olk, on**i**on
kw	**ch**oir, **qu**ick	z	ro**s**e, si**z**e,
l	**l**id, need**l**e, ta**ll**		**x**ylophone, **z**ebra
m	a**m**, **m**an, du**mb**	zh	gara**g**e, plea**s**ure,
n	**n**o, sudd**en**		vi**s**ion
ng	thi**ng**, i**nk**		
p	**p**op, ha**pp**y		

VOWEL SOUNDS

ă	p**a**t, l**au**gh	o͝o	f**u**ll, b**oo**k, w**o**lf
ā	**a**pe, **ai**d, p**ay**	o͞o	b**oo**t, r**u**de, fr**ui**t,
â	**ai**r, c**a**re, w**ea**r		fl**ew**
ä	f**a**ther, k**o**ala, y**a**rd	ŭ	c**u**t, fl**oo**d, r**ou**gh,
ĕ	p**e**t, pl**ea**sure, **a**ny		s**o**me
ē	b**e**, b**ee**, **ea**sy,	û	c**i**rcle, f**u**r, h**ea**rd,
	p**ia**no		t**e**rm, w**o**rd
ĭ	**i**f, p**i**t, b**u**sy	yo͝o	c**u**re, p**u**re
ī	r**i**de, b**y**, p**ie**, h**igh**	yo͞o	c**u**be, m**u**sic, f**ew**,
î	d**ea**r, d**ee**r, f**ie**rce,		c**ue**
	m**e**re	ə	**a**go, sil**e**nt, penc**i**l,
ŏ	d**o**t, **o**n		lem**o**n, circ**u**s
ō	g**o**, r**ow**, t**oe**,		
	th**ough**		
ô	**a**ll, c**augh**t, p**aw**		
ôr	c**o**re, f**o**r, r**oar**		
oi	b**oy**, n**oi**se, **oi**l		
ou	c**ow**, **ou**t		

STRESS MARKS

Primary Stress ´: biology [bī•**ŏl**´•ə•jē]

Secondary Stress ´: biological [bī´•ə•**lŏj**´•ĭ•kəl]

A

abandoned (ə•**băn'**•dənd) *adj.* If a place is abandoned, it is no longer cared for or used. There is an abandoned car left in the field.

abandoned

accentuated (ăk•**sĕn'**•chōō•ā'•tĭd) *v.* If something is accentuated, it has attention drawn to it. She accentuated her pigtails by wearing pink hair bands.

adventurous (əd•**vĕn'**•chər•əs) *adj.* Someone who is adventurous tries to do new things. The adventurous family was excited about their bike ride up the mountain.

ancestors (**ăn'**•sĕs'•tərz) *n.* Your ancestors are the people in your family who lived long ago. My grandfather told me that my ancestors came from several countries on the continent of Europe over one hundred years ago.

Word Origins

ancestors The word *ancestors* comes from the Latin word *antecedere*. The prefix *ante-* means "before" or "to precede." Thus the meaning of *ancestors* came to be "the people in your family who came before you."

---

appointed (ə•**poin'**•tĭd) *v.* If you are appointed to a job, you are assigned to or chosen for it. Kaito was appointed as the caretaker for the classroom plants.

assess (ə•**sĕs'**) *v.* If you assess something, you think about it carefully and judge it. On the way to school, we stopped to assess the safety of the street before crossing.

assumed (ə•**sōōmd'**) *v.* If you assumed something, you believed it without proof. When Matthew went to bed, Mom assumed that he would stop reading and go to sleep.

astonishment (ə•**stŏn'**•ĭsh•mənt) *n.* If you look at something with astonishment, you feel very surprised by it. Penny had a look of astonishment when she saw what was inside the box.

astounded (ə•**stoun'**•dĭd) *v.* If you are astounded by something, you are completely surprised by it. We were astounded by the show on TV.

ă **r**a**t** / ā **p**a**y** / â **c**a**re** / ä **f**a**ther** / ĕ **p**e**t** / ē **b**e / ĭ **p**i**t** / ī **p**ie / î **fie**rce / ŏ **p**o**t** / ō **g**o / ô **p**aw / ôr **for** / oi **oil** / ōō **b**oo**k** /

attitudes (ăt′·ĭ·tōōdz′) *n.* Your attitudes are the ways you think and feel about something. The coach gives our team a pep talk to help us keep positive attitudes as we play the game.

autonomous (ô·tŏn′·ə·məs) *adj.* If something is autonomous, it controls itself. The autonomous machines in the factory are assembling cars.

B

blog (blŏg) *n.* If you write a blog, you are writing regular and informal updates, or entries, on a website. The students created a blog about how to care for a community garden.

blunt (blŭnt) *adj.* Something that is blunt is flat or rounded, rather than sharp. The blunt pencil still needs to be sharpened.

broadcast (brôd′·kăst′) *n.* A broadcast is a program or speech on the television or radio. Robert listened to the radio broadcast of the concert.

C

canopy (kăn′·ə·pē) *n.* A canopy is a rooflike covering, like the top branches of trees in a forest. A canopy of trees shades the dirt road.

canopy

canyon (kăn′·yən) *n.* A canyon is a deep valley that has steep sides. He felt dizzy as he looked down into the canyon.

character (kăr′·ĭk·tər) *n.* A person's character is the kind of person he or she is. Peter has an outgoing character, as he is easily able to talk to anyone he meets.

chasm (kăz′·əm) *n.* A chasm is a deep crack or opening in the ground. The hikers enjoy the beauty created by the chasm.

> **Word Origins**
>
> **chasm** The word *chasm* comes from the Greek word *khasma*, which means "gaping hollow."

clamped (klămpt) *v.* When something is clamped, it is closed tightly. The puppy clamped its teeth tightly onto the tasty bone.

ōō b**oo**t / ou **ou**t / ŭ c**u**t / û f**ur** / hw **wh**ich / th **th**in / *th* **th**is / zh vi**s**ion / ə **a**go, sil**e**nt, penc**i**l, lem**o**n, circ**u**s

369

collision (kə•lĭzh′•ən) *n.* A collision happens when a moving object crashes into something. Rubber bumpers softened the collision between bumper cars.

commendable (kə•mĕnd′•a•bəl) *adj.* If you do something commendable, you do it well and earn praise. The officer received many medals for his commendable service in the military.

compost (kŏm′•pōst′) *n.* Compost is decayed plant waste that can be used to fertilize soil. The compost we make will be used in our vegetable garden.

conservation (kŏn′•sər•vā′•shən) *n.* Conservation is the act of saving and protecting the environment. People are working hard for the conservation of wildlife in this area.

convenient (kən•vēn′•yənt) *adj.* If something is convenient, it is handy and useful. My dad takes the train because it is the most convenient way for him to get to work.

core (kôr) *n.* The core of something is its center. Daniel ate every bite of the delicious apple and left only the core.

correspond (kôr′•ĭ•spŏnd′) *v.* When you correspond with someone, you exchange letters or emails with that person. The class was assigned to correspond with their pen pals for the entire school year.

crestfallen (krĕst′•fô′•lən) *adj.* If you are crestfallen, you are sad and discouraged. As Zach sees his grade on the math test, he has a crestfallen look on his face.

culinary (kŭl′•ə•nĕr′•ē) *adj.* Something that is culinary is connected to cooking. Jackie plans to go to culinary school when she gets older because she really enjoys cooking.

currents (kûr′•əntz) *n.* Currents are flowing movements of water in a lake, river, or ocean. The strong water currents quickly move the kayak down the river.

D

decay (dĭ•kā′) *v.* When things decay, they slowly break down and rot. The apple looked like it was brown and starting to decay.

decay

ă **r**a**t** / ā **pay** / â **care** / ä **father** / ĕ **pet** / ē **be** / ĭ **pit** / ī **pie** / î **fie**rce / ŏ **pot** / ō **go** / ô **paw** / ôr **for** / oi **oil** / o͞o **book** /

demonstrated (děm′•ən•strā′•tĭd)
v. If you demonstrated something,
you showed how it is used or done.
The ballet instructor demonstrated
the pose to the students.

devastation (děv′•ə•stā′•shən) *n.*
Devastation is terrible damage
or complete destruction. Many
buildings were destroyed due
to the devastation caused by
the tornado.

devastation

digest (dĭ•jĕst′) *v.* When you
digest food, it moves through your
body to your stomach. Some
foods, like meats and cheese, take
longer to digest than others.

disoriented (dĭs•ôr′•ē•ĕn′•tĭd) *v.*
Creatures that are disoriented are
confused about where they are.
The tourist was disoriented and
needed to look at a map.

disposable (dĭ•spō′•zə•bəl) *adj.*
If something is disposable, it is
meant to be thrown away once it
has been used. The trashcan was
overflowing with disposable
cardboard boxes and wrappers.

disposition (dĭs′•pə•zĭsh′•ən) *n.*
Your disposition is the way you
tend to act or feel. I really enjoy
spending time with my friend
Juanita because she has such a
happy disposition.

diverse (dĭ•vûrs′) *adj.* If something
is diverse, it is made up of things
that are different from each other.
The marine life in the ocean is so
diverse that I saw over forty types
of fish at the aquarium.

E

ecology (ĭ•kŏl′•ə•jē) *n.* Ecology is
the relationship between the living
things in their environment. I
wrote about the ecology of the
rainforest for my science project.

edible (ĕd′•ə•bəl) *adj.* If something
is edible, it is safe for people to eat.
Some flowers are edible.

> **Word Origins**
>
> **edible** The word *edible*
> comes from the Latin word
> *edere*, which means "to eat."

embedded (ĕm•bĕ′•dĭd) *v.* If a
thing is embedded, it is firmly set
into something else that surrounds
it. An oyster will create a pearl
when a grain of sand becomes
embedded in the soft tissue within
its shell.

---

o͞o b**oo**t / ou **ou**t / ŭ c**u**t / û f**u**r / hw **wh**ich / th **th**in / *th* **th**is / zh vi**s**ion / ə **a**go, sil**e**nt, penc**i**l, lem**o**n, circ**u**s

enabled (ĕn·**ā**'·bəld) *v.* If you are enabled to do something, you are given a chance to do it. The crutches enabled Darla to walk with her hurt leg.

envision (ĕn·**vĭzh**'·ən) *v.* If you envision something, you picture it in your mind. Charlotte likes to envision herself becoming an astronaut in the future.

eroding (ĭ·**rōd**'·ĭng) *v.* If something is eroding, it is slowly wearing away, often from wind or water. The rocks have been eroding for years as a result of the daily rush of water.

estimate (**ĕs**'·tə·mĭt') *n.* If you give an estimate, you give an amount or size that is not exact. Our teacher taught us that finding an estimate first can be a helpful step when solving a math problem.

eternal (ĭ·**tûr**'·nəl) *adj.* If something is eternal, it has no end and lasts forever. There is an eternal flame at Arlington National Cemetery.

Word Origins

eternal The word *eternal* comes from the Latin word *aeternus*, which means "age."

---

exaggeration (ĭg·**zăj**'·ə·rā'·shən) *n.* An exaggeration describes something as more important or larger than what it really is. Saying that your sister is twice as tall as you are is an exaggeration.

expectantly (ĭk·**spĕk**'·tənt·lē) *adv.* If you do something expectantly, you are excited that something good is about to happen. Gregory looks in the box expectantly, eager to see what is inside.

F

fascinated (**făs**'·ə·nā'·tĭd) *v.* If you are fascinated by something, you are very interested in it. Ella is fascinated with searching for places on the globe.

fathom (**fă***th*'·əm) *v.* If you fathom something, you understand it. Roberto could not fathom how the goat got stuck in the fence.

forbidden (fər·**bĭd**'·n) *adj.* If something is forbidden, it is not allowed or accepted. My little sister sneaks into my mom's room and uses her makeup, even though she knows that it is forbidden.

frequent (**frē**'·kwənt) *adj.* If something is frequent, it happens often. I take frequent trips overseas.

ă r**a**t / ā p**ay** / â c**are** / ä f**a**ther / ĕ p**e**t / ē b**e** / ĭ p**i**t / ī p**ie** / î f**ie**rce / ŏ p**o**t / ō g**o** / ô p**aw** / ôr f**or** / oi **oi**l / ŏŏ b**oo**k /

G

generous (jĕn'•ər•əs) *adj.* A generous amount of something is larger or more plentiful than is usual or necessary. I was amazed by the generous number of gifts at my birthday party.

gestures (jĕs'•chərz) *n.* If you make gestures, you make movements with your hands or arms to share a message. As my teacher talks, she makes a lot of gestures with her hands.

glimpse (glĭmps) *n.* A glimpse is a very quick look at something. We saw a glimpse of two orcas as they surfaced.

glistens (glĭs'•ənz) *v.* If something glistens, it sparkles or shines. The dew-covered spider web glistens in the early morning sunshine.

gratitude (grăt'•ĭ•tōōd') *n.* When you show gratitude, you show that you are thankful. Theresa shows her gratitude by giving her mom a big hug.

H

hydrated (hī'•drā'•tĭd) *v.* Something that is hydrated has taken in plenty of water. The players are given water before, during, and after the game so they stay hydrated.

hydrated

I

idle (īd'•l) *adj.* If something is referred to as idle, it is not doing anything. An idle boast is bragging about something that cannot happen. It is no idle boast that she can lift almost 100 pounds.

immaculate (ĭ•măk'•yə•lĭt) *adj.* Something that is immaculate has no mistakes or faults. Benji's performance is immaculate and precise.

impact (ĭm'•păkt) *n.* Impact is the effect that one thing has on something else. The heavy snow makes an impact on our travel plans.

influence (ĭn'•flōō•əns) *v.* If you influence people, you use your power or ability to change what they think. Daria's teacher was able to influence her to play the clarinet.

ōō b**oo**t / ou **ou**t / ŭ c**u**t / û f**u**r / hw **wh**ich / th **th**in / *th* **th**is / zh vi**si**on / ə **a**go, sil**e**nt, penc**i**l, lem**o**n, circ**u**s

inspect (ĭn•**spĕkt'**) *v.* If you inspect something, you look at it carefully to judge its quality. To ensure the safety of the children at our school, an official came to inspect all of the fire extinguishers and alarms.

installing (ĭn•**stôl'**•lĭng) *v.* If you are installing something, you are setting it up so it is ready to use. He is carefully installing a stained glass window.

instinct (**ĭn'**•stĭngkt') *n.* An instinct is something you do or know naturally, without being taught. Most animals, including humans, are born with the instinct to do whatever is necessary to survive, such as eating.

intensive (ĭn•**tĕn'**•sĭv) *adj.* Something that is intensive uses a lot of effort to complete a task. We know it is an intensive task to clean up the backyard.

intriguing (ĭn•**trē'**•gĭng) *adj.* Something that is intriguing is very interesting. Isabelle thinks that space is intriguing and hopes to be an astronaut one day.

L

landform (**lănd'**•fôrm') *n.* A landform is a natural feature, such as a mountain, of a land's surface. The tallest landform in the world is Mount Everest.

landscape (**lănd'**•skāp') *n.* When you look at a landscape, you are looking at the area of land around you. The landscape of a forest is thick with trees.

landscape

legendary (**lĕj'**•ən•dĕr'•ē) *adj.* If something is legendary, it is very famous and has had many stories told about it. Many people have read the legendary story of Hercules.

linguists (**lĭng'**•gwĭsts) *n.* Linguists are people who study languages and the way they are put together. My aunt and her co-workers are linguists who speak and study many languages.

liveliest (**līv'**•lē•ĭst) *adj.* The liveliest person or animal is the one that is the most active or full of energy. We picked our puppy, Luna, because she was the liveliest one in the litter.

luscious (**lŭsh'**•əs) *adj.* A food that is luscious is tasty and often juicy. Marco and Valentina thoroughly enjoy the sweet taste of the luscious strawberries.

ă **r**a**t** / ā **pay** / â **c**a**re** / ä **f**a**ther** / ĕ **p**e**t** / ē **be** / ĭ **p**i**t** / ī **pie** / î **fie**rce / ŏ **p**o**t** / ō **go** / ô **paw** / ôr **for** / oi **oi**l / ŏŏ **bo**ok /

N

nutrition (nōō•**trĭsh'**•ən) *n.* If you have good nutrition, you eat the right foods to help you stay healthy and grow. Good nutrition includes eating fresh fruits, vegetables, and lean protein.

nutrition

O

oasis (ō•**ā'**•sĭs) *n.* An oasis is a relaxing or peaceful spot in an area that is unpleasant in some way. My dad enjoys going to the park because it is an oasis where he can relax.

obsessed (əb•**sĕsd'**) *adj.* If you are obsessed with something, you think about it all the time. My sister is obsessed with taking pictures.

offense (ə•**fĕns'**) *n.* An offense is something that makes you feel hurt, annoyed, or insulted. My mom takes offense when a hairdresser gives her a bad haircut.

> **Word Origins**
>
> **offense** The word *offense* comes from the Latin word *offendere*, which means "strike against."

operation (ŏp'•ə•**rā'**•shən) *n.* An operation is a set of actions that are carried out to meet a goal. My dad is an engineer at a facility where the main operation is to clean the water that will be used in homes around the city.

opted (**ŏp'**•tĭd') *v.* If you opted for something, you chose it. After careful thought, Mason opted to wear a long sleeved shirt and jeans to school.

organic (ôr•**găn'**•ĭk) *adj.* If something is organic, it is made up of living matter. Soil is made from minerals and organic matter.

outspoken (out•**spō'**•kən) *adj.* If you are outspoken, you say what you think even when others do not agree. Grace is outspoken and is not afraid to give her opinion.

P

partial (**pär'**•shəl) *adj.* If you are partial to something, you prefer it more than other things. Mom made pasta for dinner because she knew that Nicholas was partial to it.

ōō b**oo**t / ou **ou**t / ŭ c**u**t / û f**u**r / hw **wh**ich / th **th**in / *th* **th**is / zh vi**s**ion / ə **a**go, sil**e**nt, penc**i**l, lem**o**n, circ**u**s

patent (păt'·nt) *n.* If you have a patent for an invention, you are the only one who is allowed to make or sell the invention. My uncle is a lawyer, and he works to help inventors write a patent for their inventions.

peak (pēk) *n.* A peak is the highest point of something. This restaurant's business is at its peak during lunchtime.

permission (pər·mĭsh'·ən) *n.* If you get permission, someone who is in charge allows you to do what you asked to do. David asks permission to open his gift.

pests (pĕsts) *n.* Pests are insects or small animals that harm crops or annoy people. There are many pests in the forest.

plucked (plŭkd) *v.* If something is plucked, it is pulled away from where it is. Ana plucked the apple from the highest branch of the tree.

> **Word Origins**
>
> **plucked** The word *plucked* is from the Old English word *ploccian*, which means "pull off, cull."

practical (prăk'·tĭ·kəl) *adj.* If something is practical, it has a useful purpose. My younger brother dressed in a raincoat and boots, which were very practical in this weather.

prehistoric (prē'·hĭ·stôr'·ĭk) *adj.* Something that is prehistoric is very old, from a time before history was recorded. Prehistoric animals, like dinosaurs, roamed the Earth long before people.

proposed (prə·pōzd') *v.* If you proposed an idea, you suggested that it was useful or true. Mom proposed that the family go for a bike ride since it was such a beautiful day.

prosper (prŏs'·pər) *v.* If you prosper, you succeed and do well. The tree was able to prosper over the years.

publication (pŭb'·lĭ·kā'·shən) *n.* A publication is something that has been printed and made available for sale. My favorite publication is a newspaper that contains stories from local authors.

publication

ă r**at** / ā p**ay** / â c**are** / ä f**ather** / ĕ p**et** / ē b**e** / ĭ p**it** / ī p**ie** / î f**ie**rce / ŏ p**ot** / ō g**o** / ô p**aw** / ôr f**or** / oi **oil** / ōō b**oo**k /

R

react (rē·**ăkt'**) *v.* When you react to something, you act in a way that shows you are aware of it. The baseball player had to react quickly to tag the runner out.

recall (rĭ·**kôl'**) *v.* If you recall something, you tell about something you remember. Sienna had a look of concentration as she tried to recall the information.

reckless (**rĕk'**·lĭs) *adj.* Someone who is reckless does not care how his or her actions affect others. It is reckless to drive and text at the same time.

recruiting (rĭ·**krōō'**·tĭng) *v.* If you are recruiting people, you are asking them to help do something. Akari began recruiting her friends to help collect canned goods for the food drive.

recycle (rē·**sī'**·kəl) *v.* If you recycle something, you put it through a process so that it can be reused. Remember to recycle the newspaper after you read it.

remotely (rĭ·**mōt'**·lē) *adj.* If you use something remotely, you control it from a distance. The toy car can be controlled remotely.

resourceful (rĭ·**sôrs'**·fəl) *adj.* If you are resourceful, you are good at solving problems quickly. My grandfather is very resourceful because he is able to fix almost anything that is broken.

S

sanctuary (**săngk'**·chōō·ĕr'·ē) *n.* A sanctuary is where people or animals go to be safe from danger. The elephants are safe living in the animal sanctuary.

scenic (**sē'**·nĭk) *adj.* Something that is scenic has beautiful scenery. The scenic cliffs towered over the beach.

scorching (**skôrch'**·ĭng) *adj.* Something that is scorching is very, very hot. As the volcano erupted, scorching lava flowed down its sides.

scorching

sentries (**sĕn'**·trēz) *n.* Sentries are guards or lookouts who stand in a place to keep watch. The palace has sentries standing guard in front of the gates.

ōō b**oo**t / ou **ou**t / ŭ c**u**t / û f**u**r / hw **wh**ich / th **th**in / *th* **th**is / zh vi**s**ion / ə **a**go, sil**e**nt, pen**ci**l, lem**o**n, circ**u**s

shatter (**shăt'**·ər) *v.* When things shatter, they explode or suddenly break into pieces. Grayson saw the window shatter.

shrewd (shrōōd) *adj.* Someone who is shrewd is able to quickly understand a situation to gain an advantage. Her shrewd decisions helped us get out of a difficult situation.

significantly (sĭg·**nĭf'**·ĭ·kənt·lē) *adv.* If something changes significantly, the change is great enough to be noticed or important. When Kari practiced for thirty minutes each day during the summer, her playing improved significantly.

sneered (snîrd) *v.* If you sneered, you showed disapproval and lack of respect by the look on your face. Mia sneered when she found out that she could not go to her friend's party.

splendor (**splĕn'**·dər) *n.* The splendor of something is its great beauty or impressive appearance. When we walked into the wedding reception, we were amazed by the splendor of the decorations.

stammered (**stăm'**·ərd) *v.* If you stammered, you spoke with many pauses and repeated words. Lilly was so nervous about reciting her poem to the class that she stammered through the first few lines.

stranded (**străn'**·dĭd) *v.* If you are stranded, you are stuck somewhere without a way to leave. Mom is stranded because her car broke down on her way to work.

submersible (səb·**mûr'**·sə·bəl) *adj.* If something is submersible, it can go or work under water. A submersible camera is nice to use when scuba diving.

succulent (**sŭk'**·yə·lənt) *adj.* If food is succulent, it is juicy and tasty. I enjoyed the taste of the succulent watermelon, as the sweet juices ran down my chin.

--- **Word Origins** ---

succulent The word *succulent* comes from the Latin word *succulentus*, which means "juice."

sufficient (sə·**fĭsh'**·ənt) *adj.* If something is sufficient, it is just what is needed and no more. The smaller suitcase is sufficient to fit all of Leah's clothes for the weekend.

ă r**a**t / ā p**ay** / â c**a**re / ä f**a**ther / ĕ p**e**t / ē b**e** / ĭ p**i**t / ī p**ie** / î f**ie**rce / ŏ p**o**t / ō g**o** / ô p**aw** / ôr f**or** / oi **oi**l / ōō b**oo**k /

summit (**sŭm′·ĭt**) *n.* The summit of a mountain is its top or highest point. The summit of the Matterhorn has a unique shape.

summit

sustainable (sə·**stā′**·nə·bəl) *adj.* If you use a natural resource that is sustainable, it is able to stay at a certain level and not cause harm to the environment. Farmers are trying to grow food in a sustainable way.

swirled (swûrld) *v.* If something swirled, it moved quickly around in circles. My mother swirled the cream into her coffee.

T

thrifty (**thrĭf′**·tē) *adj.* If you are thrifty, you save your money and buy only what you need. By being thrifty, Neal was able to save lots of money.

thrive (thrīv) *v.* When living things thrive, they grow well and are healthy. Many types of plants thrive in a rainforest.

transmitted (trăns·**mĭ′**·tĭd) *v.* If something is transmitted, it is sent electronically from one place to another. After I finished my book report, I transmitted the assignment to my teacher by email.

Word Origins

transmitted The base word of *transmitted* is the verb *transmit*. It comes from the Latin word *transmittere*. *Trans-* means "across" and *mittere-* means "send."

---

transported (trăns·**pôr′**·tĭd) *v.* If something is transported, it is taken from one place to another. Most of the fruit we buy is transported from international farms to the United States by ships.

trench (trĕnch) *n.* A trench is a long, narrow groove or ditch. Heavy machinery is used to dig a long trench.

trench

trickster (**trĭk′**·stər) *n.* A trickster is a character who deceives or tricks others, usually to get something from them. The fox is often portrayed as a crafty trickster in folktales.

ōō b**oo**t / ou **ou**t / ŭ c**u**t / û f**u**r / hw **wh**ich / th **th**in / *th* **th**is / zh vi**s**ion / ə **a**go, sil**e**nt, penc**i**l, lem**o**n, circ**u**s

U

unique (yŏŏ·nēk') *adj.* Something that is unique is different or one of a kind. Every snowflake is unique because it has its own special pattern.

unique

V

vital (vīt'·l) *adj.* If something is vital, it is needed or very important. Water is vital to all living things.

vividly (vĭv'·ĭd·lē) *adv.* If you remember something vividly, you have a clear, detailed memory of it. As she wrote a story about her summer vacation, Nora vividly remembered her family's trip to the beach.

W

withered (wĭth'·ərd) *v.* If a plant has withered, it has dried up and died. The flowers hanging on the porch have withered.

wrath (răth) *n.* Wrath is strong anger. My older sister was filled with wrath when she forgot to email her writing assignment to her teacher.

ă rat / ā pay / â care / ä father / ĕ pet / ē be / ĭ pit / ī pie / î fierce / ŏ pot / ō go / ô paw / ôr for / oi oil / ŏŏ book /

Index of Titles and Authors

Acknowledgments

"Aurora Borealis" by Steven Withrow from *Book of Nature Poetry* edited by J. Patrick Lewis. Text copyright © by Steven Withrow. Reprinted by permission of Steven Withrow.

"Bug Bites" from *ASK Magazine*, Nov. /Dec. 2004. Text copyright © 2004 by Carus Publishing Company. Reprinted by permission of Cricket Media. All Cricket Media material is copyrighted by Carus Publishing d/b/a Cricket Media, and/or various authors and illustrators. Any commercial use or distribution of material without permission is strictly prohibited. Please visit http://www.cricketmedia.com/info/licensing2 for licensing and http://www.cricketmedia.com for subscriptions.

Cooper's Lesson by Sun Yung Shin, illustrated by Kim Cogan. Text copyright © 2004 by Sun Yung Shing. Illustrations copyright © 2004 by Kim Cogan. Reprinted by permission of Children's Books Press, an imprint of Lee & Low Books Inc.

"Eco Friendly Food" (excerpted and retitled from *A Teen Guide to Being Eco in Your Community)* by Cath Senker. Text copyright © 2013 by Heinemann Library, an imprint of Capstone Global Library, LLC. Reprinted by permission of Capstone Press Publishers.

Grand Canyon: A Trail Through Time by Linda Vieira, illustrated by Christopher Canyon. Text copyright © 1997 by Linda Vieira. Illustrations copyright © 1997 by Christopher Canyon. Reprinted by permission of Bloomsbury Publishing LLC.

"The Great Barrier Reef" by Robert Schechter from the *Book of Nature Poetry*, edited by J. Patrick Lewis. Text copyright © by Robert Schechter. Published in 2015 by National Geographic Society. Reprinted by permission of Robert Schechter.

How Can We Reduce Household Waste? by Mary K. Pratt. Text copyright © 2016 by Lerner Publishing Group, Inc. Reprinted by permission of Lerner Publications Company, a division of Lerner Publishing Group, Inc.

"In the Days of King Adobe" from *Watch Out for Clever Women! Hispanic Folktales* as told by Joe Hayes, illustrated by Vicki Trego Hill. Text copyright © 1994 by Joe Hayes. Illustrations copyright © 1994 by Vicki Trego Hill. Reprinted by permission of Cinco Puntos Press.

"The History of Communication" (excerpted and titled from *Inventions and Discoveries: Communication)* published by World Book, Inc. Copyright © 2009 by World Book, Inc. Reprinted by permission of World Book, Inc.

Material from *Luz Sees the Light* written and illustrated by Claudia Dávila. Copyright © 2011 by Claudia Dávila. Reprinted by permission of Kids Can Press Ltd., Toronto, Canada.

"Mariana Trench" (excerpted and titled from *Seven Natural Wonders of the Arctic, Antarctica, and the Oceans*) by Michael Woods and Mary B. Woods. Text copyright © 2009 by Michael Woods and Mary B. Woods. Reprinted by permission of Twenty-First Century Books, a division of Lerner Publishing Group, Inc.

"The Mariana Trench" by X.J. Kennedy from the *National Geographic Book of Nature Poetry* edited by J. Patrick Lewis. Text copyright © 2015 by X.J. Kennedy. Reprinted by permission of X.J. Kennedy.

"A New Language--Invented by Kids!" by Charnan Simon from *ASK Magazine*, September 2010. Text copyright © 2010 by Carus Publishing Company. Reprinted by permission of Cricket Media. All Cricket Media material is copyrighted by Carus Publishing d/b/a Cricket Media, and/or various authors and illustrators. Any commercial use or distribution of material without permission is strictly prohibited. Please visit http://www.cricketmedia.com/info/licensing2 for licensing and http://www.cricketmedia.com for subscriptions.

"On Sea Turtle Patrol" by Nancy Dawson, illustrated by Denise Ortakales, from *Cricket Magazine*, May/June 2015. Text copyright © 2015 by Carus Publishing Company. Reprinted by permission of Cricket Media. All Cricket Media material is copyrighted by Carus Publishing d/b/a Cricket Media, and/or various authors and illustrators. Any commercial use or distribution of material without permission is strictly prohibited. Please visit http://www.cricketmedia.com/info/licensing2 for licensing and http://www.cricketmedia.com for subscriptions.

"A Pair of Tricksters" (retitled from "Raven and Crayfish") from *Trick of the Tale: A Collection of Trickster Tales* by John and Caitlin Matthews, illustrated by Tomislav Tomic. Text copyright © 2008 by John and Caitlin Matthews. Illustrations copyright © 2008 by Tomislav Tomic. Reprinted by permission of Candlewick Press and Templar Publishing.

Excerpt from *Seeds of Change* by Jen Cullerton-Johnson, illustrated by Sonia Lynn Sadler. Text copyright © 2010 by Jen Cullerton Johnson. Illustrations copyright © 2010 by Sonia Lynn Sadler. Reprinted by permission of Lee & Low Books Inc.

Ten Suns: A Chinese Legend by Eric A. Kimmel, illustrated by YongSheng Xuan. Text copyright © 1998 by Eric A. Kimmel. Illustrations copyright © 1998 by YongSheng Xuan. Reprinted by permission of Eric A. Kimmel and YongSheng Xuan.

Thunder Rose by Jerdine Nolan, illustrated by Kadir Nelson. Text copyright © 2003 by Jerdine Nolan. Illustrations copyright © 2003 by Kadir Nelson. Reprinted by permission of Houghton Mifflin Harcourt Publishing Company.

Credits

5 (t) *Grand Canyon* ©Michael Busselle/Exactostock-1598/Superstock, *volcano* ©Images & Volcans/Science Source, *Rio de Janeiro* ©David Wall/Alamy, *northern lights* ©Sjoerd van der Wal/iStockPhoto.com, *Victoria Falls* ©Vadim Petrakov/Shutterstock, *Mount Everest* ©Nicole Kucera/Moment/Getty Images, (b) *coral reef* ©Sven Hansche/Shutterstock, (tc) *Managaha Island* ©Raquel Bagnol/Shutterstock, *underwater* ©Seishi Nakano/Aflo/Getty Images, *rock letters* ©dimdimich/iStockPhoto.com, (tc) *watercolor background* ©Houghton Mifflin Harcourt, *Rocky cliff* ©eurobanks/iStockPhoto.com, (bc) *Alaska* ©Daniel A. Leifheit/Moment/Getty Images; **7** (b) *eating mealworms* ©Sean Gallup/Getty Images News/Getty Images; **8** (c) *dad and son kitchen* ©Tom Werner/DigitalVision/Getty Images, (t) *paper on grass* ©malerapaso/iStockPhoto.com, *paper with flowers* ©struvictory/iStockPhoto.com, Images; **9** (t) *dots* ©artishokcs/iStockPhoto.com, *telegraph* ©Getty Images, *typewriter* ©spinetta/Fotolia, *telephone* ©autsawin/iStockPhoto.com, *1920 radio* ©PhotoDisc/Getty Images, *television* ©Silberkorn/iStockPhoto.com, *computer* ©John Robertson/Alamy, *cell phone* ©Chris Willson/Alamy Images, *www* ©chaoss/iStockPhoto.com, *email icon* ©masterzphotois/iStockPhoto.com, *smartphone* ©scanrail/iStockPhoto.com, *facebook notifications* ©JaysonPhotography/iStockPhoto.com, (tc) *Nicaraguan Sign Language* ©Susan Meiselas/Magnum Photos, (bc) *dolphin* ©Rodrigo Friscione/Cultura/Getty Images; **10** ©(c) Swapan Jha/Moment/Getty Images; **12** ©fabio lamanna/iStockPhoto.com; **16** (r) ©Michael Busselle/Exactostock-1598/Superstock, (l) ©Images & Volcans/Science Source; **17** (tl) ©David Wall/Alamy, (tr) ©Sjoerd van der Wal/iStockPhoto.com,(cl) ©Vadim Petrakov/Shutterstock, (br) ©Nicole Kucera/Moment/Getty Images, (bl) ©Sven Hansche/Shutterstock; **18–19** (bg) ©Seishi Nakano/Aflo/Getty Images; **18, 19, 21, 22, 23, 24, 25, 26, 27, 28, 30, 32** (pattern) ©supermimicry/iStockPhoto.com; **18** (inset) ©Raquel Bagnol/Shutterstock; **20** ©Planetary Visions Ltd/Photo Researchers, Inc.; **21** (b) ©filo/iStockPhoto.com; **22** (b) ©World History Archive/Alamy; **23** ©saimai saelim/Moment/Getty Images; **24, 33** (inset) ©Ron & Valerie Taylor/Mary Evans Picture Library Ltd/age footstock, **24, 25** (bg) ©TEXTURE/Alamy; **25** (t) ©Dante Fenolio/Science Source; **26, 27** (t) ©Seishi Nakano/Aflo/Getty Images; **26** (b) ©NOAA/Science Photo Library/Science Source; **27** (inset) ©Xinhua/Photoshot; **29** ©World History Archive/Alamy; **30** (r) ©Raquel Lonas/Shutterstock, **35** (l), (cr), (r) ©dimdimich/iStockPhoto.com, (b) ©eurobanks/iStockPhoto.com, (bg) ©Polina Katritch/Shutterstock, (c) ©J.D.S/Shutterstock; **36** (c) ©aimy27feb/iStockPhoto.com, (l) ©Aleoks/Shutterstock, (b) ©Polina Katritch/Shutterstock, (bg) ©J.D.S/Shutterstock; **37** (br), **38** (bl), **39** (br), **40** (t), (b), **41** (bg), **44** (bg), **45** (bg) ©Polina Katritch/Shutterstock; **37** (l) ©Dan Loh/ASSOCIATED PRESS/AP Images, (r) ©AIphotographic/iStockPhoto.com, (t), (b) ©J.D.S/Shutterstock; **38** (t) ©Deborah Callahan/Alamy, (r) ©Christopher P/Shutterstock, (t) ©kanate/Shutterstock; **39** (c) ©Animals Animals/MaXx Images, (r) ©Stephen Saks Photography/Alamy, **40** (c) ©David M. Dennis/Animals Animals/age footstock, (l), (c) ©Aleoks/Shutterstock, **41** (c) ©Gary Crabbe/age fotostock/Getty Images; **42** (l) ©FLPA/Alamy, (c) ©aimy27feb/iStockPhoto.com, (inset) ©Aleoks/Shutterstock, (bg) ©licccka/iStock/Getty Images; **44** (fg) ©Gary Crabbe/age fotostock/Getty Images; **46** ©Daniel A. Leifheit/Moment/Getty Images; **48–49** (bg) ©Auscape/Universal Images Group/Getty Images; **48** (inset) ©Daniela Dirscherl/WaterFrame/Getty Images; **49** (r) ©Sergii Moskaliuk/Dreamstime; **50** ©Jeff Rotman/Photolibrary/Getty Images; **51** ©Kenneth Koh/Adventure Nomad/Flickr/Getty Images; **52** ©Shin Okamoto/Moment/Getty Images; **54** ©Daniel A. Leifheit/Moment/Getty Images; **70** ©Ariel Skelley/Blend Images/Getty Images; **73** ©wavebreakmedia/Getty Images; **76** ©Menno Schaefer/Shutterstock; **124, 140** (b), (t) ©yangzai/iStockPhoto.com; **124, 140** *Video still from Ten Suns* ©Time to Know, Limited; **144** ©Erik Isakson/Tetra Images/Getty Images; **147** ©Syda Productions/Shutterstock; **148** ©Ales-A/E+/Getty Images; **150** ©xamtiw/iStockPhoto.com; **154** ©ChooseMyPlate.gov/USDA; **155** ©chaluk/iStock/Getty Images Plus/Getty Images; **158** ©a_namenko/iStock/Getty Images Plus/Getty Images; **160** ©Lefthand666/iStock/Getty Images Plus/Getty Images; **161** ©Yuri Samsonov/Shutterstock; **162** (tl) ©yoshi0511/Shutterstock, (tr) ©stigmatize/Shutterstock, (bl) ©Michelle Lee Photography/Shutterstock, (br) ©SeDmi/Shutterstock; **163** ©nickpo/iStock/Getty Images Plus/Getty Images; **164** ©RedFoxBrush/Shutterstock; **166** ©Lefthand666/iStock/Getty Images Plus/Getty Images; **167** ©nickpo/iStock/Getty Images Plus/Getty Images; **168** ©Tom Werner/DigitalVision/Getty Images; **170, 172, 173** ©twomeows/Moment/Getty Images; **174** (l) ©HugoB4106326/iStockPhoto.com, (r) ©Stig Alenas/Shutterstock; **175** ©Sean Gallup/Getty Images News/Getty Images; **176** ©NZSteve/iStockPhoto.com; **177** (b) ©©fitopardo.com/Moment/Getty Images, (t) ©aon168/Shutterstock; **178** (t) ©Artville/Getty Images, (c) ©©fitopardo.com/Moment/Getty Images, (b) ©Lakhesis/iStockPhoto.com; **179** ©Devrimb/iStock/Getty Images Plus/Getty Images; **180** ©Charoenkrung.Studio99/Shutterstock; **182** ©aon168/Shutterstock; **183** ©Stig Alenas/Shutterstock; **198** ©Syda Productions/Shutterstock; **201** ©Getty Images; **202** ©Photo by Supoj Buranaprapapong/Getty Images; **204** ©R_Tee/Shutterstock; **208** (c) ©malerapaso/iStockPhoto.com, (l) ©TukkataMoji/Shutterstock; **209** (bg) ©struvictory/iStockPhoto.com, (t) ©Sichon/Shutterstock; **244** *Video still from Saving the Kemp's Ridley Sea Turtle* ©Texas Parks & Wildlife Department; **246** ©Thomas Barrat/Shutterstock; **247** ©Carus Publishing Company; **248** ©Matt Jeppson/Shutterstock; **250** ©Carus Publishing Company; **252, 253** ©Roger de la Harpe/Gallo Images/Getty Images; **254** *Video still from Saving the Kemp's Ridley Sea Turtle* ©Texas Parks & Wildlife Department; **254** ©AnkNet/iStockPhoto.com; **256** ©Aneese/iStockPhoto.com; **257** ©loonger/iStockPhoto.com; **258** ©millraw/E+/Getty Images; **261** (b) ©Phovoir/Shutterstock, (t) ©Photodisc/Getty Images; **262** ©Mitrija/Shutterstock; **263** (b) ©millraw/E+/Getty Images,(t) ©piotr_malczyk/Getty Images; **264** (t) ©Jonathan Alcorn/Bloomberg/Getty Images, (b) ©David W. Leindecker/Shutterstock; **265** (b) ©JohnKwan/Shutterstock, (t) ©asife/